DEFENDING BEDFORDSHIRE

THE MILITARY LANDSCAPE FROM PRE-HISTORY TO THE PRESENT

MIKE OSBORNE

FONTHILL

Fonthill Media Language Policy

Fonthill Media publishes in the international English language market. One language edition is published worldwide. As there are minor differences in spelling and presentation, especially with regard to American English and British English, a policy is necessary to define which form of English to use. The Fonthill Policy is to use the form of English native to the author. Mike Osborne was born and educated in England; therefore British English has been adopted in this publication.

Fonthill Media Limited
Fonthill Media LLC
www.fonthillmedia.com
office@fonthillmedia.com

First published in the United Kingdom and the United States of America 2021

British Library Cataloguing in Publication Data:
A catalogue record for this book is available from the British Library

Typeset in 10pt on 13pt Sabon
Printed and bound in England

Acknowledgements

A special thank you must go to Maurice Nicholson at Bedford Local Studies Library for all his help in digging out obscure (and fascinating) facts and sources; I must also acknowledge the work of Stephen Coleman and Trevor Ball during the Defence of Britain Project back in the 1990s; my thanks go also to the following: Albion Archaeology; Stuart Antrobus; John Jordan and Jon Miles at Elstow; Richard Luscombe and John Wallace at Wrest Park; Alan Judge and the guys at Chicksands; Julie Lawrence and colleagues at Electrolux, Oakley Road, Luton; Clive Makin at Barton-le-Clay; Delia Gleave at Leighton Buzzard; Kevin at Crawley Crossing; members and staff at the Gliding Club in Dunstable; Alan Bailey and Gareth Wilcox at Sandy; the numerous people who have given directions or granted access; and my wife, Pam, who has, as ever, helped the project along in so many ways. My thanks must also go to Alan, Jay, Jamie, and Josh at Fonthill Media for their editing and publishing expertise.

Contents

List of Abbreviations

AA	Anti-aircraft
AA	Automobile Association
AALMG	Anti-aircraft light machine-gun
ACF	Army Cadet Force
ADGB	Air Defence Great Britain
AFDD	Air Force Distribution Depot (fuel)
AFRD	Air Force Reserve Depot (fuel)
AFS	Auxiliary Fire Service
AI	Airborne Interception (Radar)
AMWD	Air Ministry Works Department
ARC	Army Reserve Centre (formerly TA Centre)
ARD	Aircraft Repair Depot
ARG	Airfield Research Group
ARP	Air Raid Precautions
ASU	Aircraft Storage Unit (RAF)
A/T	anti-tank
ATA	Air Transport Auxiliary (civilian ferry pilots)
ATC	Air Training Corps
ATS	Auxiliary Territorial Service (1938–49, then WRAC)
AW	Albright & Wilson (phosphorus bombs)
BAC	British Aircraft Corporation
BEF	British Expeditionary Force
BHQ	Battle Headquarters
BLEU	Blind Landing Experimental Unit
BSA	Birmingham Small Arms
CAVTC	Central Association of Volunteer Training Corps (First World War)
CBA	Council for British Archaeology
CCF	Combined Cadet Force (successor to OTC)

CCS	Casualty Clearing Station (RAMC)
CD	Civil Defence
CIA	Central Intelligence Agency (successor to OSS)
C-in-C	Commander-in-Chief
CLB	Church Lads' Brigade
COB	Co-located Operations Bases (RAF and USAF)
CRU	Civilian Repair Unit (aircraft repair workshops)
CTA	County Territorial Association
Cwt	hundredweight; 20 cwt = 1 ton
DFW3	Directorate of Fortifications & Works, Department 3
DL	Defended Locality
DoD	Department of Defence (USA)
EARE	East Anglian Royal Engineers (pre-1908)
ERD	Engine Repair Depot
(E&R)(S)FTS	(Elementary & Reserve)(Service) Flying Training School
ESR	Essential Service Route
FAA	Fleet Air Arm (reformed in 1938)
FANY	First Aid Nursing Yeomanry
FFD	Forward Filling Depots (ordnance supply)
FRIBA	Fellow of the Royal Institute of British Architects
GC&CS	Government Code and Cipher School
GCI	Ground-Controlled Interception (radar system Second World War onwards)
GDA	Gun-Defended Area (AA defences)
GHQ	General Headquarters (GHQ Line, GHQ Reserve, etc.)
GOC	General Officer Commanding
GPO	General Post Office
GS	Grammar School
HAA	Heavy Anti-aircraft
HCU	Heavy Conversion Unit (pilot training)
HD	Home Defence (RFC Squadrons and Infantry Divisions, First World War)
HE	High explosive
HER	Heritage Environment Record (ex-Sites and Monuments Record)
HT	Horse Transport
ICI	Imperial Chemical Industries
ITC	Infantry Training Centre
IWC	Italian Working Company (POWs in the Second World War)
KRRC	King's Royal Rifle Corps
LAA	Light Anti-aircraft
LADA	London Air Defence Area (AA scheme First World War onwards)
LDV	Local Defence Volunteers, later Home Guard (Second World War)

LG	Landing ground
MAFF	Ministry of Agriculture, Fisheries & Food (post-Second World War)
MAP	Ministry of Aircraft Production (Second World War)
MEW	Ministry of Economic Warfare (controlled SOE in the Second World War)
MGB	Motor Gun-boat (RN, Second World War)
MI5, MI8, etc.	Military Intelligence departments
MI(R)c	Military Intelligence (Research) later became MD1 (Second World War)
MOS	Ministry of Supply
MRRS	Military Road Route System
MT	Motor Transport
MTB	Motor Torpedo Boat (RN, Second World War)
MU	Maintenance Unit (RAF)
NAAFI	Navy, Army and Air Force Institute
NAD	Naval Air Department (at Thurleigh post-Second World War)
NAE	National Aircraft Establishment
NFS	National Fire Service (Second World War)
NRA	National Rifle Association
OC	Officer Commanding
OCTU	Officer Cadet Training Unit
OP	Observation Post
ORP	Operational Readiness Platform
OSS	Office of Strategic Services (US equivalent of SOE)
OTC	Officer Training Corps (school or university cadet corps)
OUT	Operational Training Unit (RAF Bomber/Training Commands)
PH	Public House
PIAT	Projectile Infantry Anti-Tank (bazooka-type weapon)
PID	Political Information Department (Foreign Office)
PTSD	Post-Traumatic Stress Disorder
PWE	Political Warfare Executive
QF	quick-firing (gun)
RA	Royal Artillery
R&D	Research and Development
RAuxAF	Royal Auxiliary Air Force (until 1957)
RAE	Royal Aircraft Establishment (Farnborough, Hampshire)
RAF	Royal Air Force (from 1 April 1918)
RAFVR	Royal Air Force Volunteer Reserve
RAMC	Royal Army Medical Corps
(R)AOC	(Royal from 1918) Army Ordnance Corps (until 1993)
(R)ASC	(Royal from 1918) Army Service Corps
RBL	Royal British Legion

RCHM(E)	Royal Commission on Historical Monuments (England)
RE	Royal Engineers
REME	Royal Electrical and Mechanical Engineers (formed 1942)
REU	Radio Engineering Unit (RAF)
RFA	Royal Field Artillery
RFC	Royal Flying Corps (up to 31 March 1918)
RFCA	Reserve Forces and Cadets Association (successor to CTAs)
RGHQ	Regional Government Headquarters
RHQ	Regimental Headquarters
RN	Royal Navy
RNAS	Royal Naval Air Service (until 31 March 1918)
(R)OC	(Royal from 1941) Observer Corps
ROF	Royal Ordnance Factory
RSM	Regimental Sergeant-Major
RSPB	Royal Society for the Protection of Birds (Sandy Lodge)
RVC	Rifle Volunteer Corps (1859–80)
SAA	small arms ammunition
SAC	Strategic Air Command (USAF, post-Second World War)
SAM	Surface-to-Air Missile
SF	Special Fires (Bombing Decoy—'Starfish')
SIP	Self-Igniting Phosphorous (grenade)
S/L	searchlight
SLG	satellite landing-ground
SMLE	Short Magazine Lee Enfield (0.303-inch rifle)
SOE	Special Operations Executive
STS	Special Training School (SOE)
TA	Territorial Army (from 1920–39 and 1947–2014)
TAC	Territorial Army Centre (drill hall 1947–2014, see ARC)
tb	temporary brick (single brick with buttresses in RAF buildings)
TF	Territorial Force (from 1908–1918)
TNA	The National Archive (formerly Public Record Office, Kew)
u/g	underground
UHF	Ultra High Frequency (radio wavelength)
UKWMO	United Kingdom Warning and Monitoring Organisation
USAAC	United States Army Air Corps (Second World War)
USAAF	United States Army Air Force (Second World War)
USAF(E)	United States Air Force (Europe) (post-Second World War)
VAD	Voluntary Aid Detachment (First World War)
VHF	Very High Frequency (radio wavelength)
VP	Vulnerable Point
VTC	Volunteer Training Corps (First World War Home Guard)
WAAC	Women's Auxiliary Army Corps (First World War)

WAAF	Women's Auxiliary Air Force (later WRAF)
WAC	Women's Army Corps (US, Second World War)
WLA	Women's Land Army
WRAC	Women's Royal Army Corps (from 1949–92)
WRNS	Women's Royal Naval Service
W(R)VS	Women's (Royal) Voluntary Service
W/T	Wireless telegraphy
YM/WCA	Young Men's/Women's Christian Association

Introduction

Though a small, inland county, Bedfordshire has consistently punched above its weight in the military sphere. Criss-crossed by the Jurassic Icknield Way, the Roman Ermine and Watling Streets, and the River Great Ouse, it was inevitable that campaigning armies would leave their physical marks on the ground as they manoeuvred between battles and sieges. Bedfordshire contains a higher density of earthwork castles and moated sites than most other English counties, and ancient Britons, Romans, Saxons, Danes, and Normans all played out their conflicts in everything from minor skirmishes to pitched battles. The Mercian *burh* of Bedford lay on the edge of the Danelaw, and Viking fleets are believed to have over-wintered beside the Ouse. Medieval times witnessed power struggles as kings put down rebellious subjects or attempted to fight off rival claimants. During the Civil War of the seventeenth century, Bedfordshire once again constituted a borderland between two factions. In more recent conflicts, the county has helped to lay the foundations of the RAF; has provided the industrial muscle to equip armies; and, in the Second World War, represented the core of Britain's secret and covert activities. Since then, new aeronautical technologies have been developed here.

This is the tenth volume in a series I started with *Defending Lincolnshire* in 2010. It has been a delight to explore those ten very different counties as, in each one, I have discovered a wide range of emphases, similarities, and contrasts. Each county displays unique features influenced by location, politics, population, geology, personalities, or communications, and this is visible in those elements of the military landscape that predominate. It may seem very obvious that a coastal county will exhibit evidence of measures taken to counter threatened invasion and inland counties are more likely to have more of an industrial focus producing munitions and providing the conditions for training soldiers or aircrew. Heavily populated counties will furnish more recruits to the colours whether regular, militia, territorials, or volunteers. The secret war was fought in the most unlikely of places, often in full view of those able to recognise what was going on around them. All these factors are reflected in the military landscape whether as fortifications, airfields, army camps, naval installations, battlefield sites, military hospitals, training areas, or munitions factories.

Norman castles often necessitated the demolition of large numbers of dwellings as they were inserted into Saxon towns, and this cavalier attitude to people's homes would continue through the centuries, with houses being demolished to clear fields of fire in the Civil War. One particular theme that emerges in every corner of the country is the use to which buildings were put as they were requisitioned, leased, commandeered, or borrowed for temporary, but often destructive military use. Many, but by no means all of them, were country houses, but many were ordinary humble suburban houses, the only requirement being four rooms or more on the ground floor and preferably an electricity supply. The Defence of the Realm Act of 1914 and the Defence (General) Regulations of 1939 permitted the government to acquire millions of acres of land, millions of square feet of industrial storage, and tens of thousands of buildings, often earmarked in peacetime for future use. The War Economy dictated what factories manufactured, what jobs people did, and what they could eat. No less than those medieval people embroiled in the violence around them, few could remain untouched by the wars of the twentieth century.

While some sites are preserved, many others are fast disappearing: medieval earthworks are ploughed out; brownfield sites such as airfields or camps become housing estates; and buildings intended for only a short lifespan gradually collapse. Other, more substantial buildings continue in use, while their previous purpose—however important at the time—is often forgotten. The humble pillbox at the Interchange Retail Park between Bedford and Elstow has recently been preserved through local efforts. The RAF stations at Cranfield and Henlow appear to have achieved a functional balance between preservation and development. The great airship hangars at Cardington have been successfully repurposed. The recording studios at Milton Bryan may hope for a new lease of life. The military landscape is an integral part of our national heritage and deserves to be acknowledged as such.

Mike Osborne
Market Deeping
August 2019

1

Fortification in Bedfordshire before 1066

This chapter begins by examining defensive structures from earliest times, through the period of Roman invasion and occupation, and on into the so-called Dark Ages, when the remnants of Romano-British society first resisted and then absorbed the Anglo-Saxon immigration, itself to be devastated by the Danish invaders and settlers. These centuries saw both change and the *status quo* in terms of defensive works with an emphasis on fierce resistance to incursion, and the dogged retention of land gained on the battlefield.

Prehistoric Fortifications in Bedfordshire

The earliest enclosures form one of a series of innovations that appear in the Neolithic Age. These are Causewayed Camps, which have generally been dated to the Neolithic Period, 3700–3500 BC. Enclosures of this type, as were found at Maiden Bower near Dunstable and at Cardington, consisted of rings of concentric banks pierced by openings for the transit of people and animals. Although these causewayed camps have sometimes been regarded as having a defensive purpose, the gaps would suggest that they were anything but defensible. An analysis in British Archaeology 119 (July to August 2011) suggests that they were in use possibly only intermittently to meet mainly social needs—trade, clan, or tribal gatherings, and feasts or festivals—and that the fashion lasted only a few centuries, after which the collective construction effort went into the monumental cursus. However, it was not uncommon for later settlements to overlay causewayed camps, as indeed was the case at Maiden Bower, so one might infer some common element of site selection, satisfying a variety of needs. Though thoroughly unlikely to have been primarily defensive, these 'camps' represented an organised communal effort, which must have absorbed a significant output of the available labour, if not quite as much as would the later construction of the hillforts.

The earliest likely defensible site in Bedfordshire is that on the site of the former hospital at Fairfield Park, Stotfold. A Bronze Age hilltop enclosure of *c*. 800 BC was actually found in recent excavations to be empty, so its purpose remains a mystery. It could have been a refuge or have met a completely different need. One that will most likely never be known. However, the site was later developed as a much larger village.

Hillforts

The Iron Age introduced the notion of the defensible structures generally referred to as hillforts. Within this category, every possible variation of size, plan, and location may be found. Forts could be enclosed by one or more circuits of rampart and ditch; they could cover small or large areas; and they could occupy the summits of hills, promontories, or low-lying sites. The construction of hillforts necessitated enormous investments in time and labour, and it has been estimated that a fort covering around 20 acres (8 ha) would consume the labour of over 100 workers for an entire building period of seven months. This suggests that the effort would be considered worthwhile for social, cultural, or religious purposes or overriding ones of security or prestige. While several of the county's hillforts, such as Craddock's Camp under Leighton Buzzard golf course, destroyed as early as the sixteenth century, and Dunstable hillfort largely quarried away, have disappeared, others remain. Billington Camp, whose last remnants were bulldozed in 1959, provided the location, as did a large number of prehistoric sites, for a medieval chapel, now the parish church.

A number of hillforts were built along the Chiltern Ridge in the late Bronze Age and early Iron Age, among them Sharpenhoe Clappers and Ravensburgh. The Clappers, a name derived from the French for rabbit-hole, is a promontory fort of roughly rectangular shape measuring 170 yards (150 metres) across and 270 yards (250 metres) from end to end. The fort is built on a prominent spur standing 290 feet (90 metres) above the lower ground on each of three sides, with a relatively level plateau running along the spine. The southern side forms the neck that was fortified with a rampart, 10 feet (3 metres) in height and 490 feet (150 metres) long with a ditch and a timber palisade. A gateway, marked by the post-holes of substantial timbers, was defended by outer ditches. Often the entrance to a hillfort incorporated a dog-leg passage overlooked by the defences of the gateway and banks, which channelled attackers into an approach parallel to the ramparts, thereby creating a killing zone. Here, though, the existing banks and ditches outside the gateway represent medieval adaptations to form a rabbit warren, where packed chalk was used to strengthen terraces. A couple of miles to the east, straddling the Bedfordshire–Hertfordshire boundary, near to Barton-le-Clay and Hexton, is Ravensburgh Castle. On a hilltop site, 500 feet (150 metres) above sea level, this large, oval enclosure covers 22.5 acres (9 ha), and measures 230 yards (210 metres) across and 475 yards (440 metres) north to south. It is defended by double banks and ditches on three sides, and a stronger rampart on the east side where the valley sides are less steep. The ramparts, generally rising

16–22 feet (5–7 metres) above the bottoms of the ditches, command a natural glacis. The original entrance, with out-turned banks, is in the north-west corner. The eastern rampart exhibits traces of burning, an indication that it might have been attacked. Its original construction dates back to around 400 BC, but it was refortified in the mid-50s BC. It has been suggested that it was a stronghold of Cassivellaunus attacked by the Romans in 54 BC.

Maiden Bower, to the west of Dunstable, built over an earlier causewayed camp, occupies a site 500 feet (150 metres) above sea-level, and is described by Historic England as a 'plateau fort'. It takes the form of a roughly circular enclosure, around 245 yards (225 metres) in diameter, and has a single rampart with a V-section ditch, 10 feet (3 metres) deep and 25 feet (7.6 metres) wide, enclosing 12.25 acres (4.9 ha). An inner bank enclosing a smaller area may represent an earlier structure. The main rampart is of the standard box-type construction in which timber uprights, braced by lateral timbers create a continuous run of boxes, which are then filled with the spoil from the ditch, and reinforced with chalk, clay, or whatever material is available on site. The rampart may then be turfed and a palisade and wall-walk erected on top. There are two entry points, and the gateway on the south-west, found by excavation to be original, was revetted with timber uprights and palisade slots. These features have been interpreted as one wall of a funnel-shaped gateway. Coin finds indicate later Roman occupation. At some time in its life, there was a

Sharpenhoe Clappers: the bulk of this Iron Age hillfort at the end of a ridge, looms over the surrounding area, thoroughly dominating it.

small building, possibly Romano-British in origin, inside the western part of the fort. Danesborough Camp at Aspley Heath was also univallate but enclosed a smaller area of 6 acres (2.4 ha). Roughly oval, measuring 227 by 140 yards (210 by 130 metres), its defences followed the 500-foot (150-metre) contour and were scarped with an outer rampart thus increasing the depth of the ditch to a height of nearly 13 feet (4 metres) from the bottom of the ditch to the top of the lower inner rampart. The original entrance was in the south-west corner approached over the causeway, which still crosses the ditch. It would appear to date from between 100 BC and AD 100, and may never have been completed.

At Leagrave, Waulud's Bank is a semi-circular Iron Age fortified earthwork enclosure around a single hut dwelling, which was then abandoned for 1,500 years before being reoccupied for a short while (*Bedfordshire Archaeology* 1.1, 1955 and *Bedfordshire Archaeological Journal* 2, 1964). It enclosed 17.5 acres (7 ha) with a bank now 8 feet (2.5 metres) high and an external ditch 30 feet (9 metres) wide and 6 feet 6 inches (2 metres) deep. Evidence from an excavation in 1953 suggests that the bank was revetted with turves and maybe timber stakes, although traces of only one such stake was found. The bank may have carried a wooden palisade, although, again, no post-holes were uncovered. Its location is significant in that it lies close to the Icknield Way and its banks enclose the natural springs, which provide the source of the River Lea. The site was reoccupied in both Anglo-Saxon and post-Conquest times, possibly in connection with a watermill. Mowsbury Hill, Ravensden, a short distance to the north of Bedford, is another univallate hillfort measuring 220 yards (200 metres) across by 330 yards (300 metres) diagonally north to south, and enclosing an area of 7 acres (2.8 ha). It was excavated in 1971 but not apparently written up. The ditch is 14 feet (4.3 metres) wide and some 6 feet 6 inches (2 metres) deep with a clay and timber rampart, which had been destroyed by fire. The site was reused in Roman times and later still a medieval moat occupied the north-west part.

There are no fewer than three Iron Age hillforts in Sandy. Two of them were what are known as promontory forts, where a spur of land is isolated by a rampart and ditch across its neck, providing an effective and economic solution to the problem of being secure. Galley Hill lies in the grounds of the RSPB. It is a small univallate fort of 3 acres (1.25 ha) with an entrance in the north side and an earlier fort in the south-west corner, and is seen as being the best preserved of Sandy's forts. A mere 160 yards (150 metres) away, The Lodge is the second promontory fort cut off by an artificially deepened dry valley and an interior bank. It is thought to be early in date and possibly unfinished. Caesar's Camp, north-east of the railway station, is a contour fort enclosing 7 acres (2.8 ha). It has strong defences on its southern side with a rampart, 8 feet (2.4 metres) on the inside and 20 feet (6.1 metres) on the outside, with a possible entrance in the south-east corner. It has been connected to both the Belgae and the Catuvellani and may date from the Early Iron Age. In its current damaged state, it presents as an earthwork of only slight strength.

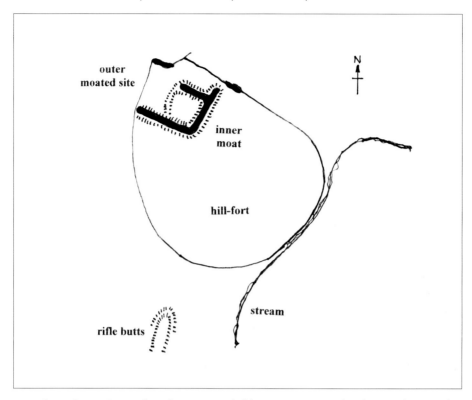

Mowsbury Camp, Ravensden: the Iron Age hillfort contains a medieval moated site with a smaller moat within it. To its south lie the rifle butts used by the Highland Division in 1914–15.

Like other sites lying along the corridor of the Icknield Way, Puddlehill, to the north of Houghton Regis, was a small settlement with a cluster of roundhouses surrounded by a protective bank and ditch, probably designed more to keep stock safe from predators than to defend against hostile neighbours. At Fairfield Park, the earlier settlement was reworked sometime in the fifth to fourth centuries BC to become a much larger village of up to forty roundhouses sprawling along a low ridge and possibly surrounded by a double rampart and ditch. Another site where evidence of Iron Age occupation has been found is Bury Hill Camp, Thurleigh, later the site of a Norman castle. At Odell, two circular timber buildings inside a fence, dating from the time before the Roman invasion, were in occupation into the fourth century AD, but the site was then abandoned for 200 years or more.

The late Iron Age saw a move into the counties of the East Midlands by the Catuvellauni, who expanded into previously settled areas but brought an abrupt transition into enlarged settlements, evidenced by the distribution of coinage. These settlements consisted of larger clusters of roundhouses contained within ramparts and ditches, as have been investigated at Kempston, fully excavated at Odell and made visible by aerial photography at Wyboston.

Linear Dykes

Apart from hillforts, the other characteristic Iron Age defensive structure is the linear dyke or rampart, often employed to define tribal boundaries. Lying between Warden Hill and the A6 road out of Luton, and overlaying an earlier ditched area of unknown purpose, Dray's Ditches, were dug *c.* 500 BC, at right-angles to the Icknield Way. This dyke appears to represent the south-western boundary of the Catuvellauni, a tribe whose centres of power lay over the Hertfordshire border at Wheathamstead and St Albans. The most visible remnant of the dyke's former length of 1,100 yards (1 km) can be seen south of the clubhouse of the South Bedfordshire golf club. The bank still stands about 4 feet (1.25 metres) high. The dyke originally comprised a double bank and three V-shaped ditches, each 6 feet (1.8 metres) deep and 15 feet (4.6 metres) wide. Between the central and southern of these three ditches were located the post-holes of a double palisade joined at regular intervals by tie-beams.

Historians are divided over the provenance of Grim's Ditch, which appears to consist of isolated stretches of dyke between Oxfordshire and the eastern end of the Chilterns. While there is certainty that Dray's Ditches were dug in the Iron Age, opinion is split as to whether Grim's Ditch has a similar origin or belongs to the Anglo-Saxon period. Just as hazy are ideas about its purpose: boundary or defence? And if its purpose related to defence, was it defending London against the hostile intentions of those to its north or was it seeking to hold those stroppy Londoners at bay? Although it is clear that though Grim's Ditch represents a discontinuous feature, there is little agreement as to whether all the separate lengths are, in fact, parts of the same whole. Having said all that, there are two stretches of dyke near Whipsnade and Dunstable, which have been identified by at least one writer as integral to Grim's Ditch. Both sections are cut by Roman roads that would irrefutably place them in the Iron Age. The proponent of this theory, J. Dyer, adheres to the single monument theory, so, for him, Grim's Ditch is a singular Iron Age structure. However, recent excavations have cast doubt on this interpretation, generally supporting the notion of unrelated lengths of dyke marking agricultural boundaries, but most likely all still emanating from Iron Age times.

The Romans in Bedfordshire

Although Watling Street defined the western frontier of Roman penetration while they began to consolidate their invasion of Britain, there are no Roman military remains in the county. In this region formerly ruled by the Catuvellauni, farmsteads occupied by small extended family groups had been established prior to the invasion and continued to thrive afterwards. The Romans developed St Albans into the important town of *Verulamium*, which would become a target during Boudicca's revolt in AD 60. Although she appears to have caused little material damage to property in the county, it is possible that the occupants of the Dunstable area may have witnessed the end of her rampage. While material evidence for her final battle is lacking, there have been several theories as to its location. One scenario sees Paulinus with the 14th Legion, returning south from his successful campaign against the Druids on Anglesey, meeting the Iceni advancing up Watling Street. Another, based on archaeological evidence of the burning at Silchester, sets the confrontation in the Kennet valley, west of Silchester. William Foot has recently suggested that Paulinus prepared a trap on the Icknield Way, catching Boudicca's army on its triumphant but wearied return to Norfolk, citing a corridor between Great Chishill and Heydon in Cambridgeshire as a possible pinch-point. A fourth suggestion is that of Barry Horne, which has Boudicca's army of up to 40,000 Iceni warriors, leaving St Albans in ruins, and striking out north up Watling Street. However, possibly strung out along a 4-mile (6.4-km) stretch of road, which cuts through the Chilterns at this point, they would have been vulnerable were they to meet the army of Paulinus marching south to prevent them gaining the junction with the Icknield Way. Despite lacking the evidence of

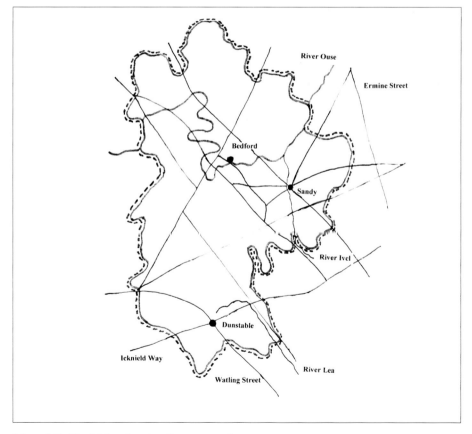

Map of Bedfordshire showing Roman roads.

archaeological finds to support this thesis, he nevertheless stands by his conviction that Boudicca met her end in the fields a mile or so to the south-east of Dunstable.

The preamble to *Wessex Archaeology*'s report on its excavation of the Roman villa at Colworth Science Park (2009) highlights the absence of signs of conflict right across Roman Bedfordshire, pointing out the rewards to be gained from the production of food for the local populace as well as for the legions. One aspect of this continuity related to the status of the wealthy families of the Iron Age who may have managed to retain their position under Rome, another factor encouraging stability. It suggests that there may have been a local administrative centre at Sandy, a Roman settlement on the road from Godmanchester to St Albans, which apparently developed directly from an Iron Age settlement rather than via a Roman military installation. It stretches southwards down both sides of the River Ivel and the Roman road to Biggleswade, and on to Baldock, an alternative route to Ermine Street. Another area of Romano-British settlement lay between the River Ouse and the Roman road, which ran west from Sandy. Bedfordshire, therefore, may be seen as a land of comfortable villas and farmsteads, rather than rugged fortresses. As an analogue of the Roman forts higher up Watling Street at major crossing points such as High Cross where the Fosse Way meets Watling Street, the existence of a fort could quite plausibly be inferred at Dunstable (*Durocobrivae*). Here, Watling Street and the Icknield Way cross, at a point halfway between St Albans (*Verulamium*) in Hertfordshire to the south-east along Watling Street, and Fenny Stratford (*Magiovinium*) to the north-west. This settlement thrived from AD 50–350, with stone buildings, and served as a market for the produce of the surrounding farms, and for the exchange of imported goods. Some of the inhabitants must have done well out of this trade as, following the breakdown of the *Pax Romana*, hoards of coins were buried for safekeeping. Villas such as that at Totternhoe had been at the centres of large estates producing grain surpluses to feed the legions across the Empire. They were already declining by the end of the fourth century and would have no comparable importance after the Romans left. However, no evidence for a Roman fort has been found at Dunstable, although the outline of a possible Roman fort near Sandy, another perfectly feasible location, has been revealed by aerial photography. A further suggested Roman military site is Quince/Quint's Hill at Old Warden, which has been put forward as the site of a Roman watchtower. Other instances of Warden Hills, a name often assigned to lookout positions, are on the north-east edge of Luton, overlooking the junction of the Icknield Way with Watling Street; and at Everton, around 3 miles (4 km) or so north-east of Sandy, overlooking the Roman road to Godmanchester.

Anglo-Saxon Bedfordshire

For many people in Bedfordshire, the departure of the Romans made little difference to their lives. In Toddington, four of eight Romano-British sites examined continued in use after AD 400, and sites in Kempston have offered up evidence for continuity of occupation from Roman to late Saxon times. Subsequent occupations by Britons, Danes, or Anglo-Saxons seem not to have represented definable dominant influences on the pattern of settlement and cultivation that evolved in the county. Squatters took over a Roman villa at Totternhoe; there is evidence for a fifth-century settlement at Sandy; and a few 'ing' and 'ham' place-names exist in the main river valleys on land that had already been farmed for upwards of 2,000 years, and had now received the earliest Saxon settlers. Pots and other grave goods found in a pagan cemetery at Kempston are similar to those found in the graves of mercenary *foederati* outside York and Cambridge. The *foederati* originated as tribal warriors, usually from Saxony, who operated alongside the regular Roman Army in the last century of the Empire. Some remained in Britain after the legions had gone, in a similar role to today's private security companies. It has been suggested that Studham, on the Dunstable Downs, was a centre for breeding horses for the *foederati* cavalry. It is likely that Stotfold and Stodden could make similar claims. By 575, however, the whole of southern England had been colonised by the Saxons and Angles, and it is possible that Saxon incursions into Bedfordshire in the second half of the sixth century could, in effect, have been the result of a pincer movement, with incomers arriving from East Anglia via the Icknield Way, to link up with a similar move from the West Saxons entering from the south-west.

The *Anglo-Saxon Chronicles* record a battle in 571, fought at *Bedcanford* by Cuthwulf of Wessex. The king of Wessex at the time was Ceawlin who named a son Cutha or Cuthwulf, so the Cuthwulf of the battle might have been a member of the royal house. Although assigning the location of the battle to Bedford would be neat, place-name experts have pointed out that it would be wrong to do so. Slightly less speculative is the association of Lygeanburgh, one of the four places mentioned as being captured by Cuthwulf, with Limbury or Waulud's Bank.

Unlike many settlements that would become shire towns, Bedford had no Roman heritage, being named for a Saxon chief called Beda, who established his settlement in the eighth century at a ford of the River Great Ouse. Offa, king of Mercia, died in 796 at Offley near Hitchin, and his body was brought to Bedford to be buried in a chapel on the south bank of the river. His widow, Cynethryth, became abbess of the monastery at Bedford, whose charter is dated 796. Unfortunately, the chapel, and Offa's remains with it, was washed away when the river flooded. Over the ninth and tenth centuries, an artisan class developed alongside merchants and traders defining the settlement as a town, which would contain industrial premises producing pottery, metal-working, and textiles, housing, and shops.

Three years before Offa's death, the Danes or Vikings, referred to in *Chronicles* as 'the Force', a generic for invaders of Scandinavian origin, had commenced their raids on the north-east coast of England. By 835, to a background of warring

Anglo-Saxon kingdoms, the Danes had stepped up their raiding to the level of a full-scale invasion. Over the next sixty years, dominance teetered between Mercia and Wessex under the constant threat of Danish conquest. Battles were regularly fought with victories to be won by both sides, but the tide gradually turned in favour of the Danes who had occupied East Anglia; established a capital in York; defeated Northumbria; and, by 870, found only Wessex holding out against them. But after six years' campaigning, Alfred of Wessex had subdued the Danes and the negotiated Peace of Wedmore drew up new boundaries. The Danish leader Guthrum ruled what became the Danelaw, extending up the east side of the country; Wessex and Mercia were allied through marriage; and a period of peaceful co-existence lasted, with periodic interruptions until Alfred's death in 900. The boundary of the Danelaw ran along the Thames, up the River Lea to its source at Leagrave in the north-west corner of Luton, then in a straight line ensuring the inclusion of Bedford, and up the Ouse as far as Watling Street. Mercia retained an odd triangle of land between Luton, Bedford, and Stony Stratford, possibly to memorialise the former burial place of King Offa.

It has been suggested that Bedford was specifically retained by Alfred as of very definite strategic value on this frontier. Alfred's son-in-law, Aethelred of Mercia, was responsible for restoring the defences of London and Worcester, and it is possible that he also established Bedford as a *burh*. An area of Bedford was called Aldermanbury, and the only other application of this name is in London where it was associated with Aethelred. There are two, not necessarily mutually exclusive, suggestions for the limits of the northern *burh*. One theory, building on the evidence of an Anglo Saxon-period ditch excavated in Midland Road, posits an area bounded, on its northern side, by Lime Street and Lurke Lane. The other suggests a larger area, possibly a later development, taking in St Peter's church as part of its northern defences. Churches served just such an overtly defensive function at Oxford and Wareham. Thus, Bedford may have constituted an established fortified centre as an element of the defences of Wessex, prior to its subsequent occupation by the Danes. Whoever controlled it, Guthrum's East Anglia took Bedford as marking its western edge, separating his territory from the non-aligned Scandinavian settlers of the Midlands and, along with Cambridge and Huntingdon, defending the line of the River Ouse.

Edward, known as 'the Elder', Alfred's son and heir, in concert with his brother-in-law, Aethelred of Mercia, initially ratified a treaty in 905 with the Northumbrians and the Danish Host at a place recorded as Tiddingford, usually identified as Linslade. Responding to a flagrant breach of the treaty by the Northumbrians, Edward, having opportunistically routed a Danish army in 910, embarked on a mission, along with Aethelred, to regain the Danelaw. Over the next two years, Edward and Ethelfreda, his sister, and by now a widow, instituted a building programme of strategically sited *burhs*. These fortified centres had become the basis for defence, particularly under Alfred in Wessex. A *burh* was a fortified town or camp defended by earthen ramparts and deep ditches. The ramparts were topped by timber palisades and gateways were usually defended by wooden towers. Each *burh* was designed to be defended by the numbers of men available based on formulae, which determined the length of the perimeter, and defined the acreage that supplied the garrison. Bedford, as a potential *burh* of Alfred's build, conforms to this formula. Its defence perimeter would have needed a force of around 1,200 men to defend it. The Domesday survey of 1086 assessed Bedfordshire at 1,200 hides. These men constituted the *fyrd* or militia and were under an obligation to turn out when summoned.

In 914, Viking raids were launched from Northampton, penetrating as far south as Luton, but in 915, Edward captured the Danish *burh* of Bedford, receiving the submission of jarls from Bedford and Northampton. As a way of strengthening the defences, he ordered the digging of the King's Ditch, thus forming a southern *burh* on the south bank of the river, a technique he had previously applied at Hertford and Buckingham, and would later on carry out at Stamford and Nottingham. Several lengths of this ditch survive, with traces found at Bedford College, reported in *South Midlands Archaeology* 10. This double *burh* afforded the garrison control of the river crossing of the Ouse and ensured that the Viking longships were denied passage. Bedford up until the tenth and eleventh centuries was easily approachable by the Viking boats with their shallow draught of only 2 feet (60 cm), so a bridge supported by fortified areas on each bank effectively limited invaders' movements. The southern *burh* was more than merely a fortified bridgehead as it would have had three gates through which streets lined with domestic buildings converged on the bridge. A further element in Edward's strategy was borrowed from the Franks. In 890, Odo, the leader of the West Franks, had provided a defeated Danish Army with ships in order to export the menace to England. Edward now found himself in a position to return the compliment by assisting the Bedford Jarl Thurcytel to depart for Francia with his people. Edward's *burh* at Bedford now conformed to the principles developed by his father in Wessex. It had a defended perimeter of 250–350 poles (1,375–1,935 yards). This perimeter was assessed on the basis of the 'hide', which, depending on the quality of the land, represented that land necessary to support a man and his dependants, anything between 60 and 120 acres (24 and 48 ha). Each pole (5.5 yards or 5 metres) would be defended by four men, each responsible for just over 4 linear feet (1.25 metres). If we assume that Bedford's agricultural hinterland was of average quality, an area of 90,000–126,000 acres (36,000–50,000 ha) or 140–197 square miles (224–315 square km) would generate the 1,000–1,400 men necessary for its garrison. Edward also, around this time, constructed a *burh* at the unidentified *Wigingamere*, suggested as Old Linslade, one of several new sites designed to protect Watling Street. The notion that the inhabitants of Wessex and Mercia enthusiastically welcomed the *burhs* with their attendant commitments to construct, garrison, and defend them has been greatly overplayed within the context of Alfred as a 'national' leader. Asser records people's reluctance and the need to cajole, instruct, urge, and command, finally resorting to sanctions and chastisement; that was necessary to get the ealdormen, bishops, nobles, thegns, and reeves on side. The 'official' *burhs* are mainly mentioned in the various *Chronicles* but others may have existed, noted by the survival of the word 'bury' in place-names. Numerous examples survive including Stanford Bury and Ickwell Bury both near Southill; Bury End, near Stagsden, near a moated site; Bury Leys Farm and Bury Farms near Houghton Conquest; Medbury Farm, Elstow; Apsley Bury Farm and Shillington Bury; and Newbury Farm and Gagmansbury Farm, both in Silsoe, associated with moated sites.

Only in 942 was there any mention of the 'Five Boroughs' as a significant entity, so there appear to be few reasons for not regarding Northampton and Bedford as warranting equal importance as sometime *burhs* of the Danelaw, since they share common criteria: a strategic location on a river; those urban characteristics that relate to commerce and industry; and the provision of defensive features. These are just those qualifying criteria that were applied to York, Lincoln, Derby, Nottingham, and Stamford. Additionally, both developed into shire towns, which Stamford did not.

In 917, a renewed threat arose with a Danish Host advancing westward up the Great Ouse from Huntingdon, and establishing a fortress at Tempsford, where the rivers Great Ouse and Izel meet, using it as a springboard for an attack on Bedford. This was repulsed by the *fyrd*, but in order to relieve pressure on *Wigingamere*, which was also under siege, Edward gathered an army and marched on Tempsford, where the fort was taken, the Danish leaders were killed, and their warriors perished or became prisoners. The Danish *burh* at Huntingdon was also taken by Edward's troops and its defences repaired. By 921, the Vikings had abandoned Huntingdon entirely as a wintering camp and had developed Tempsford for that purpose. Gannocks Castle at Tempsford is a medieval fortified manor house site, built close to the site of that former Danish camp. Nearby at Willington, 'Danes Camp', despite its name and evocative publicity featuring Vikings, is a medieval moated site containing the foundations of buildings. What are sometimes described as docking facilities alongside the river are most probably medieval fishponds. Wintering sites for the Viking fleets such as Tempsford usually consisted of a defensible D-shaped enclosure backing on to the riverbank. The ships would be beached for the winter and their crews would erect timber huts for domestic use and for the necessary facilities, such as smithies, necessary for maintaining the ships. Other reputed Danish camps have been attributed to Arlesey, Eaton Bray, and a mysterious earthwork between the Ouse and the A421 south of Howbury Hall and marked, somewhat imaginatively, on an eighteenth-century map as a Roman amphitheatre.

Edward's successes in unifying the major part of England under his kingship were consolidated by Aethelstan through the 920s and 930s, and the fall of Viking York in 954 brought a period of relative peace. However, that peace would not last, and

Bedford as a fortified centre would, several times, come under attack again over the succeeding decades. Intensive Viking raids picked up again in 980, culminating in a full-scale invasion in 992. In 1010, the Force ravaged southern England, and Bedford was destroyed, with the whole county under Danish rule by the end of the next year. In 1013, Swein, king of Denmark, landed and secured the whole of England, being universally recognised as king. The Anglo-Saxons put up a spirited resistance under Aethelred against Swein's son, Cnut, and Bedford was sacked again in 1016 during the ensuing fighting. In the end, it was agreed that Aethelred's son, Edmund, would rule England south of the Thames, while Cnut ruled the rest, but with Edmund's premature death, Cnut took over the whole kingdom.

It was the *burh*, the derivation of the words 'bury', 'burgh', and 'borough' in British place-names, which provided the basis for territorial and communal defence in these times. Edward the Elder added nineteen *burhs* between the Thames and the Mersey, and his sister established a further ten, all these complementing the work of their father in Wessex, and of Offa in Mercia. There were, however, two other elements of national defence on land. The first was the use of a network of beacons in the 890s linking the Thames Valley and the Chilterns with the south coast, and many of these can be inferred from place-names. The use of 'Warden' to mean lookout and hill, for instance, as well as 'Tot', meaning hillock or tump, were widespread. Warden Hill, outside Luton, and Old Warden with, in Quince Hill, the legend of a former use as a lookout or signal station, may provide us with examples in Bedfordshire. The second element was the private residence of the *thegn*. Kempston Manor is known to have been held by Tostig, banished by Edward the Confessor in 1065. Excavations have found evidence of occupation in Saxon times signified by the post-holes and sill beam slots of three timber buildings laid out to standard Saxon proportions. The largest one measures around 40 by 16 feet (12 by 5 metres) and pottery finds point to an occupation date in the tenth or eleventh centuries. One of the qualifications for *thegn*-hood was the possession of a (generally) timber hall surrounded by a 'hedge' or defensible wall, and a *burhgeat*. This last could be a belfry or tower, and would, in some instances, be the tower of a church, closely associated with the *thegn*'s hall, and often within the hedge. There are a number of Anglo-Saxon church towers in the county that may have figured in this scenario. Such towers are also known to have played a part in lordly ritual. Across the country, a number of Anglo-Saxon church towers have first-floor doorways either opening out to the field or inwards to the nave or chancel, and it is thought that these enabled the *thegn* to assert his dominance by showing himself to his people, a tradition maintained to this day, if only symbolically, from the balcony of Buckingham Palace. The Anglo-Saxon church of St Peter de Merton, in Bedford, originally had a west tower, the present chancel representing the original nave. This tower retains its long-and-short work quoins on the outer, western face, now visible within the nave. It has an interior doorway, also still visible, in its east wall at first-floor level, originally giving access to an internal timber platform. The tower is now a crossing tower with the later nave to its west, and its twin bell openings are 1850 copies within a Victorian restoration. St Thomas's, at Clapham, has a Saxon west tower, 85 feet (26 metres) in height, its top storey added post-Conquest. Above the tower arch is a triangle-headed doorway, which may possibly have afforded the only access to the tower with its 4-foot-thick (1.2-metre-thick) walls. In the tenth century, the inhabitants of Clapham lived on the very edge of the Danelaw and may well have felt it advisable to build a defensive element into their church. Similarly, All Saints' church at Turvey has an Anglo-Saxon nave and a tower with an eastern door into the nave at first-floor level, and St Mary's, at Stevington, has an Anglo-Saxon west tower with a blocked doorway over the tower arch, and an internal south door into the former *porticus*. This was a built-up porch, a feature that in churches of this period might sometimes be wrapped around the west end of tower and nave. At St Peter's, Thurleigh, a southern side door led into another former *porticus* linked to its Anglo-Danish west tower. St Mary's, Bedford, is a further church with blocked Anglo-Saxon openings in its crossing tower, probably dating from *c*. 1050. Here, an external stair accessed the tower at first-floor level through a round-headed doorway, set where the eastern face of the south transept meets the junction of the tower and chancel. The much-expanded St Mary's, Carlton, started life as a two-cell Saxon church with a west tower. A late Saxon minster has been inferred at Flitton, and such sites were often associated with royal manors. At least one of these towers, at St Peter de Merton, would later fulfil a significant function in the defences of Bedford.

St Mary's Church, Bedford, the doorway into the Saxon tower.

Clapham church has a Saxon tower with defensive features and a slightly later top storey.

2

Bedfordshire in the Medieval Period, 1066–1500

At the time of the Norman invasion and conquest, Bedfordshire was characterised by a patchwork of small estates and would for the most part remain so throughout the medieval period. The barony of one Norman beneficiary, Nigel d'Albini of Cainhoe, took in the lands of twenty-five Saxon *thegns*; Bedford itself had been earlier assessed at 50 hides, which translated into ten knights' fees; and over 90 per cent of the county's population were serfs or other categories of non-free men. Coupled with an absence of large royal or monastic holdings, these factors allowed plenty of scope for small estates to develop. This may account for what appears to be a relatively high density of defensible sites in the county. The number of sites definable as 'castles' in the two centuries following the Conquest was twenty-three, an extremely high density in a small county a long way from either the coast or land borders. There were already a number of semi-defensible moated homesteads marking the beginnings of what would become a positive rash of such structures over the next few centuries. Almost 300 moated sites have been identified across the county, again, the highest density in the country, serving hundreds of smallish manorial holdings. Although a number of important thoroughfares crossed the county, apart from Bedford itself, where a royal castle was built in the years after the Conquest, there were few obvious strategic points to be secured. Bedfordshire, however, was clearly a successful place since it was one of the two most rapidly expanding counties with a population increase of 300–400 per cent between 1086 and 1275. In 1297, there were 122 taxpayers in Dunstable and 100 in Bedford. It is estimated that by 1500, there were 300–400 manors in Bedfordshire.

Early Castles in Bedfordshire

All the county's early castles began life as structures of earth and timber, and most of them never achieved the dignity of masonry. As we have seen, both Anglo-Saxon and Danish landowners had built hall complexes surrounded by banks, palisades, and ditches, so the imposition of Norman castles on to the landscape was not in itself entirely alien to the subject population. What the castle represented, however, might have been perceived as an unwelcome symbol of foreign domination. It was usual for Norman castles to take one of two common forms. The first was the motte and bailey consisting of a mound of earth surmounted by a stockade enclosing a timber tower. The attached courtyard or bailey contained the domestic buildings of hall, kitchen, chapel, barns, stables, workshops, and forge. The alternative to this was the ringwork, a flat platform surrounded by a bank and ditch, and large enough to accommodate the main buildings of the castle. There might additionally, as with the motte, be one or more baileys attached. These castles served a whole range of functions: defensible lordly residence; administrative centre and estate office; court of justice; and symbol of lordly power. As well as tactical considerations, an element of local fashion might dictate which model was chosen. Across the country, there were around twice as many mottes as ringworks, the motte providing greater dominance, while the ringwork afforded more comfort.

In Bedford, Ralph de Taillebois, the new Norman lord, chose a motte, with which he might overawe the townsfolk, with another to the town's east at Risinghoe, close to the Ouse. Similarly, d'Albini raised a motte at Cainhoe, as did Walter de Wahull at Odell and Totternhoe, his brother, Hugh the Fleming, at Thurleigh, Albert de Loring (or Lorrain) at Chalgrave, and Geoffrey de Trailly at Yielden. Each of these eight mottes had between one and three associated baileys, not all contemporaneous with their mottes. Even though these mottes all shared similar principles, both of design and construction, they were very different in several respects. It is almost certain that the motte at Bedford had masonry fortifications from an early date, probably effected by Hugh de Beauchamp who had married the daughter of de Taillebois and was in possession of the castle by 1087. The most likely form would have been a shell-wall around the edge of the motte-top. This might either have enclosed an original timber tower, its replacement in stone, or else pentice buildings ranged around the inside of the wall with a central open courtyard. The inner bailey may also have been walled in stone by the beginning of the twelfth century. The motte at Cainhoe was 30 feet (9 metres) in height with a diameter across its flat top of 33 feet (10 metres), sufficient area to accommodate a substantial tower and an encircling stockade. Even after the erosion of centuries, Cainhoe's motte retains a very dominant aspect. In contrast, Chalgrave, destroyed for agricultural development, was always very low. In its first form, built on top of an earlier manor, it supported a timber structure, 33 feet (10 metres) square. Such a residential tower could have been constructed in one of several ways. It could have been built on stone or timber foundations, or it could have sat on timber posts, which would either have been sunk into the motte, or had the motte built up around them. In all cases, the earth from the surrounding ditch was used to form the motte, sometimes supplementing a natural hillock. Depending on the material involved, the motte might need to be layered with clay or rock, or to be revetted with stone or timber. Access could be via a causeway across the ditch, or more often by a flying bridge supported on posts. If the defences of the bailey joined up with those of the motte, then access might be via steps on the wall-walk of the palisade ascending the motte. Once it had settled, a more permanent structure might be built on the summit, but in Bedfordshire, only at Bedford is the motte known to have acquired a stone keep at a later date, although at Totternhoe and Yielden there are indications that a stone structure might have occupied the motte top. Odell Castle, of which barely a trace remains, appears to have consisted of an oval motte with a rectangular bailey. Masonry ruins were recorded by Leland round about 1540, and the motte is reported to have been revetted in stone. The castle was obliterated when a new house was built. Just as homes have always been altered or extended over the years, castles were no exception. At Chalgrave, towards the end of the twelfth century, the original timber tower was dismantled, the motte extended, and a new single-storey building constructed. This, in turn would be abandoned for a more convenient site nearby.

There are far fewer ringworks in Bedfordshire. At Quince Hill, Old Warden, only the southern defences of William Speke's castle survive, suggesting that the ringwork was about 260 feet (80 metres) across, with a high bank inside a deep and wide ditch. There is an outer bank and ditch, pierced by an entrance, possibly representing a small bailey or even a barbican. Renhold, or Howbury, is a ringwork of unknown date, with an interior space around 130 feet (40 metres) across. Ridgmont Castle, Segenhoe, may have been built by Walter de Wahul. It was a ringwork, 150 feet (45 metres) in diameter, of which only two vestiges of bank remain, standing 400 feet (122 metres) above sea-level. On one side lay a bailey, while a wide bank and ditch defended the other. Seymour's Mount at Steppingley has been put forward as another possible ringwork on a spur cut off by a ditch. At least two sites previously thought to have been ringwork castles— Etonbury at Arlesey and Palace Yard at Roxton—have since been reassigned as later moated sites.

The provision, size, and shape of baileys differed for reasons to do with situation and importance. Totternhoe occupies the flat top of a promontory, so a kidney-shaped inner bailey and a second, smaller one are both wrapped around the base of the motte. A much longer outer bailey extends toward the end of the spur, terminating in a strong bank and ditch. At Yielden, a bailey was built to the south and west of the motte and was apparently walled in stone. At a later date, another bailey was added to the north of the motte. The western ditch was probably fed by the river. Cainhoe's three baileys surround the motte almost completely and are demarcated by high banks and deep ditches. In contrast to these three sites with dominant earthwork features is Chalgrave, with an insignificant bank and ditch enclosing the bailey on the east, and on the west, a ditch 15 feet (4.7 metres) in width, but only 4 feet (1.1 metres) deep. Bedford Castle, according to

Cainhoe Castle, the motte seen across the ramparts of the inner bailey.

Yielden Castle, the motte viewed from the north looking across one of the outer enclosures.

a recent reconstruction based on excavated evidence, had two powerful baileys, one fronting the riverbank, and the other behind it, occupying the angle of the old *burh*. Opposition to the Norman conquerors continued well into the twelfth century. Dunstable is supposed to memorialise Thomas Dun, a notorious criminal gang leader in the Robin Hood tradition. His men would terrorise travellers along Watling Street and the Icknield Way before disappearing into the chalk caverns of the Chilterns. He was eventually captured and, so the story goes, clinically dismembered by the troops of Henry I.

Those earth and timber models continued in use for over a century after the Conquest and examples would continue to be constructed during the reign of Stephen (1135–54), usually, if misleadingly, remembered as the Anarchy. When Henry I died, Matilda, or Maud, his daughter and appointed heiress, despite having the sworn support of the country's nobility, found herself opposed by her cousin, Stephen. For nearly twenty years, periods of intermittent civil war saw localised breakdowns of law and order and outbreaks of actual warfare, which often provided opportunities for the exploitation of the populace by armed gangs. Both Stephen and Matilda sought to gain allies by grants of land. King Stephen's allies, the Beaumont twins, Waleran and Robert, had a brother, Hugh, who had previously missed out on sharing his brothers' inheritance in 1118. When Simon de Beauchamp, castellan of Bedford Castle, died in 1137 leaving only his young daughter to inherit, Hugh le Poer seized his opportunity. He became betrothed to Simon's daughter and was granted Bedford Castle by Stephen. However, Simon's nephew, Miles de Beauchamp objected, and his resistance provoked an unsuccessful assault by the king and a long siege by Hugh. In December 1137, Stephen brought siege engines to beat down the castle's defences, but the strength of the stone walls, especially the keep on the motte, described as 'unshakable', proved too difficult to overcome, and Stephen moved northwards to meet a Scottish threat, leaving his troops to starve the garrison into surrender, an unduly long process where the castle under siege was well provisioned. Eventually, an intervention by Stephen's brother, Bishop Henry of Winchester, brought about a settlement that ousted Miles. Later on, he returned and evicted the Beaumonts, retaining the castle for his descendants. Right through the reign of Stephen, Bedford was one of a handful of places that continued to mint all four issues of Stephen's coinage, and the area is one in which significant hoards of coins have been uncovered with peak periods reflecting the uncertainties of the 1060s after the Conquest and the 1140s.

The castle at Bedford saw further action during this period of unrest, when it was captured in 1146 by Stephen and the recently reconciled earl of Chester. This most probably involved another siege and assault as the word 'manfully' was applied to the earl's actions, intending, presumably, to impress his new master. Seven years later, Henry of Anjou, Matilda's son, the future Henry II, sought refuge in Bedford Castle, and would later deprive the Beauchamps of their custodianship. Meppershall Castle appears to be one of those fortresses that might have been erected during this time. William de Meppershall declared for Matilda in 1135, and it may have undergone a siege by Stephen who was on his way to besiege Bedford Castle. Meppershall consisted of a motte and two baileys in line, and would appear to have been inhabited only briefly as its owners moved to a moated site adjacent to the church. Walter de Wahul, lord of Odell, was described as an 'invader of Ramsey Abbey' by the archbishop of Canterbury. This may refer to an episode in 1142 when Geoffrey de Mandeville, earl of Essex, who had fallen out with King Stephen, saw an opening when the abbot had been dismissed. This power vacuum allowed him to seize Ramsey Abbey near Huntingdon and fortify it as one of his castles guarding his base at Ely, possibly aided by Wahul. Walter's son, Simon, also backed the young king in 1172 when he rebelled against his father, Henry II, and was taken prisoner. Robert de Wauderi, a mercenary captain employed by King Stephen, was granted Luton where he built a castle in 1139. It appears to have been of the motte and bailey design, with the motte possibly surviving into the nineteenth century as Holly Lodge, but only reappearing during building operations, first in 1963, and then again in 2005. The castle occupied an area of around 2½ acres or 1 hectare measuring a very generous 375 by 290 feet (115 by 90 metres). The extent of the motte was defined by a V-shaped ditch, 14 feet (4.5 metres) wide and 7 feet (2.3 metres) deep. This ditch would appear to have been rapidly backfilled with substantial quantities of chalk rubble after only a short period of occupation, possibly indicating deliberate slighting after the succession of Henry II. It may be significant that de Wauderi chose a site some 200 yards south of the established manorial centre, which would be the site of a later castle. His chosen location was strategic in that it would dominate the town and overlook the road to London, but would also diplomatically avoid trespassing on a traditional royal manor. The whole site now lies under the bus station.

Other castles from this period include The Mount at Flitwick, a small motte and bailey; a similar structure at Podington; and the supposed mottes at Sutton known as John of Gaunt's Hill, and Warren Knoll at Tilsworth. At Cardington's Cotton End, a low motte in Exeter Wood is barely 6 feet (1.8 metres) high, 65 feet (20 metres) in diameter, and surrounded by a ditch. It appears to date from the late eleventh or early twelfth centuries and belonged to the Beauchamps. Old Warden Castle, across the river from Biggleswade has, in recent times, only appeared as a crop mark, observed from the air by the Cambridge Air Survey in 1954. It occupied a gravel island, surrounded by low-lying land liable to flood, with the river on the eastern side and a stream on the west. Two circular, concentric ditches, 150 feet (45 metres) in diameter, enclose a low, mounded platform, signifying a ringwork rather than a motte. It may date from the twelfth century, probably being built by Alexander, bishop of Lincoln, in defiance of King Stephen following a difference of opinion. The ringwork and its two associated baileys all carried timber defences and domestic structures, and evidence of deliberate burning suggests that the castle was destroyed either during Stephen's reign, or as the result of Henry II's policy of eradicating such fortresses lacking his seal of approval. At Toddington, the large, flat-topped motte of the castle survives, but its associated bailey has disappeared beneath encroaching farm buildings. More substantial than many of the other castles of this period (early to mid-twelfth century), it probably existed well into the next century as its owner was recorded as living in a moated manor nearby by 1251, and the castle had become a rabbit warren. Although it is convenient to assign any slight earthwork of the twelfth century to the period of unrest under Stephen, without specific hard evidence from documents or excavation, this is impossible to verify.

Henry II had reasserted his right to Bedford Castle as a royal possession during the 1160s, but there is little evidence of royal interest in this period. In one of the very few writs issued by the young king in around 1170, the reeves and burgesses of Bedford were warned against molesting people attending the fair mounted by the monks of Elstow abbey. Other tensions between the secular and church authorities were also present in Bedford. When a canon of St Paul's was accused of murder by a civil authority, Thomas à Becket, archbishop of Canterbury, and already involved in similar disputes with Henry II, objected to his undergoing a civil trial. He permitted him to be tried and acquitted by the ecclesiastical court in Lincoln. The canon was, however, subsequently tried at the Assizes, found guilty, and deprived of two years' income. Such cases, so clearly defining the conflict between King Henry II and his archbishop, were at the root of Becket's troubles. Having been forbidden to leave the country by the king, Becket spent some time in hiding at Chicksands Priory.

It would appear that at Bedford Castle, only minimal work to maintain or strengthen the defences was financed by the royal exchequer during this period of nominal royal tenure. At some time, possibly by the 1180s, the Beauchamps, in the person of Simon, nephew of Miles, had resumed their occupation of the castle and may have invested considerably more in the buildings. Simon was succeeded by his nephew, William, who fought in Ireland in 1210 and in France in 1214, but John's mismanagement of the French campaign was one of the contributory factors that, along with his refusal to respect the provisions of *Magna Carta*, alienated many of the barons. By 1215, William de Beauchamp was in rebellion against King John, and Bedford Castle became a meeting place for his fellow rebels. This attracted the attention of King John who despatched Fawkes (or Falco, or Falkes) de Breaute to seize the castle. After only a week, Fawkes prevailed and, as a reward, was made custodian of the castle and sheriff of Bedfordshire. The rebel barons who had sought to replace John with the dauphin of France, were defeated at Lincoln in May 1217, where William de Beauchamp was captured. On their retreat south, the survivors stopped off in Dunstable, damaging the church, and extorting 200 Marks from the town.

Fawkes de Breaute has been described as a mercenary, one of King John's 'alien' captains, denounced by the barons, and as a tyrannical enforcer of the king's will. Contemporary chronicles report his rapacious exploits and his high-handed treatment of anyone who crossed him. He attacked the abbeys of St Albans and Warden in 1217 for their accommodation with the Dauphin Louis. A dispute with the monks of Warden Abbey over property resulted in the death of one monk, serious injuries to several others, and the abduction of thirty more who were dragged through the mud and imprisoned in Bedford Castle. He secured his hold on the area by raising castles at Eaton Bray and at Luton. In 1221, he had acquired the manor of Luton, securing an area of 150 acres (60 ha) to the south of St Mary's church for his castle, on a different site from that used by de Wauderi eighty years earlier, and displacing twenty houses. In order to fill his impressive moat, 40 feet (12 metres) wide and 10 feet (3 metres) deep, he dammed the Lea. This caused problems for his neighbour, the abbot of St Albans, whose mill stopped working and whose cornfields were flooded. De Breaute seemed quite untroubled by this, expressing his satisfaction with the abbot's discomfort. The castle appears to have consisted of a rectangular area bounded by a rampart and wet moat, and excavations have revealed the post-holes of a rectangular timber-framed building measuring 39 feet (12 metres) by 11 feet (3.3 metres) on the site. Following de Breaute's exile in 1227, the castle's defences were dismantled but the building itself may have survived as a courthouse.

Although it is also possible to see de Breaute as a loyal, if ruthless, servant of the crown, a combination of rivalry between Henry III's ministers; aristocratic snobbery regarding his base birth and lack of inherited wealth; his reputation for savagery and corruption; his perceived attempt to start a rebellion against the king; and his snub in not attending a royal consultation finally precipitated his fall from favour in 1224. An attempt to bring back into royal control those castles delegated to his supporters by King John roused anger among those castellans who regarded themselves as loyal servants of the crown, especially during the minority of Henry III. Refusing to give up Bedford Castle, de Breaute was faced with trumped up charges of breach of the peace, of which he was found guilty and fined heavily. Meanwhile, his brother, William, had rashly rushed an armed band to Dunstable to abduct the three royal justices concerned in order to convey them for imprisonment in Bedford Castle. Two escaped but Henry of Braybrooke, who had dismissed his brother's defence, was taken. The scene was now set for one of the longest sieges of medieval England, and one which would produce some of the most graphic descriptions of the times.

During his time in Bedford, de Breaute had considerably strengthened the defences of the castle, which he had made his main base. The basic layout of the Beauchamp's castle had been enhanced by masonry towers on the stone walls of both inner and outer baileys. The keep on its mound appeared even more impregnable than it had previously and wet moats, paved and lined in stone, and surrounding both baileys, were fed by the river. A strong gatehouse and barbican towards the town, and a postern on the riverside frontage, would allow sallies and make possible resupply by boat. A contemporary depiction of the castle shows sockets around the tops of the towers, possibly to carry brattices, overhanging timber platforms that allowed the defenders to dominate the bases of the walls and so discourage under-mining. The castle, commanded by William de Breaute, was strongly garrisoned by a dozen knights and up to seventy men-at-arms, and the castle was equipped with artillery firing stone balls and oversized crossbow-bolts.

In June 1224, Henry III brought his army to invest Bedford Castle, and it was clear that the king, having postponed an expedition to France to be there, meant business. He had gathered a force of 3,000 men including siege engineers, crossbowmen, and miners from the Forest of Dean. Materials, provisions, and craftsmen were summoned from all over the country, and huge amounts of weapons and munitions were stockpiled. Timber was purchased from Warden Abbey to construct on site the great siege engines it was so difficult to transport. The siege began with an exchange of fire from the catapults and the besiegers gradually began to have an impact on the walls of the outer bailey. First a breach appeared in the barbican and then in the adjacent walls. With great loss of life, particularly to the attackers, the outer bailey fell, with the loss to the garrison, of livestock, grain, and materiel. Timber belfries or siege towers were brought up so that bowmen could fire down into the inner bailey, picking off anyone who broke cover. The miners, protected by a tortoise, an open shed on wheels, dug under the walls of the inner bailey, supporting their excavations with pit-props that, when set alight, brought the wall crashing down. Once this technique was applied to the keep, the defenders were forced to surrender after a siege lasting two months. Early in the siege, Henry had vowed to hang the garrison and the de Breaute brothers had all been excommunicated by the Pope. As the last of the defenders emerged from the ruins, the king's orders would be carried out. In fact, it is possible that very few of them were hanged. Certainly William de Breaute and some of his fellow defenders were, but two other brothers bought pardons and three supporters were pardoned provided they joined the Templars. In the royal army, over 200 men including six knights had been killed. Justice Braybrooke was released unharmed as were the ten royalist soldiers captured in an assault. The king ordered the immediate slighting of what remained upstanding of the castle. Fawkes de Breaute was induced to travel from Chester to face the music. He received absolution and a conditional pardon from the king, giving up all his lands and property. His wife divorced him saying she had been forced to marry him in the first place, and he was exiled to France in 1227 where he was persecuted by his enemies who held him responsible for the fate of the dauphin's men killed at Lincoln. This continued for two years before, allegedly, he was fed poisoned fish. Given that virtually all the chroniclers of these events were monks, and that abbeys had been the targets for much of the de Breautes' offensive behaviour,

Bedford Castle, the castle mound encased in modern masonry and given a gazebo.

Bedford Castle, the model that stands on the site today shows the view from the north toward the Ouse; it is based on investigations and informed conjecture and shows the keep, inner and outer gatehouses, domestic buildings, and mural towers.

then they were always going to get a bad press. It is likely that the castle at Luton was destroyed by order of Henry III around this time.

Once the de Breautes had been dealt with, Bedford Castle, or what was left of it, was handed back to William de Beauchamp. He would be allowed to rebuild a manor house out of the ruins but much subsequent development on the site was industrial rather than domestic or military. History would go some way to repeating itself as John de Beauchamp, lord of Bedford, was among the barons who supported the rebellion of Simon de Montfort. Three other rebel Bedfordshire knights were taken prisoner, but he was one of those unfortunates slaughtered in cold blood after the Battle of Evesham in 1258, marking the end of another chapter in the Barons' Wars.

With the demolition of Bedford, the county's only substantial masonry castle, the age of the early medieval castle came to an end. The insubstantial earthworks of the Anarchy had gone by the late 1100s; the owners of Chalgrave, Toddington, and Cainhoe had migrated to more spacious and comfortable sites nearby; Toddington and Tilsworth had become rabbit warrens; Risinghoe and Ridgmont are both referred to as 'old' in medieval documents implying disuse; Luton's second castle was destroyed in the 1220s; and Yielden's moats were turned into fishponds and nesting islands for wildfowl. Only Odell might have survived into Tudor times. When a new house was built in 1623, it appears to have incorporated medieval masonry, perhaps the twelfth-century revetment of the motte, and this may account for the great thickness of the walls in the basement on the south-west and north-west sides. But this house, too, has gone.

Blow's Down at Dunstable was one of those relatively few places in England permitted to hold tournaments during periods of calm when insecure kings felt they could trust their barons to gather without goading each other into rebellion. A tournament had been held in 1214, but further such events were banned in 1244 after Henry III suspected that rebellion was in the air. This ban was renewed through 1245, 1247, 1248, 1254, 1256, and 1264, only resuming when Edward I was present in 1273. The tournament scheduled for 1290 was abandoned, and three years later an armour-bearer was killed during a tournament. A rule was then introduced prohibiting anyone on foot from carrying weapons, apart from a small shield for protection against the horses, and in 1301, normal service was resumed. In 1309, Piers Gaveston, the hated favourite of Edward II was out of the country, still temporarily banished to Ireland, and the Dunstable tournament served as a cover for a large assembly of knights airing their grievances, possibly contributing to the petition demanding reform, which was submitted to parliament that summer. Many of the 240 knights assembled were prominent members of the nobility forming the opposition to the king, expressing distaste for his infatuation with Gaveston. Among them were Roger Damory and Hugh Despenser the Younger who would both succeed to the position of royal favourite. Probably as a direct result of this opportunity for subversion, in 1312 the ban was reintroduced by King

Edward and then extended to 1319, and the next year, a royal sergeant-at-arms was expressly appointed to arrest anyone attempting to organise tournaments.

In September 1326, Edward's mother, Isabella of France, and her ally and consort, Roger Mortimer, landed in England with an army of mercenaries. They linked up with Henry of Lancaster and the earl of Norfolk, Thomas of Brotherton, at Dunstable, causing the king to flee London. The next year, Edward was effectively deposed, shut away and ultimately murdered. Power now lay in the hands of Isabella and Mortimer, technically acting as regents for the fifteen-year-old Edward III. Henry of Lancaster had been accused of rebellion after he had joined up with Isabella's army and would only be cleared at an Inquisition held in Dunstable in 1329. Mortimer was generally hated by the nobility for his presumption and armed conflict had barely been avoided in Bedford in January 1329 when Henry of Lancaster submitted to arbitration but some of his compatriots were forced into exile. Mortimer employed the old formula of bread and circuses to deflect the hostility of his peers, and to conceal his grip on them from the young king. As a moratorium on tournaments was often a sign of a ruler's insecurity, by continuing to permit tournaments, Mortimer demonstrated confidence in his position. His round of tournaments climaxed at Dunstable in October 1329 when the newly-married seventeen-year-old Edward III, his mother, and her consort, Mortimer, attended. Edward was kitted out by his wife in sumptuously covered armour from her native Hainault, and took part in the jousting.

Edward III's famous love of chivalry meant that once he had disposed of Mortimer and was ruling in his own right, the tournaments would continue. In 1331, he jousted at Bedford, and held seven tournaments in 1334 to celebrate the victory over the Scots at Halidon Hill. At that held in Dunstable, eighty-nine of the 134 knights taking part were members of the royal household and would be accompanying the king on the Crécy campaign. In 1342, he fought incognito as a 'simple knight' at Dunstable where the Shrovetide tournament was held by Edward and Philippa to celebrate the betrothal of their three-year-old son, Lionel, to Elizabeth de Burgh. This event was not only marked by lavish expenditure in the jewellery and textile departments but, more perilously, featured the very last melee to be featured in an English tournament. The melee was a very entertaining but highly dangerous free-for-all, with the last knight standing taking the plaudits.

While knights used the tournament as a surrogate battle to gain attention, martial experience, and prize money, there was also more purposeful fighting to be done. The Hundred Years' War (1338–1453) brought new demands for military service. Fifty Bedfordshire squires worth more than £5 *per annum* were each required to provide one fully equipped archer for the royal army fighting in France. Many lords made their fortunes in the early campaigns of the war. Nigel (or Neil) Loring of Chalgrave fought at the sea-battle of Sluys, after which he was knighted by Edward III, and on mainland France at Crécy and Poitiers. In 1341, a tournament in his honour was held in Dunstable to celebrate those military achievements. He went on to serve with the duke of Lancaster in France and then undertook a diplomatic mission to Rome. In the service of Edward, the Black Prince, he fought at Crécy and, along with his patron, he was one of those twenty-six prominent warriors to be chosen as the king's Knights of the Round Table at Windsor Castle, becoming a Knight of the Garter in 1348. He was second in the retinue of the Black Prince during his time as prince of Aquitaine and fought beside him in 1356 at Poitiers, and at Najera. In the absence of any fighting going on in France in 1351, he fought with the Teutonic Knights in Prussia, retiring from military service in 1370. Between periods of official military activity, Sir Nigel had led one of the Free Companies, bands of otherwise redundant soldiery, which terrorised the French countryside as they burnt and pillaged at will. He was adopted by Sir Arthur Conan Doyle as the hero of his sanitised accounts of these ventures in books such as *Sir Nigel*, and its sequel *The White Company*. A benefactor of Dunstable Priory, he was rewarded for his royal service with land, armour, horses, agricultural produce, and mineral rights and received licence to enclose a deer park at Chalgrave in 1365. At the time, his manor, next to the church, was described as a substantial, probably timber-framed hall-house over a stone cellar, with numerous outbuildings all occupying a compound defended by a stout mud wall with a gatehouse.

The Social Context of Bedfordshire in the Later Middle Ages

Homicide figures for thirteenth-century Bedfordshire suggest a level twenty times higher than for the region today at 22 per 100,000 compared to 0.9 now. Most murders were the result of sudden disputes where the use of a weapon, usually a knife, would cause wounds that, in times of minimal medical treatment, would often prove fatal. Perpetrators tended to come from the higher ranks of the commonalty—servants, clerks or clergy, and tradesmen. Criminal gangs also operated such as that which invaded Honeydon in 1267, killing four people and seriously wounding as many more while robbing their houses and burning one down. The gang moved on to repeat their depredations in another village, managing to stay clear of any pursuit. Murders and other instances of violence were the most common crimes coming before the Justices of the Peace in the fourteenth century. Many of these crimes would now be described as aggravated burglary, as theft, particularly of livestock, was carried out by armed gangs using threats and actual violence to seize property.

Three major catastrophes would dominate the fourteenth century, bringing social dislocation and widespread insecurity. The first of these was the Little Ice Age, which brought consecutive years of crop failure and consequent famine in the early years of the century. The second was the Great Plague or, more commonly, the Black Death of 1349, which claimed the lives of up to half the population and a very precise fifty-four of the county's 123 clergy. Plague appears to have carried off the entire population of Cainhoe, including the lord of the manor and his son. Cainhoe is probably unique as an example of a community totally unable to recover from the Black Death, becoming deserted shortly after 1350, but other villages lost enough souls to make them barely viable. By the 1370s, stone was being removed from Cainhoe castle, and villages were put under pressure to give way to sheep pasture. The Cistercians of Warden Abbey had been granted pasture for 200 sheep, increased by a further 600 in 1205. They also accrued extensive woodlands with the right of felling the valuable timber and bringing the land into cultivation, but gained further woodland in the Forest of Huntingdon, which was managed for timber production. The abbey converted the village of Putnoe into a grange, exploiting the fluctuations in local populations, a process which accelerated. For others, the clearances came later, as when the village of Higham Gobion was depopulated for the running of sheep in the mid-fifteenth century. The third event was the Great Rebellion or Peasants' Revolt, an apparent misnomer as most of those in rebellion were from the merchant or artisan class. In 1381, a mob of townsmen attacked Dunstable Priory expressing mounting opposition to its hold over the town, and achieving the award of a new Charter by the Prior. Fortunately, only isolated instances of trouble occurred elsewhere in the county. Bedfordshire only ever contained relatively small settlements with few meriting the name of township, places large enough for trouble to be fomented. It has been estimated that by 1500, there were 300–400 manors in Bedfordshire, an average of three per parish, with an average size of 2,250 acres (900 ha).

As we have seen, it was down Watling Street that Paulinus marched his legionaries to bring Boudicca to battle, and it was this route that many armies took during the medieval period, causing brief, but often serious, disruption to the lives of those whose homes they despoiled. In 1326, Queen Isabella landed in Suffolk with an army of around 5,000, and chased Edward II to Gloucester via Dunstable; and Edward IV marched his army from Daventry to Dunstable and on to St Albans on Good Friday 1471, prior to the Battle of Barnet.

Town and Village Defences

Several of the earlier earthwork castles appear to have had village enclosures. The manorial earthworks at Etonbury, Arlesey with the river Ivel on their west, prior to their virtual destruction, had an extensive outer enclosure to the east. This had banks and ditches on two sides, and a stream on the fourth, enclosing an area measuring 400 by 200 yards (370 by 185 metres), and this may have contained the village. At Thurleigh, there was a very large outer bailey measuring 215 by 290 yards (200 by 270 metres) within which stood the church and, presumably, the village. A similar arrangement existed at Meppershall where the castle and later moated site, along with the church and manor house, all stand within a banked enclosure. Additionally, Cainhoe, Totternhoe, and Yielden have been suggested as castles whose outer earthworks enclosed settlements. The only defended town in the county was Bedford. Here, the two *burh* enclosures defined almost separate townships, each with church and market. While only banks and ditches surrounded these areas, the tower of St Peter de Merton's has been seen as having a defensive function, and the stone bridge linking the two halves of the town assumed a greater significance. The present bridge dates only from 1811, but its predecessor carried two gatehouses, one of them, the more northerly, serving as a chapel and a jail. The lack of a stone wall around the town is underlined by the complete absence from the records of the murage grants, which constituted enabling mechanisms for levying tolls to fund the construction of town defences.

Moated Sites

The major upheavals of the later Middle Ages, as we have seen, added to the general lawlessness caused by armed criminal gangs; by demobilised soldiers returning from the Hundred Years' War; and by rootless peasants turned out of depopulated villages. These factors together forced those who stayed put with something worth protecting to invest in security measures. The equivalent of today's gated enclave was the moated site. This was usually a raised earthen platform surrounded by a wet moat, crossed by a removable, timber bridge. Bedfordshire contains the highest density of moated sites of any county, with 297 known moats of which only twelve have been scheduled as Ancient Monuments. For such a small county, it has the fifth highest total in England, comparable to the much larger Lincolnshire. The greatest number of sites are found on the claylands, although moats can be found everywhere in the county. The moat in Tempsford Park has over twenty moated neighbours within a radius of 5 miles (8 km), lying on all types of soils. Clearly, landscapes providing well-drained, flat areas, with plentiful springs, streams, and rivers, and with soil which retains the water in ditches and pools, were exploited to a greater extent. Often dams and high banks were constructed to aid water retention. Moated platforms were most often rectangular but could come in all shapes and sizes, and were built right through the medieval period from the twelfth to the fifteenth centuries. Moats are predominantly found in villages, sometimes more than one where, as in much of Bedfordshire, there were multiple manors, but there are examples of isolated moats, some of them, as at Potsgrove, on high ground, remote from water sources, reliant on rainfall alone. Besides Bedfordshire's rectangular moats, there is a circular moat at Westoning; a pentagonal one at Cranfield; a parallelogram at Biscot; one of at least six sides at Ruxox Farm, Flitwick; moats within moats at Moggerhanger and Staploe; a moat inside a hillfort at Mowsbury; and a complex of moats at Gagmansbury Farm, Pulloxhill. There is almost as much variation in size as there is in shape: a square with sides of under 100 yards at Barton-le-Clay but another with sides over twice as long at Sharpenhoe;

Cotton End measures 215 by 110 yards (200 by 100 metres) and Ruxox measures over 325 yards (300 metres) across. Several explanations exist for the functions of moated sites. While not primarily dug with defence paramount, moats nevertheless conferred a significant element of defensibility. They would keep casual marauders at bay; protect the livestock from predators; and keep animals from straying. The moat would provide fish for the innumerable non-meat days required by religious rules; water for stock and industrial processes; and would drain the domestic and garden areas. There was also an element of social cachet to having a moat around a home, demonstrating status in the community.

Buildings on the moated platform would include a house, often of timber, but perhaps on stone foundations, containing a hall, open to the roof, and an adjoining solar block of family rooms. A kitchen would stand adjacent but separate to counter the risk of fire, along with all the other barns, stables, brewhouse, forge, stores, and so forth, the moat defining the nucleus of the manor. A manorial site in Tempsford Park had an aisled, timber-framed hall measuring 60 by 26 feet (18.5 by 8 metres), dating from the twelfth century with detached kitchen and workshop. A century on, and a moated complex, 108 by 75 yards (100 by 70 metres) developed, containing a new, more elaborate timber hall with a solar-range to one side and a service wing to the other. The new hall measured 29 by 21 feet (9 by 6.5 metres), with a two-storey block at one end with a parlour below a solar. At the opposite end of the hall was a kitchen. The walls were built on stone foundations with sill beams running between vertical posts lodged on stone pads, the whole strengthened with clay. The hall was roofed with tiles of coloured ceramic and graduated limestone slates, suggesting different roof-coverings, including thatch, for different parts of the building. Subsequent centuries added extensions. The Camps at Staploe shows evidence of building stone across the site suggesting that the hall, at least, might have been constructed in masonry.

At both Cainhoe and Meppershall, moated sites replaced the castle as a dwelling, affording more comfort and space than the cramped conditions of a motte and bailey castle. Moat Farm at Biscot, now swallowed up by Luton's suburbs, is a fourteenth-century house built of brick, flint, and local stone. The hall was originally open to the roof but has since been floored, and the timber roof dates to *c.* 1500. Calcutt Farm at Houghton Regis was owned by Dunstable Priory. Close to two tributaries of the River Ousel, the moats contained a late sixteenth-century timber-framed house. Not all moats contained buildings as, sometimes, the so-called 'empty moat' might protect a cash crop of fruit or honey from pilferage.

Very few of these moats have ever been excavated, Milton Ernest, Harlington, Tempsford, and Willington being exceptions. Willington is a mistakenly-named site based on a false interpretation of its location and layout, and misleadingly named 'Danish Camp'. The main construction consists of a D-shaped enclosure backing on to the banks of the Ouse, and a raised rectangular area measuring 230 by 65 feet (70 by 20 metres). The idea of the D-shaped enclosure, thought at one time to be a dock for longships, and a possible analogue of the Danish camp at Repton in Derbyshire, was clearly seductive, but has been shown to be false. It is now thought that the rectangular enclosure was an outer court, entered through gates with drawbridges, containing the entrance and domestic buildings, and that the D-shaped enclosure, linked by the moat and also accessed via a gate and drawbridge, was an inner court in which wall footings and post-holes have been found, possibly representing the main domestic buildings. Post-holes have also been discovered in the outer enclosure. The outer earthworks are now thought to represent fishponds. The manor was held by the Mowbrays in 1265 but was decayed by 1376. Mavourn Farm in Bolnhurst, is a trapezoidal moat enclosing a platform with a post-medieval house, while a secondary moat contains the farm buildings. The main moat has a submerged, outer berm lying under 2 feet (61 cm) of water before falling away abruptly to a depth of 9 feet (2.75 metres) in an apparent attempt to provide a nasty surprise for the malicious trespasser. Another moated site at Bolnhurst occupies the northern half of an Iron Age hillfort. On Mowsbury Hill, Ravensden, the Iron Age hillfort became the basis for a medieval moat, which occupies the central and north-western part of the earlier camp. The moated area measures 120 by 85 yards (110 by 80 metres) with a strong outer bank, especially on the eastern side, and, though on top of a hill, a wet moat, supplied by a stream. The outer ditch of the camp accommodated fishponds in the medieval period. In the south-east corner of the medieval moated area is a smaller moated island. The ditch of the stronger inner enclosure is 50 feet (15 metres) wide and 9 feet (2.5 metres) deep. This moated manor of 'Morinsbury' is mentioned up until 1465. Ducksworth Farm at Stagsden is a moated site dating from at least the fourteenth century but abandoned by 1600 and now overlain by farm buildings. No buildings are shown within the moat on an early nineteenth-century map so the present buildings must be post-1839, most likely reusing earlier materials. The original manor house probably occupied a central position within the moated area, but no traces were found in the survey conducted up to 2012 and reported in *South Midlands Archaeology* 43, in 2013. Eaton Bray is a site previously fortified by Fawkes de Breaute. Here the house, surrounded by a stone wall and moat was accessed by two gates with two drawbridges. The original moat was circular but was enlarged into a rectangular shape in the sixteenth century. Until later research provided more evidence, Eaton Bray, The Creakers at Great Barford, and Gannock's Castle at Tempsford have all been described as castles or, in the case of the last named, another Danish camp. In fact, all three are better described as moats where the defensive element is more pronounced than at most other such sites. Tilsworth Manor stands in a large moat and superseded the earthwork castle near the church. Repairs to the house were recorded in 1474. It has a fifteenth-century gatehouse consisting of a square tower with an un-vaulted entrance passage. The house was substantially remodelled in the seventeenth century and again in 1955.

Right: Tilsworth,
the gatehouse to this
late-medieval moated manor
house.

Below: Sharnbrook, the
moat and inner rampart of
this medieval manor site.

Some moats are associated with parks, embanked for hunting. Areas of woodland at Carlton and Harrold, were emparked by the de Pabenhams and more such parks could be found at Stevington. A licence to crenellate was granted to Baldwin Wake at Stevington in 1281, but this is now thought to relate to the park rather than to the timber hall Wake was planning to build prior to his early death. Keysoe's park with its boundary bank partly preserved can be found in woodland. A farmhouse lies nearby, just outside the banks of a large semi-circular moat.

Ecclesiastical

It must be remembered that the medieval church maintained a foot in the secular camp. It was normal for monasteries, either in towns or rural locations, to be walled and entered only through a gatehouse that controlled access for visitors, and egress for the monks. Dunstable Priory retains part of its fifteenth-century gatehouse to the outer court with carriage and pedestrian arches, to the south-west of the church. The website of Elstow Abbey suggests that the detached tower acted as 'a flanking tower to guard the western entrance to the Abbey like the Abbott's [*sic*] Tower at Buckfast Abbey' in Devon, but is more likely to have been a detached campanile. The military orders owning granges that financed their

Dunstable Priory, the outer face of the gatehouse with carriage and pedestrian entrances; originally, porters' lodges would have stood each side and upper storeys might have held apartments for visiting dignitaries.

crusading activities are well represented in Bedfordshire. The Knights Templar occupied Sharnbrook from 1199, and the local names of Temple Wood, Temple Spinney, and Temple Closes indicate their woodland clearances providing areas for cultivation and an income from the sale of the timber for building. After the suppression of the Templars, their property was made over to the Knights Hospitallers of St John who also maintained a preceptory at Melchbourne, described as being solidly built of stone over masonry vaults.

Later Castles

If a moat was good enough for the majority of lords of the manor, then the upper classes required something more substantial to impress neighbour and visitor alike. There were few magnates in Bedfordshire and those with pretensions were largely self-made men enjoying the benefits of royal patronage or the spoils of foreign war.

Sir John Cornwall (*c.* 1364–1443) whose father had been in the service of Francis II, duke of Brittany, served four kings himself. In 1400, he married the newly widowed Elizabeth of Lancaster, sister of Henry IV. Her first husband had been John Holland, duke of Exeter, who had been rewarded by Richard II for supporting him against his political opponents. On usurping the throne, Henry IV stripped him of his title. One of a group of nobles considering themselves hard done by, Holland conspired with the others to seize Henry at Westminster at the feast of the Epiphany in 1400. One of them, however, spilt the beans and his fellow conspirators were forced to flee. Holland was captured at Pleshey Castle in Essex and summarily beheaded. Sir John Cornwall and his new bride were in trouble for not seeking the king's permission to marry, but his status as a distinguished soldier carried them through. Sir John's military career had included fighting for Richard II in Scotland; for the duke of Lancaster in Brittany; and for Henry IV against Owen Glyndwr in Wales. He would go on to fight for both Henry V and VI in the Hundred Years' War in France, leading the English vanguard on the march from Harfleur prior to the Battle of Agincourt. Here he captured and ransomed valuable prisoners, including the duke of Orleans. It was with the proceeds from these prisoners that he reputedly financed the building of his castle of Ampthill, where Orleans was comfortably imprisoned for three years. Sir John excelled in tournaments, particularly in single combat. His advantageous marriage, coupled with prizes won in tournaments and ransom money won in battle, brought him titles, riches, and lands. He was created Baron Fanhope in 1432 and Lord Milbroke ten years later. One of his sons was killed beside him at the siege of Meaux in 1421, which was where Henry V apparently contracted the illness from which he would shortly die. Sir John built his palatial, fortified residence of Ampthill Park on the site of an earlier castle, which had a great tower or keep. His new castle comprised four ranges around a central courtyard measuring 210 by 180 feet (65 by 55 metres) with a gatehouse on the east and a great hall on the north; a smaller court enclosing a well-house lay outside the north wing and a larger base-court containing stables, workshops, and other services lay to the south. A description of a visit in the 1530s referred to four or five stone towers in the inner ward and a chapel with stained glass, as well as the outer court. In 1444, Ampthill came into the possession of Edmund Grey following the death of Baron Fanhope. It was one of Henry VIII's numerous acquisitions for its attractions as a hunting lodge, and it was occupied by Katherine of Aragon during her divorce proceedings in 1533. Despite improvements under Henry VIII, and its role as the centre of a large royal estate administering the disposal of monastic properties, by 1555, it was decayed; a partial demolition had been planned by 1567; it was ruinous by the end of the sixteenth century; and had completely disappeared by 1649.

Traditionally, one way of demonstrating the depth of royal favour one enjoyed was to obtain a licence to crenellate, granting royal approval for the provision of a wall of stone and lime, and usually a moat, around one's property. While not strictly necessary, possession of such a licence acted as a sign of royal approval and esteem. In 1327, John de Pateshull was rising in the social scale, was granted a licence for his house at Bletsoe, and married his daughter to Roger Beauchamp. A descendant, Margaret Beauchamp, married John Beaufort, duke of Somerset, a great-grandson of Edward III, and their daughter, probably born at Bletsoe in 1443, was Margaret Beaufort, mother of Henry VII. Given these connections, it is likely that the castle here would have been a substantial pile and, given the turbulence of the times, a well-defended one. Very little remains, even of subsequent rebuildings, but the moat is traceable and short lengths, with a later bridge, survive. It surrounded a square platform with rounded corners on which stood the mediaeval house and inner court. A southern base court held stables, barns and all the other ancillary buildings. Contained within an outer bank are several other enclosures that have been interpreted as 'pleasaunces' or garden features, added from the 1500s onwards. Although the moat has been landscaped over the years up to recent times, it appears to have been an impressive 55 feet (16.7 metres) wide, 15 feet (4.5 metres) deep, and water-filled.

By 1284, Reginald de Grey was lord of the manor of Silsoe and Flitton, held from the Wahull Barons of Odell, and Wrest Old House was probably begun at this time. Ground plans drawn in the eighteenth century at the time the house was being given a make-over which included a classical South Front, show a great hall, chapel, kitchen, and screens passage in the layout typical of a late medieval manor house. Edmund, Lord Grey of Ruthin, is notorious for having changed sides at the Battle of Northampton, thereby enabling Edward IV to assume the crown of England. Grey was rewarded by being given the office of lord high treasurer in 1463 and the title of earl of Kent two years later. He was sword-bearer at Richard III's coronation in 1483. It is likely that this swift increase in both income and status will have been reflected in his homes. A sixteenth-century inventory mentions a chamber over the gate, which would suggest that Wrest was walled and also refers to moats, while a century later, double moats are described in a poem. Later garden developments mention water features developed from ponds, which might have represented the vestiges of the moats. Given that the earlier building had been extended several times into an agglomeration of buildings exhibiting little cohesion, it is unsurprising that the new house of 1830 was built on a new site and that the old house, with its original core, fifteenth-century extensions and successive remodelling, should be demolished piecemeal as the new build progressed. A resistivity survey in 2004 found traces of the moat on two sides, with a later bridge crossing it on the west, just as was depicted in an engraving of 1705. The foundations of several buildings including the chapel were identified.

Sir John Wenlock was a protégé of Sir John Cornwall, and fought in the French Wars taking ransoms and gaining royal patronage. According to an account written in 1648, he began to build Someries Castle from 1464, out of the money he gained from his exploits in France. It was thought that there may have been an earlier manor house on a site adjacent to Wenlock's new build but the remaining earthworks, 110 feet (35 metres) square, are now seen as representing later landscaped gardens. Having fought for Lancaster at St Albans and for York at Towton, Wenlock now threw in his lot with the earl of Warwick and was in command of the Lancastrian centre at Tewkesbury. It would appear that the agreed plan of battle failed to work out and Wenlock missed an opportunity to punish the Yorkists' tactical errors. A legend persists, perpetuated by the chronicle of Edward Hall, published in 1548, upon whom was placed so great a reliance by Shakespeare, that Edmund Beaufort, duke of Somerset, having received a severe mauling from the unopposed Yorkists, blamed Wenlock's inactivity for the defeat. Most probably attributing this to Wenlock's track record for changing sides, he is supposed to have split his head in two with a single blow of his pole-axe. Whether killed by the hand of his fellow commander or in the chaos of a rout, Wenlock died on the battlefield in 1471, and Somerset was executed shortly afterwards. A helmet in St Mary's church in Luton, purporting to be Wenlock's, however, exhibits no evidence of such violent treatment. Someries ended up with Bishop Rotherham in 1475 and, given his enthusiasm for and experience in building in brick, he has been credited with continuing Wenlock's building works. However, another school of thought sees it all as Wenlock's achievement in the seven years prior to his death. The remains consist of a gatehouse with a vaulted gate passage flanked by projecting semi-octagonal turrets, possibly once four storeys in height, the western one of which has a newel stair attached. To the east of the gatehouse is a large chapel measuring 34 by 18 feet (10.5 by 5.5 metres). A difference in the bricks used may indicate two building periods but both could lie within that seven-year span after 1464. The gatehouse uses one type of brick while the chapel is built of a different type, large quantities of which were reused in the nearby farmhouse. The final build consisted of twenty-six rooms around two courtyards with further farm buildings. Only the existing gatehouse and chapel survived the demolition of 1742.

Above: Someries Castle, the rear face of the gate-house range and chapel built by Sir John Wenlock in the middle years of the fifteenth century.

Left: Someries Castle, a doorway showing the quality of the workmanship here at the earliest brick building in Bedfordshire.

The Wars of the Roses

Throughout the first half of the fifteenth century, squabbles and feuds among the nobility acted as precursors to the struggles over the throne, which would cost the lives of so many of those nobles. In 1437, an argument over where the assizes should be held prompted a confrontation between Baron Fanhope from Ampthill and Lord Grey of Ruthin from Wrest Park in which each fielded dozens of armed retainers. This particular fracas ended in no more than recriminations, but the future would be less rosy for many. In 1455, the first Battle of St Albans saw the Lancastrian forces moving north from London in an attempt to prevent the Yorkist advance down Watling Street. On this occasion, the Yorkists proved the better streetfighters. Since then, the fortunes of both Yorkists and Lancastrians had waxed and waned. In February 1461, the Lancastrian army under Margaret of Anjou, Henry VI's queen, surged down the country, looting and pillaging, fresh from its overwhelming victory at Wakefield, expecting to meet up with their western allies. However, this army of Welshmen under Jasper Tudor had been defeated at Mortimer's Cross by a Yorkist army under the earl of March, the future Edward IV, son of the late duke of York. Unaware of this victory, the Yorkists remained desperate to stop the queen from reaching London. The earl of Warwick therefore deployed his army across the enemy's expected line of approach by heavily defending the northward approaches to St Albans astride the Great North Road. Warwick's defences are believed to have extended from Nomansland Common, south of Wheathampstead, south and west to Sandridge and Bernards Heath and Beech Bottom on the northern edge of St Albans.

Margaret's army advanced from Royston, down the Icknield Way to Luton and then down Watling Street, appearing unexpectedly in Dunstable, causing mayhem and quickly subduing the 200 men manning this isolated Yorkist outpost. Margaret took stock and quickly detected the vulnerability of the Yorkist positions to her east. Despite losing many of her troops who had decided to call it a day and to carry their loot back home, the appearance of a deserter confirmed that her Lancastrian army had effectively bypassed the Yorkist defences. So making a 12-mile (19-km) night march down Watling Street, she pressed her advantage and entered the southern edge of St Albans, marking the extent of Warwick's defences. These had been established in strength utilising the ancient Belgic dyke, reinforcing it with barricades of mantlets, stakes, caltrops to spike horses' hooves, and even some primitive cannon. However, perceiving themselves outflanked and outnumbered, the Yorkists unwisely abandoned their secure, but by now redundant, position and, unable to regroup quickly enough, were rolled up from their left flank. Warwick fled the field, Henry VI was repossessed by his queen, and the interminable struggle would stutter on for another twenty-five years.

Henry V's brother, John of Lancaster, was created 1st duke of Bedford in 1414. He held many senior military and administrative appointments in England and France, especially after his brother's death in 1422, but is best remembered for his role as commander of the English army in France during the Hundred Years' War. Since he had died in 1435 with no legitimate heir, the era of the Wars of the Roses produced two unrelated holders of the dukedom. George Nevill held the title for a year prior to his father's attainder after the Battle of Barnet in 1471 but was deprived of the dukedom in 1477 on the grounds that he was in possession of insufficient lands to justify the title. Jasper Tudor, uncle to Henry VII, was duke of Bedford from 1485 until his death, without issue, in 1495. After a fifty-year hiatus, the dynasty which continues to this day was begun by John Russell (1486–1555) who performed noteworthy military and diplomatic service for Henry VII, Henry VIII, and Edward VI. He was created earl of Bedford in 1550 and passed extensive lands including Woburn on to his son, Francis.

3

Bedfordshire's Military Landscape, 1500–1900

The sixteenth century saw the building of a number of country houses perpetuating the mediaeval tradition, with ranges around a courtyard entered, often across a moat, and through a turreted gatehouse. Following the Dissolution of the Monasteries, the former abbot's lodging at Old Warden was converted into the gatehouse of a new house built by John Gostwick, the king's auditor, who had, himself, been instrumental in the dissolution of local monasteries. The rest of his house was demolished in the eighteenth century, and the house is now owned by the Landmark Trust. Toddington Manor, built in 1560–80 for Sir Henry Cheyne, took the form of a quadrangle around a courtyard with round towers at the corners and turrets flanking the gatehouse, all in brick. It was remodelled in the early seventeenth century but one corner remains with its circular turret. Henry VIII added country houses at Ampthill and Dunstable to his extensive property portfolio. Ampthill came to Henry in 1508 when Richard Grey, 3rd earl of Kent, got into debt, and it was while Katherine of Aragon was detained there in May 1533 that the official announcement of the annulment of her marriage to Henry VIII was made by Cardinal Wolsey in the Lady Chapel of Dunstable Priory. Dunstable and Ampthill had both been included in the 300-mile (480-km) royal progress made by Henry and Katherine in 1526, and Dunstable was again visited by Henry and Ann Boleyn in 1529 on their way to Ampthill for the hunting. Kingsbury Palace at Dunstable, its site now marked by the Old Palace Lodge on the north side of Church Street, had been established by Henry I in 1109 but had been given to the Priory by King John. In 1525, Cardinal Wolsey's secretary pre-empted the Dissolution of the Monasteries by buying Kingsbury. Queen Elizabeth preferred to stay in other people's homes, so on her 1575 Progress to Stafford, she stayed at Luton Hoo on the way out from Greenwich, and at Woburn on the last leg of her return to Windsor.

Sir John Russell had risen from his roots in trade to become a soldier who, having lost one of his own at the siege of Morlaix in 1522, caught the eye of Henry VIII. He

Old Warden, the former abbot's lodging became the gatehouse of a new grand house built by John Gostwick, the king's auditor.

became Lord Privy Seal and was given, at the Dissolution, several choice properties. These included some rich abbeys in the West Country; Westminster Abbey's former produce gardens, later known as Covent Garden in London; lands formerly belonging to Chicksands Priory; and the priory at Woburn. He was an executor for Henry VIII, and was made earl of Bedford by Edward VI, moving the family home from Chenies in Buckinghamshire to Woburn Abbey, while retaining a London palace on the Strand. The real development of Covent Garden and Woburn was only started by the 4th earl in 1630, and nothing earlier than this date survives at Woburn.

The Tudor Militia

In the tradition of the Anglo-Saxon *fyrd* and the feudal system, men could be called up to serve whenever the king needed to raise an army. Such a Muster was announced by Royal Commission, on 1 March 1539, in the name of Henry VIII who was facing the threat of foreign invasion. Records of several Hundreds have survived, with the numbers of men and their weapons and armour, or 'harness':

Hundred	Archers	Billmen	Pairs of Harness
Bereford/Barford	44	130	20
Stoddon	32	122	12
Wylly/Willey	67	179	24
Bedford Town	75	97	12
Totals	218	528	68

These totals show the number of men, from those particular Hundreds, present at the Muster of April 1539. Archers hardly differed in dress or appearance from those who had fought at Agincourt. Billmen carried the standard infantry weapon, which was a spear with an axe-blade pointing in one direction, and a spike in the other. A set or 'pair' of harness consisted of a steel cap or 'sallet'; a 'gorget', which protected the throat; a 'jack', which was a leather coat sewn with small steel plates; and a pair of 'splints', which protected the elbows. An alternative to the jack was the 'brigandine', which was formed by lacing together back- and breastplates, hence the 'pair'. Nobles and squires were required to contribute sets of harness. Lord Mordaunt of Turvey, high sheriff of Bedfordshire, supplied harness for twenty men; Sir John St John of Bletsoe for fifty men; and Nicholas Hardyng and his fellow commissioner Thomas Fitzhugh supplied two sets each.

In 1598, Bedfordshire men were impressed for service in Ireland, providing sixty Pikes; twenty 'Halbertes [*sic*]'; sixty 'Muskatiers [*sic*]'; and sixty Calivers, or muskets with shorter barrels than normal. The armouries at Bedford, Shefford, and Ampthill were reported as being well stocked, which was just as well as some of those meant to be ready to contribute arms, armour, or horses on demand were refusing to honour their obligations. In 1625, the Trained Bands were not mustered owing to a recent outbreak of the plague. A levy by Charles I for war against the Scots in 1640 required an army of 23,000 men. Bedfordshire was lumped in with the other East Anglian counties to produce a total of 2,450 men between them. They would gather at Great Yarmouth to be shipped to Newcastle, being allowed to take five days to cross the intervening counties, which would be required to maintain them at a cost of 8*d per diem* for each man.

The Civil War

In the years leading up to the Civil War, Bedfordshire was one of those counties where the Anglican Church was finding itself increasingly side-lined by the Puritan, non-conformist movements. In 1619, Dunstable's minister was being persecuted for his High Church stance. His gardens were wrecked and his produce destroyed; he was threatened with violence; and an attempt was made to lure him out at night so that he might be physically attacked. As parliament enforced puritan practices, more priests would lose their livings. A total of nine Bedfordshire gentry with puritan leanings sat in the House of Commons, and Lord Bolingbroke and the earls of Kent and Bedford were on the anti-royalist side in the Lords. Thomas Wentworth, inherited Toddington Manor in 1614, and was created earl of Cleveland in 1626. In 1627, he served on Buckingham's disastrous expedition to La Rochelle, and attended the execution of his relative, Thomas Wentworth, earl of Strafford. A thoroughly committed royalist, he was appointed lord lieutenant of Bedfordshire.

In 1625, a dispute between Charles I and a group of aristocrats, which included Lord Francis Russell, over the sale of titles, laid the foundation for a noble opposition to the king, its focus being the hated duke of Buckingham. Russell's barony had been created only in 1603, but he was heir to his cousin's earldom of Bedford, which he inherited in 1627 as the 4th earl of Bedford. He had previously served as a MP and as lord lieutenant of Devonshire, and had briefly been imprisoned when he was accused of circulating a subversive pamphlet. In 1638, Ship Money was levied in Bedfordshire, and in 1640, he voted against Charles and his attempts to raise money outside parliament, allowing his London home to be the centre of a cabal of lords plotting resistance. As Charles I's foremost opponents in the House of Lords, this group of English aristocrats was accused of colluding with those who were resisting the king's efforts to impose bishops and a prayer-book on Presbyterian Scotland. They were accused of apparently encouraging a Scottish invasion, which might force the king to resolve the crisis by recalling Parliament. The 4th earl found himself in the middle of conflicting situations. On his estates in Thorney, in Cambridgeshire, he had spent enormous sums of money in Fen drainage, antagonising the Fen Slodgers who lived off the wildfowl and fisheries. He also came up against a young lawyer named Oliver Cromwell who was defending the interests of the fen-dwellers. In 1638, the king had taken over Bedford's investments and may have thereby stoked up the anti-royalist stance of those living in the Fenland. After his father's death from smallpox in 1641, his son, William, became the 5th earl.

At the beginning of the war, Bedfordshire's parliamentarian gentry dislodged the earl of Cleveland as lord lieutenant. Cleveland, however, remained a staunch supporter of the monarchy to the bitter end, serving as a general in the royalist army, leading the decisive cavalry charge at Cropredy Bridge in 1643, being taken prisoner at the Second Battle of Newbury in 1644, and commanding a regiment of cavalry with Prince Charles, at the Battle of Worcester in 1651. Baron St John of Bletsoe, created earl of Bolingbroke in 1624, served as lord lieutenant, but his heir, summoned to the House of Lords in 1641 by a writ of acceleration, was killed at the Battle of Edgehill the next year, fighting for parliament. Their Wiltshire kinsmen fought on the royalist side. The 5th earl of Bedford was appointed to the parliamentarian army in 1642 as general of the horse with the experienced Scottish soldier Balfour as his minder. After an unsatisfactory campaign in the West Country, he joined the Peace Party in 1643 and defected to the king. However, despite being pardoned by Charles, he quickly became disillusioned with the royalists when peace negotiations failed, and rejoined parliament but would never be fully trusted again and, disapproving of the radicals' treatment of the king, withdrew to Woburn where, once again a friend to Charles I, he would host several royal visits.

Bedfordshire's main role as a member of the parliamentarian Midland Association under the leadership of Lord Grey of Groby was to supply men, materiel, and cash to the anti-royalist cause. The county's first contribution to the parliamentarian army was 500 men of the Trained Bands, or militia, along with 500 extra volunteers. While puritan Bedfordshire might have morally supported parliament against the king, when it came to taking up arms and going off to fight, there was less enthusiasm. In 1642–3, even before they had been clothed and armed, eighty out of a cohort of 150 men levied as parliamentarian troops had absconded. The county also raised a regiment of dragoons, soldiers who rode on to the battlefield but fought on foot. Under the leadership of Sir Samuel Luke in June 1643, this regiment suffered fifty deaths and 120 injured in camp at Chinnor in Oxfordshire. They had been surprised by a force of cavalry under Prince Rupert, who went on to rout his parliamentarian pursuers at the Battle of Chalgrove Field, in large part due to the treachery of John Hurry. In each successive year, the numbers of troops levied increased, up to a peak of 700 in 1645. The parliamentarian troops represented a further drain on local resources as they were billeted across the county including in such grand houses as Chicksands Priory whose owner, Sir Peter Osborne, was away holding Castle Cornet on Guernsey for the king.

The Bedfordshire Committee petitioned parliament for supplies, and raised taxes for the maintenance of garrisons, which would secure the association's borders against attacks from royalist Oxfordshire. The most important of these would be the fortified town of Newport Pagnell, which kept Watling Street, the road to London through Dunstable and St Albans, open. Across the county, some twenty royalist estates were sequestered to bolster the parliamentarian treasury. Cromwell is recorded as having been in Dunstable in November 1642, possibly on a recruiting or a fundraising mission. In 1643, soldiers under the command of Sir Thomas Fairfax destroyed the Eleanor Cross at Dunstable, but the fate of that at Woburn is unknown.

Sir Lewis Dyve of Bromham received a sword-cut in his first skirmish and then distinguished himself by getting Prince Rupert out of a tight corner. Early in the war he fortified his mansion at Bromham, but, isolated in parliamentarian territory, it quickly fell, and he was forced to escape across the river. He fought at Newbury but then resorted to raiding, attacking Ampthill as the Bedfordshire Sequestration Committee was in session, and moving on to Newport Pagnell, which he occupied in September 1643, securing it by building earthwork fortifications. The next month, a royalist force took Bedford, capturing its 300-strong garrison, and making an unsuccessful attempt to secure the bridge by refortifying the castle. However, its leader, Sir John Hurry, knighted after Chalgrove Field, was wounded in the fighting and withdrew his force to Oxford and Bedford returned to parliamentary control for the rest of the war. Seeking to secure Bedford Bridge from future attacks, a loop-holed palisade was erected on the castle mound, similar to the parliamentarian fortification of Rockingham castle in neighbouring Northamptonshire. This fort at Bedford was garrisoned by 100 locally raised men under a Captain Hudson. Pitching their tents on the castle mound and living off the town, they remained there to the end of the war, apparently failing to gain the support or the goodwill of the townsfolk, who may have taken the line: '… with friends like these, who needs enemies?'

Bromham Hall, the moated stronghold of the cavalier leader Sir Lewis Dyve.

As Sir Philip Skippon advanced toward Newport Pagnell with a force of London trained bands, Sir Lewis Dyve is reputed to have evacuated the royalist garrison having misread a message and embarrassingly left the town open for Sir Samuel Luke to secure. After his *faux pas* at Newport Pagnell, Dyve resorted to hit-and-run raids at the head of 400 cavalry. In 1644, a force of royalist cavalry descended on Dunstable, plundering the town, taking pot-shots at the minister in his pulpit, and killing the landlord of the Red Lion who attempted to prevent them from requisitioning horses. Evidence of this assault may still be seen in the oak doors of the Priory where musket balls are lodged. Dyve, however, was forced to evacuate Abingdon in May 1644 and to join the royalist army in the West Country.

In June 1644, the king is reported as staying over at Woburn House, the Russell family's home on the priory site. His intention had been to journey from Aylesbury to Bedford but he changed his route to Leighton Buzzard instead. He was pursued by Luke with 200 of his Newport Dragoons but managed to hold him off, and was afterwards lodged in Buckingham from 22–26 June. Luke's pursuit is recorded as involving two of the parliamentarian top brass: Sir William Waller, who was reported as being camped at Great Brickhill, and Major-General Browne. Waller had force-marched from Gloucester, arriving in the vicinity of Banbury on the 27 June; and Browne marched out of London on 24 June with 4,500 men, probably bound for his base at Abingdon, so their involvement is likely to have been slight.

In 1645, as the opposing forces converged on Naseby in Northamptonshire, on his journey north, Charles I stayed at that same Red Lion in Dunstable. A short while later, the Eastern Association forces, including the Ironside cavalry under Cromwell, met up with Fairfax, commander of the parliamentarian forces, at a rendezvous in Bedford, before moving on to the battlefield in June. Through the preceding year, Cromwell had been in the habit of using Bedford's Swan Inn as an accommodation address for correspondence. After Naseby, King Charles I and Prince Rupert gathered a force of several thousand of their surviving cavalry around them and attempted to head north to join up with Montrose in Scotland. Blocked by the Northern Association army in Yorkshire, he set off back south, sacking Huntingdon in August 1645. The king and Rupert, with a force numbering 300, then mustered at Great Barford and moved on towards Bedford, getting involved in skirmishes in Goldington where the royalist officer Major Baskerville was reported killed, and then with the garrison around the bridge in Bedford. A large force of parliamentarian cavalry under Poyntz and Rossiter pursued Charles and Rupert as they headed away westwards. On 26 August, the king is said to have stayed at Woburn House again on his way to Oxford. Passing through Luton, he attempted to extort money and goods from the citizens but parliamentarian troops intervened and the royalists lost four killed and twenty-two taken prisoner. The king arrived back in Oxford on 28 August.

In November 1645, a large body of royalist cavalry from Oxford occupied Woburn via Leighton Buzzard. The townsmen had resisted the advance guard and killed their leader and several of his soldiers. When the main body arrived, they set about taking reprisals. Using fire-pikes to set fire to the thatch on half the houses in the town and setting alight haystacks, they then plundered the rest. Having caused an enormous amount of damage, they were finally chased off by a body of Bedfordshire Horse, but pillaged Great Brickhill on their way back to Oxford. The townsfolk of Woburn then set about fortifying their town with trenches and a barricade across the main road, and also raising a troop of 100 cavalry. Upon receiving a petition from the townspeople describing their ordeal and consequent loss, Colonel Whalley, a cousin of Cromwell, was despatched with 1,000 horse to safeguard the town. A further scare occurred in January 1646 when news of a projected royalist raid was received, but this false alarm allowed Whalley to take his force to join the main army in Banbury leaving a small garrison behind to protect Woburn. The town's petition to parliament obviously paid off as it was, unusually, permitted to open a public subscription to recompense those who had lost home and property. During the time he spent in captivity prior to his execution, Charles passed one further night at Woburn House in June 1647. While there, his host, the earl of Bedford who had returned to the royalist fold, made an attempt, along with the earl of Cleveland, an experienced royalist cavalry commander, to promote peace and reconciliation.

In the Second Civil War, following their defeat at St Neots, fleeing royalist soldiers were found hiding in the fields and hedges around Luton. Royalist soldiers made their way into town and were involved in a skirmish with parliamentarian troops on Bridge Street, where nine of them were killed. The earl of Cleveland, credited with engineering Charles II's escape from his defeat at Worcester in 1651, was himself captured and incarcerated in the Tower until 1658. Sir Lewis Dyve fared little better. He fought a number of successful actions in the west but was captured at Sherborne by Cromwell in August 1645, and was imprisoned in the Tower of London. Though he managed to escape to Scotland in 1648, he was recaptured at the Battle of Preston, escaping once more only to go into exile to await the Restoration of 1660. Although his Bromham estate had been sequestrated, it was returned to his son but, ruined by his other losses in the wars, he lived out a quiet retirement until his death in 1669. Sir John Hurry, Dyve's colleague in the attacks on Bedford, had begun the war in the army of parliament but, believing himself to be undervalued by the earl of Bedford, had changed sides early in 1643. He changed sides twice more, achieving the rank of major-general in the royalist army, but after defeats at Preston and Carbisdale, he was captured and beheaded by the Covenanters in Edinburgh in 1650.

During the period of Cromwell's Protectorate, Major-General John Okey, whose dragoons had played a key role in the parliamentarian victory at Naseby, acquired the old Ampthill Park House and Brogborough Round House where he lived. After the Restoration, he was executed by Charles II as a regicide but was allowed a Christian burial in the Tower of London. Several of Cromwell's cousins had lived in the county throughout the war and into the next decade. Some had kept their heads down at Pertenhall and Upper Dean. At Clifton, however, two of them had been killed fighting for parliament, but their brother had served as a royalist cavalry officer and survived the conflict, dying in 1658.

An Ordinance of Parliament of December 1648 includes Bedfordshire in a list of counties in which Commissioners were appointed by the Lords and Commons to ensure that the Militia was in a fit state to 'be put in a posture of Defence, for the preservation and safety of the King [*sic*], Parliament and Kingdome'. Commissioners were empowered to raise funds in order to provide arms and ammunition for those Militias to 'oppose, seize, secure, disarm, kill and slay all such persons as shall raise or cause any tumults, insurrections or invasions, or levy any force against the Authority of Parliament'. This was followed in 1650 by an Act of Parliament confirming the control of the Militia by the County Commissioners.

After the Restoration, Charles II ordered the Bedfordshire Militia, along with many other county militias, to be drawn out as a response to the threatened Dutch invasion in 1666. The 5th earl of Bedford had resumed his place in the establishment, holding various offices. In 1678, in the wake of the panic engendered by spurious catholic plots, William, Lord Russell, the earl of Bedford's heir, was the only aristocrat to be executed among several lowlier supposed members of the Rye House Plot against James II. In 1683, the trained bands or Bedfordshire Militia were composed of 120 horse, raised by the county's magnates, and 456 foot, in five companies, armed with 309 muskets, raised by the parishes. The county was assessed at £227 8s 1d per month to cover the running costs of ammunition and equipment.

Under William and Mary, the 5th earl rebooted his public career and served on the Privy Council and as lord lieutenant of Bedfordshire, and was created 1st duke of Bedford in 1694, dying in 1700. The 4th duke, Lt-Gen. Sir John Russell, served as first lord of the Admiralty and then as lord lieutenant of Ireland, and supervised its defence against a threatened French invasion during the Seven Years' War. He signed the peace treaty that brought the war to a close in 1763.

Regular, Militia, and Volunteer Troops 1688–1815

In 1688, the 16th Regiment of Foot, predecessor unit of the Bedfordshire Regiment, was formed. It fought in dozens of the actions of the War of the Spanish Succession (1701–14) under Marlborough, notably at the battles of Blenheim in 1704 and of Malplaquet in 1709. The heroic Sgt Littler, who swam a river and let down the drawbridge in a French outwork at the Siege of Lille in 1708, is claimed by the 16th Foot. After action against the Jacobites in 1745, overseas service included Canada, Florida, the West Indies, India, and Sri Lanka.

The Bedfordshire Militia

In 1697, the Bedfordshire Militia comprised five companies of foot, totalling 420 men, and two troops of cavalry with 119 troopers, all under Col. Lord Edward Russell. In 1745, the Second Jacobite Rebellion, prompted the duke of Bedford to raise a regiment and to support the Militia Act, which reorganised the Militia. At the time of the Seven Years' War (1756–63), new legislation called for a revival of the Militia, with recruitment by ballot. This unpopular move provoked rioting, and Bedfordshire, particularly the town of Biggleswade, was one of those areas where unrest caused the process to be suspended by the lord lieutenant. Concessions included a reduction amongst the exemptions enjoyed by the quality, and the acceptance of volunteers to limit the need for balloting. The Militia returns of 1757 ordered by George II had set Bedfordshire's establishment at 400 men, more than Huntingdonshire but fewer than Hertfordshire, from a pool of 8,545 eligible men, giving an over-95 per cent chance of avoiding selection. Those actually called up would serve for three years, or could find a substitute, or could pay a fine of £10. As lord lieutenant, the duke of Bedford nominated a number of his peers and local gentlemen to serve as officers and, writing from Woburn Abbey, informed the secretary of state accordingly. The marquess of Tavistock, his son, would be colonel assisted by the earl of Upper Ossory, who had remodelled Ampthill Park House and would become colonel in 1771. George Byng, Viscount Torrington of Southill Park, would, at his own request, serve as a humble ensign. His paternal grandfather had been a successful fighting admiral and first lord of the Admiralty; his father had been a major-general; and his uncle, generally accepted to have been unjustly treated, was the unfortunate Admiral John Byng, shot in 1757, in the words of Voltaire, to encourage the others. So he may have felt it sensible to avoid the pressure of military success or failure and, as a seventeen-year-old, to aspire to only humble rank.

By the terms of the new legislation, the Militia would serve only in Great Britain, and could not be sent abroad without the express consent of its members. The Bedfordshire Militia was embodied on 4 March 1760 and joined the militias of other counties at a large camp in Winchester. This was in response to the threat posed by a French invasion force of 40,000 troops across the Channel, only removed when the French fleet was defeated by Lord Hawke at Quiberon Bay. The embodiment lasted nineteen months until the end of 1761. In 1778, at the time of the American War, the Militia was quartered in Southampton for some months, before going to Winchester to guard prisoners of war, to Taunton, and to camps in Kent and Essex, not returning to Bedford, permanently, until March 1784, having been on the road for five years.

The Militia and Volunteers in the French Wars

In 1793, the Militia was ordered to the east coast, spending time at Harwich, Great Yarmouth, and other places before crossing the Thames into Kent in 1796, replacing regular troops on foreign service, by providing garrisons along the south coast. In 1798, the eight companies of the Bedfordshire Militia began light infantry training and volunteered for service in Ireland. The 702-strong Bedfordshire Militia, along with a dozen other militia regiments, therefore received orders to proceed to Ireland in September 1799, as a response to the local rising supported by the landing at Killala Bay of over 1,000 French troops. Many of the militia units were conveyed to Liverpool by canal-boat, the normal route being by road up Watling Street through Dunstable to Towcester, from whence boats were loaded at Braunston. However, the Bedfordshire Militia went by road, marching or being conveyed in wagons, from Hastings to Rock Ferry in Cheshire, whence they were shipped to Dublin. Following a large number of enlistments into the Regular Army, the reduced Militia returned to Bedford and Dunstable to recruit replacements, before being posted to the West Country, performing garrison duty in Plymouth throughout the summer of 1802 prior to a 250-mile (400-km) march back home to Bedford and disembodiment after nine years' continuous service. The establishment of the Bedfordshire Militia was then reduced to 317, with the exception of Westmorland and Rutland, the lowest figure in England, but following the short-lived Peace of Amiens, the renewed threat of invasion brought a surge to the colours, and a re-embodiment of the Militia. This entailed the return to Devon of a force numbering 363 men stationed at Lympstone Camp near Exeter under Lt-Col. Richard Gilpin of Hockcliffe. A census of carts, wagons, draught horses, and drivers was carried out in 1803, as part of the anti-invasion preparations. At Bedford Castle, a Militia Armoury/ Depot was built in 1804. This hexagonal, free-standing building survives as

Bedford Militia Armoury was built to an unusual plan as a hexagonal structure, and is now part of the Higgins Museum on the Bedford Castle site.

Woburn, the stable yard of the Bedford Arms Hotel served as a Militia barracks and, later on, a drill hall and overflow for the Ampthill Park infantry training camp.

part of the Higgins Museum. Additionally, the Bedford Arms Hotel in Woburn allocated parts of its extensive ranges of outbuildings as barracks for the Militia and had provided storage since the middle of the eighteenth century, for the baggage of troops, both regular and Militia regiments, on the move.

Watling Street constituted an important route not only for troops, but also for prisoners of war being marched from the Hampshire depots of Portchester Castle and Forton to the large purpose-built camp outside Peterborough on the Great North Road at Norman Cross. Guards were paid a bounty for recapturing escapees, and in Dunstable in 1800, two Portuguese merchants were apprehended by overzealous militiamen who mistook them for escaped Spanish prisoners. Fortunately, the misunderstanding was soon resolved and they were promptly released.

The Admiralty had always had communication problems with the fleet's squadrons scattered around the coast, and these were highlighted in times of war. The solution lay in chains of semaphore stations linking London with Portsmouth, Plymouth, Deal and the Downs, and Great Yarmouth. The southern line had been completed by 1796 but that to Great Yarmouth was still only being surveyed in 1807. The system, put in place by 1808, relied on inter-visible gantries, which could mount six shutters that, when open or closed, offered combinations spelling out words letter by letter. However ponderous this system might be, attaining six letters per minute, it was still a great improvement on messages being carried on horseback. To avoid London's smog, the north-eastern route to Great Yarmouth, with nineteen stations in all, had to start off in a westerly direction, necessitating a right-angle bend at Dunstable Downs to bring it back on track. The route taken from London was via St Albans, Dunstable, Royston, Cambridge, and Norwich Castle. The St Albans station was on the roof of the clock-tower in the marketplace (TL147073), with the next one placed high on Dunstable Downs. This has been suggested as being at the angle in the B4541 road (TL008194) where a Trig Point marks the highest point of the Downs on Haddington Hill, at a height of 797 feet (243 metres). The next link in the chain, Telegraph Hill, Lilley Hoo (TL118288), at 595 feet (183 metres), straddles the Hertfordshire county boundary with the next station on at Baldock.

Responding to appeals broadcast by William Pitt and George III, Bedfordshire quickly raised a force of Volunteers to repel a French invasion. The 1798 Return to Parliament lists four troops of cavalry, each with an approved establishment of forty troopers. These were the Harrold and Bedford troop, with ninety-five troopers; the Warden troop, under Lord Ongley of Old Warden, one-time MP for the county; the seventy-strong Woburn troop, commanded by the 6th duke of Bedford; and the Ampthill troop under the MP and Chief Justice Lord Arden, Baron Alvanly. After Alvanly's death in 1804, his son pursued a career in the British Army, being promoted captain in 1809, aged just twenty, in the Coldstream Guards, but his debts from close association with the prince regent's circle caused him to resign his commission. In 1803, all potential Volunteers aged seventeen to fifty were listed for the ballot. By 1806, there were three battalions of Bedfordshire Volunteer Infantry with 1,007 men under Colonels Trevor, Pym, and Whitbread, and a Luton Company with seventy-two men under Captain Crawley. Additionally, the Bedfordshire Dismounted Horse Artillery was raised in 1803 by Major John Harvey, deputy-lieutenant of Bedfordshire and high sheriff in 1795. Owing to the unavailability of suitable horses, it had always been described as "dismounted" and was in existence with a roll of 251 men until 1809, attached to the 2nd Battalion of Bedfordshire Volunteers under the command of Colonel Francis Pym of Sandy. From 1809, the personnel of the artillery were absorbed by the local militia. The Bedfordshire volunteer forces would eventually total nearly 200 cavalry and approaching 2,000 infantry in fourteen companies. The infantry were designated as 'Supplementary' or 'Local Militia' and were reorganised into two regiments. One was commanded by Sir Montagu Burgoyne of Sutton who had commanded the yeomanry cavalry in 1805, and published a pamphlet on defence matters in 1810. He would later serve as a colonel in the Grenadier Guards. The commanding officer of the other regiment was Lt-Col. Aubrey. Nelson's victory at Trafalgar in 1805 removed the immediate threat of invasion but the Militia remained embodied, posted to Devon, and deployed, in 1809, to Weedon Barracks and Arsenal in Northamptonshire, from which military expeditions usually drew their arms and equipment. Men of the Bedfordshire Militia were involved in loading around 10,000 muskets into narrow-boats for transportation to the Tower of London and issue to the ill-fated Walcheren invasion force. The Military Training Act of 1806 provided for a force of 200,000 men, drawn from the lists of those eligible for the militia ballot, to be trained every year. In 1812, the Bedfordshire Militia were posted to guard French prisoners of war at Norman Cross on the Great North Road between Huntingdon and Stamford, prior to another move to Ireland. In 1814, Wellington and his victorious Peninsular Army returned, and the Militia could go home to be stood down early in 1815 after twelve years' service. That final victory over Napoleon at Waterloo saw the death of John Pym of Hasells Hall near Sandy. While Bedfordshire's involvement in balloon and airship technology still lay far into the future, at least one of the Sadler family's balloon flights from Oxford ended up on the county boundary near Newport Pagnell in 1810.

The Yeomanry were armed at government expense but members provided their own horses and tack. Having added an extra troop and been designated as a regiment in 1803, the Yeomanry had been disbanded in 1810. Now mustering six troops, the Yeomanry reformed in 1817, mainly for the assistance of the Civil Power. One of its new officers in that year was eighteen-year-old William Higgins of Turvey Abbey, who was gazetted Cornet in the Harrold and Bedford troop. After 1820, there was sporadic agricultural unrest resulting in occasional riots and outbreaks of arson, and the Militia Armoury was seen as a potential target for rioters so a small residential annexe was added to house a watchman. From 1831, militiamen contracted for four weeks' annual training. The Yeomanry was disbanded in 1827, and the former cornet, Captain Higgins, was now in charge of a Militia company made up of fifty-four men aged between eighteen and thirty-five, with sixteen of them nineteen or under, and just four over thirty. By the time of the 1835 Poor Law Riots in Ampthill, the Yeomanry had been disbanded for eight years and the Militia was not mobilised. Instead, other measures were taken when, that May, ninety-six special constables were enrolled at Millbrook, but those rioters they arrested were rescued by the mob. Four Troops of Yeomanry from outside the county were stationed in Luton, but order was eventually restored by the threat of these cavalry and the deployment of police officers from the Metropolitan Police. Lord John Russell, son of the 6th duke, initiated a Royal Commission on policing, publishing its findings in 1839. Within a year, Bedfordshire had its own police force, with a chief constable and six superintendents, one for each of the assize areas. Bedford and Woburn each had eight constables, while Biggleswade, Ampthill, Bletsoe, and Luton were allocated six each. By 1847, Luton had the first police station in the county, but not until 1865, would Dunstable gain its own police force, with a police station opening two years later.

The 16th Foot in the Nineteenth Century

The 1st Battalion of the 16th Foot spent most of the French wars in the Caribbean where they lost half their strength through disease, and many of those who survived were killed at the Battle of Surinam of 1806. In 1809, the regiments of foot hitherto linked to Buckinghamshire and Bedfordshire agreed an exchange, and the 16th Foot commenced its association with Bedfordshire. A home posting in 1810 was shortly followed by a return to Canada after war had broken out with the United States in 1812. Napoleon's Hundred Days brought a precipitate scramble home, but they arrived too late to be involved in the campaign, which culminated at Waterloo. The Regiment spent the rest of the century on garrison duties and colonial campaigns across the Empire, including spells in Canada, Sri Lanka, the West Indies again, Corfu, Malta, and India, interspersed with spells in Ireland, the Channel Islands, and home stations.

Lord George Russell, second son of the 6th duke of Bedford, combined careers in both politics and the military. He entered the army as a cornet in 1806, serving in Portugal as a captain in the 23rd Dragoons in 1808. He fought in the battles of Talavera and Barossa in the Peninsular War, and served as ADC to General Graham at Cadiz; Wellington at the Battle of Vittoria; and later to William IV and to Queen Victoria. He had been MP for Bedford while serving in the Peninsula, and was returned in 1818 and in 1826. He commanded the 8th (Royal Irish) Hussars in 1825 and served with his regiment in Ireland, impressing Wellington with his writings on cavalry tactics. He commanded the 90th Foot in Corfu in 1829 but absenteeism soon lost his parliamentary seat to a home-based Russell. After his promotion to major-general in 1841, he spent the rest of his working life as a diplomat. His son, Francis, spent six years in the army and then twenty-five years as MP for Bedford, succeeding his cousin as the 9th duke of Bedford in 1872.

The Bedfordshire Regiment spent the seven years spanning the Crimean War and the Indian Mutiny in Jamaica. The 2nd Battalion was raised in 1858 in Ireland and was soon on the same course as the 1st, spending time in the West Indies, Burma, India, and Ireland. In 1873, the Cardwell and Childers reforms brought a system of localisation whereby regiments of the line assumed official titles relating to their primary recruiting communities. This was reinforced by provision of regimental barracks/depots, and the inclusion of militia and volunteer affiliates in the family, in Bedfordshire's case, the 16th Regimental District. Thus, by 1881, the two regular battalions of the 16th Foot had become the 1st and 2nd Battalions, Bedfordshire Regiment and Kempston Barracks, opened in 1876, had become the Regiment's home.

Kempston Barracks, like many of its contemporaries across the country, was built to precise specifications. The local RE officer submitted his design to Major Seddon, RE, at the War Office for his approval. Each of these regimental barracks/depots had a central 'keep' on the medieval model. That at Kempston, like its twin of Norton Barracks at Worcester, was a square, three-storied block with four massive corner towers. The purpose of this keep was to store 3,000 stands of arms, large quantities of ammunition, and other supplies such as clothing and bedding. In order to do this safely, each of the upper floors rests on a grid of rolled, wrought-iron I-beams in 7 by 14-foot (2 by 4-metre) bays, carried, in pairs, on cylindrical cast-iron columns, with the beams supporting an un-reinforced mass concrete slab. The prototype for these slabs was tested by a large body of troops marking time in order to test for weakness. None of these keeps has ever failed but some have had further strengthening added in the shape of extra beams. At Kempston, there is a two-storey wing to each side of the keep, forming a monumental north front. The West Wing was designed to accommodate the officers' mess and quarters for eleven officers and their servants. The East Wing contained the institute, canteen, sergeants' mess, quarters for four senior NCOs, workshops, and stores. The West Wing still terminates in a two-storey block with projections including a stair-tower, but the corresponding block on the East Wing has been demolished. Behind this main block was an open courtyard flanked on one side by a pair of two-storey barrack-blocks, of standard design, each accommodating 288 soldiers and eight sergeants. On the opposite side were married quarters for thirty-one families with an attached nursery, the CO's house, stabling, and stores for carts and tentage, along with a twenty-eight-bed hospital with a detached ward for infectious cases, quarters for orderlies, and a mortuary. Along the southern side were further buildings, beyond which was a large parade ground. As a consequence of the Bedfordshire and Hertfordshire Regiment's amalgamation with other regiments to form the Royal Anglians, little use was made of the barracks after 1960, and most of the buildings were demolished in 1982, having been up for just over 100 years. The main block is currently (2019) occupied by the Freemasons, but the majority of the site is covered by housing, with the Army Reserve Centre, opened in 1983, occupying a site to the east of the main block.

Kempston Barracks opened in 1876 as the depot of the Bedfordshire Regiment.

Kempston Barracks, the front façade shows where the left end was demolished at the time of the construction of the Army Reserve Centre.

The Bedfordshire Militia in the Nineteenth Century

After the end of the French wars, the Militia had been neglected. In April 1847, Major Richard Gilpin, following in the steps of his father, was promoted to be lieutenant-colonel, as was William Bartholomew Higgins to major, subsequently to become lieutenant-colonel himself, but little effort was made to encourage recruitment or to animate those already enlisted. But in 1852 there was a revival. A mandatory period of fifty-six days' preliminary training was enforced, with twenty days' drill per year. Recruitment was by voluntary enlistment with any shortfall made up by ballot. Bounties totalling £6 were payable in regular instalments throughout the five-year period of service. The Militia was now The Bedfordshire, or 18th Regiment of Light Infantry Militia. Drilling took place on St Peter's Green in Bedford and, in bad weather, in the sheds of the London and North-western Railway, and it became obvious that the Militia Storehouse in Bedford Castle was totally inadequate. In 1854, the Crimean War began and the Militia was embodied and posted to Berwick-upon-Tweed to release regular troops for service overseas. The Militia Ballot was suspended by Earl Russell and some 250 men volunteered to enlist in the Regular Army. The depleted regiment returned to Bedford and was then posted via Aldershot to Ireland. After this spell of nearly two years' service, the regiment was disembodied, and a new Militia Depot was then built on Goldington Road in Bedford. This housed the permanent staff and provided storage for weapons, equipment, and uniforms, along with stabling and workshop facilities. In 1857, a further period of service saw the regiment in Aldershot, Dover Castle, and Weymouth, while the regulars were off to India to suppress the insurrection there, and was among the last of the militia regiments to be stood down in 1860. Crimean Lodge, standing at the former eastern entrance to Hasells Hall is a prefabricated army hut brought back from the Crimea. It was supplied to Thomas de la Rue, the playing-card manufacturer, while he was the hall's tenant, in 1860–6. In 1868, regular troops passed through Dunstable *en route* for Ireland at the time of the Fenian Revolt. In 1869, the 600-strong Bedfordshire Militia assembled at Woburn to be brigaded with the militias of Oxfordshire, Hertfordshire, and Northamptonshire for inspection by the inspector-general of Auxiliary Forces. The general countrywide reorganisation of the military saw the Militia adopted by the line regiments in 1881. Thus the Bedfordshire Militia, with a current strength of 864 men, became the 3rd (Militia) Battalion of the Bedfordshire Regiment. Under the same arrangement, Hertfordshire's militia, having no county line regiment, was fostered as the 4th (Militia) Battalion.

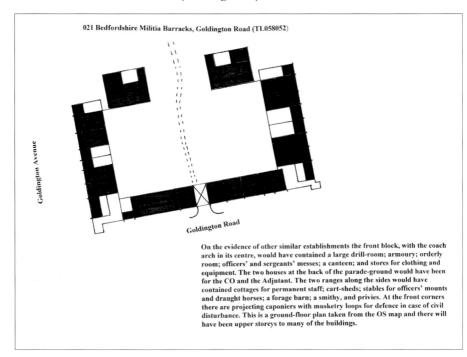

021 Bedfordshire Militia Barracks, Goldington Road (TL058052)

Goldington Avenue

Goldington Road

On the evidence of other similar establishments the front block, with the coach arch in its centre, would have contained a large drill-room; armoury; orderly room; officers' and sergeants' messes; a canteen; and stores for clothing and equipment. The two houses at the back of the parade-ground would have been for the CO and the Adjutant. The two ranges along the sides would have contained cottages for permanent staff; cart-sheds; stables for officers' mounts and draught horses; a forage barn; a smithy, and privies. At the front corners there are projecting caponiers with musketry loops for defence in case of civil disturbance. This is a ground-floor plan taken from the OS map and there will have been upper storeys to many of the buildings.

Bedford, plan of the Goldington Road Militia Barracks.

Hazell's Hall, an army hut imported from the Crimea by the tenant of Hazell's Hall.

The Rifle Volunteer Corps

Both the Indian Mutiny, or First Indian War of Independence, and the Crimean War had raised doubts about the professionalism of the Regular Army. These doubts extended to basic skills, especially musketry, and it was felt that civilians should be encouraged to develop such skills as a back-up to the military in times of national emergency. While local efforts to rectify this state of affairs such as the shooting gallery for rifles and pistols set up in the yard of the Saracens Head in Dunstable in 1856 were laudable, it was important to make such efforts parts of a nationwide system. There were two separate but related elements to this initiative. From early in 1859, the formation of local rifle volunteer corps gathered momentum, and the National Rifle Association held its inaugural shoot on Wimbledon Common in July 1860 with Queen Victoria pulling the first trigger. Bedfordshire's first RVC was raised in Bedford in February 1860, and six more corps had followed by September. These seven corps formed a 1st Administrative Battalion, Bedfordshire RVC in the August with its HQ in Bedford. The Battalion HQ moved to Toddington in 1866 and then to Woburn in 1870. The 4th (Dunstable) Corps assembled with its own band, and had the use of an outdoor rifle range in Pascombe Pit. The 6th Corps in Luton had a drum and fife band and, it too, had a range in Dallow Road where matches were held with other corps from as far away as Northampton.

Traditionally, enthusiastic enrolment in the volunteers has been put down to a sense of patriotism. However, that was not the whole story. Membership afforded little in the way of public respect, the volunteers often being derided and their parades treated with ridicule. The uniform was nothing special and a member of the 8th (Woburn) RVC went so far as to put down lack of recruitment to their unattractive uniform. Little social cachet was to be gained by membership, and members often found themselves out of pocket. It can be argued that the prime motivation came down to opportunities for recreational activity and legitimate opportunities to get out of the house with their mates. In 1865, the 7th (Biggleswade and Shefford) Corps was able to shoot for a range of prizes including silverware. Such prizes were often donated by the local gentry who saw their duty as giving support to their neighbourhood corps. Typical of such patronage was the annual dinner provided by Sir George Osborne of Chicksands Priory for the 7th (Biggleswade and Shefford) Corps. Beyond such largesse, there was a wish to provide the RVC with legitimacy by appointing their leaders from the local aristocracy and squirearchy. From the beginning there was pressure on the lord lieutenant to appoint Francis Hastings Russell as commander of the Bedfordshire RVC. He was MP for Bedfordshire and later succeeded as the 9th duke of Bedford. Lord St John of Bletsoe and Lord Wensleydale, an eminent lawyer and owner of Ampthill Park, also served on the county volunteer committee. It was also important to recruit men from the right social class as officers. The sixty-four-strong 2nd (Toddington) Corps was led from the start by Mr William Cooper Cooper, the lord of the manor. He had served in the Militia, attaining the rank of major in 1858, and was the only gentleman in a corps made up of equal numbers of farmers, tradesmen, and artisans. The 4th (Dunstable) Corps had trouble finding leaders but appointed a solicitor who was subsequently struck off and fled abroad. His deputy, the landlord of the Saracens Arms, was only appointed after authority had wrestled with the burning question of whether only gentlemen ought to be considered as officers. By 1879, half of the Bedfordshire Rifle Volunteers were drawn from Bedford's brickworks and Luton's hat makers, and the option available to the rural areas of appointing squires and parsons was not always available in towns. The 8th (Woburn) Corps was drawn from the duke of Bedford's estate where a junior Russell might have been expected to command but appears to have been led, from 1885, by Frederick Tanqueray, the local solicitor and coroner whose offices were at 5 George Street, next to the Bedford Arms Hotel. In 1864 in Bedford, the 9th Corps was drawn from the Howard Brothers' Britannia Works, which had 700 employees in 1871. James Howard started off in command but, although MP for Bedford, was living in Eastbourne in 1871. His corps was disbanded soon after 1872 after only eight years in existence.

The RVC was in receipt of subsidies from the War Department on the basis of the number of their 'efficients', i.e. trained men, competent at drill and shooting, and regular attenders on drill nights. In 1862, the 6th Corps in Luton carried out shooting practice at Leagrave Marsh with blank cartridges, and in 1871, RVC exchanged their old Enfields for breech-loading Snider rifles. In Dunstable, the corps trained on the Downs, stopping off on the way home at the Rifle Volunteer PH on West Street. It was possibly this habit that led some of the 4th Corps bandsmen to mutiny by assembling at the Saracens Head drill-shed and playing discordantly. At Easter 1877, a field day on the plain below Dunstable Downs was held for more than 10,000 Rifle Volunteers from London, Bedfordshire, and Hertfordshire. Several corps had their own outdoor rifle ranges but for those without access to a full-size range, there were miniature indoor ranges. These were used either for small-bore rifles, or for normal calibre rifles fitted with Morris Tubes, which reduced the bore and allowed smaller ammunition to be fired on these shorter ranges. Once firearms were in the hands of inexperienced young men, it was sadly inevitable that fatal accidents would occur. In June 1900, a Volunteer was shot dead by a recruit in the Luton companies' club on Park Street. Fortunately, most shooting took place under properly controlled conditions either for classification purposes or in competitions for such trophies as the Leigh Cup.

One of the stipulations for the award of the grant to RVC was the provision of suitable premises for the administration of the corps; for the secure storage of arms and ammunition; for an indoor drill space; and, eventually, for the accommodation of a permanent staff instructor, usually a retired regular senior

NCO. In the early days of the RVC, it was often convenient to have shared use of public buildings. The 6th RVC in Luton held its 1869 annual presentation of prizes for drill and proficiency in the Cheapside Plait Hall, with the armoury and stores next door in 1872. However, from 1887, 'C', 'F', and 'G' Companies of the 3rd Volunteer Battalion, Bedfordshire Regiment, are recorded in Kelly's Directory as being in premises in Park Street, Luton. It would appear that while the HQ and armoury moved to Park Street into premises that also functioned as the Volunteers' Social Club, formally opened in December 1888, many of the Volunteers' indoor activities continued to be carried out in the Plait Hall in Cheapside, until at least 1907. The advantage of the Plait Hall was that it was large enough to accommodate three companies on parade. The Park Street premises, sometimes referred to as the armoury, and at other times as the Volunteer Drill Hall, appears to have been used for smaller group activities. In Leighton Buzzard, the town hall was used, but in Dunstable, the Saracens Head public house with its shooting range and drill-shed served until the assembly rooms in Church Street were taken over in 1889. The old Militia Depot in Bedford had become available from 1857 for use by the RVC. Although Houghton House had been abandoned in 1793 and partially dismantled, the Ampthill RVC was using part of the building prior to moving into a drill room behind the King's Arms public house sometime before 1885. This move may have been prompted by more demolitions at Houghton House in 1877. In Biggleswade, a drill hall had been built on Bonds Lane, off the Hitchin Road by 1894. Major William Cooper Cooper may have offered his Toddington Park manor house as both local and county HQ. At Woburn, it is likely that the Yeomanry will have used the riding school and stables at the abbey and the grounds for squadron manoeuvres, while the 8th Corps RVC, later 'I' Company of the Bedfordshire Regiment's Volunteer Battalion, was given a dedicated space in the outbuildings of the Bedford Arms Hotel on George Street. The Shefford company had a drill hall on North Bridge Street.

The disbandment of the Bedfordshire Yeomanry in 1827 meant that the county was one of the few with no volunteer cavalry unit. One of the problems for yeomanry regiments generally was the high costs involved: for uniforms and equipment; for the provision and upkeep of horses; and for fulfilling the social obligations of the volunteers themselves, so without a very rich and enthusiastic patron, a yeomanry regiment would struggle. The establishment of Mounted Rifle Volunteer Corps was seen as having a double benefit. On the one hand, it would combine the fire-power of the rifleman with the mobility of the cavalryman thus providing tactical advantage militarily; and on the other hand, it would provide a less grand alternative to the Yeomanry in terms of both material cost and social cachet. William Montagu, 7th duke of Manchester, raised the Huntingdonshire Mounted Rifles at Kimbolton Castle in December 1859. Recruitment appears to have taken place through correspondence sent to those likely to respond

Leighton Buzzard Town Hall served as a drill hall for the Rifle Volunteer Corps and the TF.

Ampthill, the yard of the King's Arms contained a room used by the Rifle Volunteer Corps until 1912.

Biggleswade, Bonds Lane, the drill hall in a sad state behind hoardings.

Dunstable, Church Street, the assembly rooms served as a drill hall and later became the Book Castle.

positively, as Sgt Baynes circulated a letter round the hunting fraternity. He pointed out the low annual subscription of just 10*s* 6*d*; the cost of the scarlet tunic with silver facings coming in at a modest £2 2*s*; and the helmet, at an even more reasonable £1 16*s*. The clincher, as he saw it, was the fact that the breeches and boots would double as hunting attire. A second troop was raised in Bedford, and Sgt Baynes's letter was clearly successful as he was shortly promoted to captain, leading the Sharnbrook Troop he had personally recruited. In January 1861, the corps became the Huntingdonshire Light Horse Volunteers, maintaining those three established troops. It would appear, however, that the duke was not much concerned with keeping costs down, preferring to adopt expensive uniforms with all the trimmings and turning out in full splendour for every gala occasion on offer. He enlisted the prince of Wales, the future Edward VII, as honorary colonel in 1865. Although the short-lived Cambridgeshire Mounted Rifle Volunteers joined up with the Huntingdonshire corps in 1865, the combined membership was never very significant and despite outlasting most of the similar units across the country, in 1882 the corps was disbanded.

In 1881, the Childers reforms saw a new regimental structure take shape. The two battalions of the 16th Foot became the 1st and 2nd Battalions of the Bedfordshire Regiment; the Bedfordshire Light Infantry Militia and the Hertfordshire Militia became, respectively, the 3rd and 4th Battalions of the Bedfordshire Regiment; the two administrative battalions of the Hertfordshire Rifle Volunteer Corps became the 1st and 2nd (Volunteer) Battalions of the Bedfordshire Regiment; and the single administrative battalion of the Bedfordshire Rifle Volunteer Corps became the 3rd (Volunteer) Battalion. These were all part of the 16th Military District based on the new barracks at Kempston. A 4th (Huntingdonshire) Volunteer Battalion was raised in 1900, with HQ in Huntingdon, possibly in the recently-demolished Militia Barracks. Initially it mustered eight companies but these were later reduced to six.

4

The Military in Bedfordshire 1900–39

This period saw the Boer War, the establishment of the Territorial Force (TF), the First World War, the creation of the RAF, and the period of rearmament that preceded the Second World War. Much of this activity caused significant changes to both the urban and rural landscapes, and to the social fabric of the nation, particularly in the increased recognition of women's contribution to society.

The Second South African (Boer) War

The 2nd Battalion, Bedfordshire Regiment, landed in Capetown early in 1900 as part of a force that advanced into the Boer heartlands but also spent time guarding the long and vulnerable lines of communication. Once Militia units arrived in South Africa to take over much of the work of guarding the railways, the regular infantry could be released for duty in the columns that brought the Boers to battle. The Bedfordshires acquitted themselves well in these demanding campaigns, receiving praise from their leaders, mentions in despatches, and medals. In response to the extremely successful Boer tactics of forming Commandos of mounted riflemen to fight a mobile war, the War Office decided to raise a mounted volunteer force. The Imperial Yeomanry was organised in Companies, around 125 strong, many of which were drawn from existing Yeomanry Regiments, some of them having survived right through from the French Wars. In January 1900, Lord Alwyne Compton, MP for Bedfordshire and a former cavalry officer, raised the 28th (Bedfordshire) Company of the 4th Battalion, Imperial Yeomanry, for service in South Africa. There were transfers between the hundred or so companies, and two further drafts were shipped out to join the 28th Company before the end of the war. The 4th (Militia) Battalion of the Bedfordshire Regiment, formerly the Hertfordshire Militia, sent a detachment of nearly 500 officers and men to South Africa in 1900, winning plaudits from the High Command. As well as garrisoning the lines, which were set up to inhibit the movement of the Boer Commandos, they formed a Mounted Infantry Company attached to Lord Methuen's mobile column fighting in a succession of engagements, and suffering over thirty fatalities through disease and enemy action. On the Home Front, Hayward Tyler of Luton, already in receipt of government contracts relating to Woolwich Arsenal, manufactured the water supply system for military hutments in Pretoria during the Boer War as part of a consortium of local companies with War Office contracts.

On their return in 1901, the Bedfordshire Company of the Imperial Yeomanry was reformed as the Bedfordshire Yeomanry with its HQ in Bedford. It was organised in four squadrons with a mounted machine-gun section equipped with Maxim guns. One squadron was based in Dunstable using the town hall from 1902 and performing their mounted drills including lance work in the Park. Shooting was practised using Morris Tubes on an indoor miniature range. The first public schools cadet camp was held in 1899 and Bedford GS was one of four attending. In 1900, a Cadet Corps was formed at Bedford Modern School, initially affiliated to 3rd Volunteer Battalion, Bedfordshire Regiment, but later transferring its connection to the 1st Bedford Engineer Volunteers. Three years later, in Dunstable, the Ashton GS Cadet Corps was formed with RSM Odell as staff instructor. Companies of the Church Lads' Brigade, at the time a Christian paramilitary organisation whose members drilled and learned to shoot, were formed at St Martin's Church, Bedford, in 1904 and in Luton in 1905. In Oakley, two cottages, Nos 26–28 High Street, designed by Charles Holden in 1905 and paid for by the duke of Bedford were built for ex-soldiers of the Bedfordshire Regiment. The volunteer battalions continued to train regularly, and in 1907, an indoor miniature rifle range was built on the corner of Manor and Leighton Roads, in Toddington, and opened by Gen. Sir Henry Redvers Buller, VC, who had been C-in-C in South Africa. In the early years of the century, some new facilities were provided for the Volunteers. In Bedford, the 3rd Volunteer Battalion already had a HQ in Nos 44 and 46, two houses on the corner of Gwyn and Greenhill Streets. Their new drill hall stretched the entire length of Greenhill Street and connected up with No. 61 Hassett Street, on the corner, behind which was the arch 'wide enough to take the Battalion's machine-guns' giving access to the hall from Greenhill Street. This new drill hall, designed to provide all the necessary military and recreational facilities, opened in January 1904. The two-storey block, formerly Nos 44 and 46 Gwyn Street, became the HQ of the 3rd Volunteer Battalion, Bedfordshire Regiment, and No. 18 Hassett Street, the HQ of the 1st Bedford Engineer Volunteers.

Oakley, the two cottages, Nos 26–28 High Street, were designed by Charles Holden in 1905, and paid for by the duke of Bedford for ex-soldiers of the Bedfordshire Regiment.

The Territorial Force

As a result of concerns raised over the country's defences, the Secretary of State for War Richard (later Viscount) Haldane set up the Territorial Force (TF). Realising that the bulk of the professional, but tiny, Regular Army would be involved in its twin tasks of supporting Britain's allies on the continent of Europe, and of safeguarding the British Empire, there was a pressing need for a force dedicated to home defence. The TF was therefore set up on a regional basis to meet this need, absorbing as many of the old Volunteer Force as were willing to join. Across Britain there were fourteen self-contained TF divisions, each complete with three infantry brigades, artillery, medical and army service corps, engineers, and a mounted brigade of Yeomanry cavalry. The Bedfordshire Yeomanry with squadrons in Bedford, Biggleswade, Dunstable, and Godmanchester (Huntingdonshire) was attached to the Eastern Mounted Brigade for training purposes. The two Militia battalions of the Bedfordshire Regiment became the 3rd (Reserve) and 4th (Special Reserve) Battalions. The 1st and 2nd Volunteer Battalions were hived off to become the 1st Battalion, Hertfordshire Regiment, an all-TF unit. The old 3rd (Bedfordshire) and 4th (Huntingdonshire) Volunteer Battalions combined to become the new 5th Battalion (TF), whose eight companies were distributed across the county with four outliers in

Huntingdonshire. Along with the corresponding territorial battalions of the Cambridgeshire, Hertfordshire, and Northamptonshire Regiments, the 5th Battalion formed the East Midland Infantry Brigade, with its HQ at No. 10 St Paul's Square, Bedford. Additionally, based in Bedford were the 1st and 2nd East Anglian Field Companies RE, successors to the Engineer Volunteers. After 1913, when the RE Divisional Telegraph Companies were reorganised as the RE Signal Service, the East Anglian Divisional Signals Company's HQ and its No. 1 Section were Bedford based. The Eastern Mounted Brigade's Field Ambulance, RAMC, had its HQ and one section at Grove Road, Luton, with a detachment in Dunstable, and a second section in Bedford. The established cadet corps at Bedford Modern, Bedford GS. and Elstow were taken into the TF as Junior OTC units. Unusually, and possibly due to the presence in Bedford of a strong RE presence, all three schools opted for specialist engineer corps, maintaining five companies between them, while the Ashton cadets affiliated with the 5th Battalion, Bedfordshire Regiment. Companies of the Church Lads' Brigade were well established at St Martin's, and All Saints', Queens Park, churches in Bedford, in Luton, and in Dunstable. These CLB companies chose not to affiliate with the Territorial Cadet Force, and the Luton company would be dissolved in 1911 over a controversy concerning the use of dummy rifles. Could this have been a pacifist reaction to the perceived war-mongering of the Northcliffe press, or the opposite, a demand for the real Snider rifles with which many other CLB and Boys' Brigade units were visibly equipped?

Following this fundamental reorganisation of the volunteers and the increase in specialist volunteer units, the need for increased accommodation was recognised. In Ampthill, Mr Rushbrooke, the builder of Russell House in Dunstable Street, had erected a tin tabernacle for use as a gymnasium in 1889 on the opposite side of the road. Such buildings were freely available off-the-shelf from a number of fabricators and at a very reasonable cost, with many remaining in use today. Acknowledging the inadequate nature of the room behind the King's Arms, its acquisition for the volunteers was reported in the *Bedfordshire Mercury* on 26 January 1912. It was built of corrugated-iron lined with match-board, with five windows in each long side, and an apse at the east end. It measured 80 by 26 feet (25 by 8 metres), and was divided into a hall seating 350, measuring 58 by 26 feet (18 by 8 metres) and two rooms, each 22 by 13 feet (7 by 4 metres), with one serving as an armoury and lecture room, and the other as orderly room and stores. The building later served as a workshop for Mr Mann senior, builder and contractor, and, after 1922, was known as 'The Entertainment Room'. Bedford was provided with a brand-new purpose-built drill hall at Nos 32–40 Ashburnham Road, designed by J. H. Fenning, a local architect; it opened in 1912 as the HQ of the Bedfordshire Yeomanry. A very grand administrative block of nineteen bays fronted the road with a pediment with the royal arms over the archway, flanked by ornate classical pillars, leading to the inner courtyard. On

Above: Shortmead Street, Biggleswade, the drill hall used by 'B' Squadron, Bedfordshire Yeomanry in 1914.

Right: No. 10 St Paul's Square, Bedford, HQ East Midland Infantry Brigade (TF).

one side of this courtyard lay the drill hall itself measuring 100 by 50 feet (30 by 15 metres), with the riding school, measuring 150 by 46 feet (45 by 14 metres) on the other. First floor lecture and recreation rooms were provided with movable partitions enabling them to become galleries for both of these large spaces. A six-lane indoor rifle range was installed in the roof, and messes for officers and sergeants along with a canteen for ORs, an armoury, stabling, stores, and cart sheds were all included. The building would be used by the East Anglian REs and the Mounted Brigade Field Ambulance as well as the Yeomanry. The REs' previous training facilities, scattered around the town, became redundant. The Tavistock Hall in Dunstable was built in 1912 for 'C' Squadron, Bedfordshire Yeomanry. It was a large double-fronted, gabled, front-block with a hall and stabling behind and to one side. An aerial photograph on the 'Dunstable before the Bulldozers' website shows the building was still there in 1957. In Luton, the Park Street HQ, armoury, and reading room were still in use in 1912, usually known as the Volunteer Social Club, and provided the venue for machine-gun training every Wednesday evening in May 1914. In Grove Road, a new drill hall had been built by 1910, behind the Poor House, as the base for one section of the Eastern Mounted Brigade Field Ambulance. It consisted of a house with a single-storey hall and a garage behind. The three Luton-based companies of the Bedfordshire's 5th Battalion still had their HQ in Park Street, but many of their indoor drills took place in the Cheapside Plait Hall up to 1914 and, outdoors in Mr Brown's Paddock. Similarly, the Dunstable detachment drilled on the Grammar School field, and the Leighton Buzzard men at Bell Close. The Sandy detachment of the Biggleswade company used the iron-framed, concrete, and

Luton, the Grove Road drill hall used by the Eastern Mounted Brigade field ambulance.

brick prefabricated hall, which had been put up off London Road in Girtford by 1914. The TF continued to hold many of the traditional summer camps in local places such as Ampthill Park, but in 1908, the East Anglian REs went to Frinton for their annual training camp.

Flight was still in its infancy when Claude Grahame-White (1879–1959), a former pupil of Bedford GS, flew over the parental home in Bedford on a visit in 1913, landing at a Primrose League fete in Biddenham. Two days later, he flew over Luton in a Morane-Saulnier monoplane. He had started a flying school at Hendon in 1911 and sought to promote the military use of flying machines by organising exhibition events of bomb-dropping. He would later establish an aircraft factory, which was greatly enlarged in 1916 and now forms part of the RAF Museum in Hendon.

The First World War:
Mobilisation and Recruitment, August 1914

On the outbreak of war in August 1914, mobilisation of the TF and recruitment to Lord Kitchener's New Armies began immediately. The 5th Battalion mobilised at its Gwyn Street drill hall and at Goldington Road Schools. Recruits for the Bedfordshire Yeomanry left Huntingdon in October 1914 to join those already mobilised. The Bedford Rugby Club ground became a military depot for horse transport, with the Scrum Hall used as a forage store. The East Anglian RE Field Companies were accommodated in the gymnasium at the Bedford GS. By the end of August, over 500 recruits had been taken into Kempston Barracks for initial training. These represented only the first tranche of the 3,000 or so men who would become the 6th, 7th, and 8th Battalions of the Bedfordshire Regiment in Kitchener's New Armies. In October, the War Office was congratulating the CTA on attracting 2,500 men to the local TF units, and physical training teachers were recruited to improve on the low standard of the recruits' physical fitness. In Luton, the Corn Exchange was turned into a recruiting office, and the Waller Street Wesleyan Methodist Chapel was used as billets for troops. The school OTC members were enlisting in large numbers, many of them becoming infantry subalterns who, once their training was complete, would take their places in the trenches, expected to survive for just six weeks. The parish records of St Martin's in Bedford, report that the entire 1908 intake of the CLB had enlisted. But it was not necessary to go abroad to face danger. In Dunstable, in August 1914, horses of the Northamptonshire Yeomanry stampeded causing many of them to lose their lives. After that, Mr Blow's farm at Houghton Regis provided a safe base prior to their move to Winchester *en route* for France. They were then replaced there by 700 Royal Engineers from Barnet.

The Scrum Hall at Bedford Rugby Club whose Goldington Road ground became a military depot for horse transport, with the Scrum Hall used as a forage store.

The Deployment of Local Units

The Bedfordshire Regiment

Some 60,000 men served in the Regiment's nineteen battalions suffering 50 per cent casualties, over 7,000 of which were fatal, and winning seven VCs and hundreds of other gallantry awards. On the outbreak of war the 1st Battalion was at Mullingar in Ireland, and was immediately deployed to France in 15th Brigade, 5th Division, of the BEF, remaining there for the duration, fighting at Mons and Ypres in the early days; on the Somme, at Ypres again, and at Arras in the middle period; and through to the German spring offensive, the Somme again, and the Hindenburg Line in 1918. The 2nd Battalion was brought back from Pretoria, landing at Southampton *en route* for Zeebrugge, where it landed in October, also, staying for the duration. It fought at Ypres, Neuve Chapelle, Loos, and the Somme. In the second half of the war, it fought right through to the final defeat of the German army on the River Sambre. The 3rd (Reserve) Battalion from the depot in Kempston Barracks, went to Harwich Garrison for the duration, where it built a camp. For training purposes, Ampthill House and Park became a regimental training base, staffed by officers and NCOs of the Battalion. The 4th (Extra Reserve) Battalion also joined Harwich Garrison from its Hertford base, staying there until July 1916 when it was sent to France in the 63rd, formerly Royal Naval, Division. The 5th (TF) Battalion joined the 54th (1st East Anglian)

Division at Bury St Edmunds and in May 1915 was shipped to Suvla Bay for the Gallipoli campaign and then on to Egypt. The 2/5th (TF) Battalion formed at Bedford in September 1914 and joined the 69th (2nd East Anglian) Division in Newmarket. It spent time on home defence duties at Darlington before going to Carburton Camp in Nottinghamshire in May 1917 and then to nearby Clipstone Camp training drafts for the frontline battalions. The 3/5th (TF) Battalion formed in Bedford in June 1915 and then went to Windsor, Tring, and on to the East Anglian Reserve Brigade at Halton. In 1916 it became the 5th (Reserve) Battalion and merged with the 3/1st Battalion, Hertfordshire Regiment (TF), going to Crowborough and, finally, Hastings. The 6th, 7th, and 8th (Service) Battalions of Lord Kitchener's K1, K2, and K3 New Armies, served in France for the duration from July 1915. The 10th (Reserve) Battalion was part of the 6th (Reserve) Brigade for a while but, along with the 9th Battalion, was absorbed into the 6th Training Reserve Brigade at Dovercourt as the 27th and 28th Battalions, Training Reserve. The 11th (Provisional) Battalion (TF) was, from June 1915, in 225th (Mixed) Brigade in Suffolk on home defence duties. The 12th and 13th (Transport Workers) Battalions, badged as battalions of the Bedfordshire Regiment, provided working parties at ports: the 12th on the south coast from Chatham to Weymouth and the 13th on the east coast from London to Boston. The 10th (Reserve) Battalion formed the 53rd (Young Soldiers) Battalion and subsequently became the 51st and 52nd (Graduated) Battalions as their members became old enough for overseas service. The 1st, 2nd, and 3rd (Garrison) Battalions served in India and Burma from February 1916.

The Bedfordshire Yeomanry and Other Locally-Raised Units

The 1/1st Bedfordshire Yeomanry, not integral to the Eastern Mounted Brigade, was sent to France in June 1915, staying there as part of the 1st Cavalry Division, waiting in vain for the breakthrough that never came, until March 1918 when it was withdrawn to become a cyclist unit. It then combined with the Essex Yeomanry as a machine-gun battalion, but was remounted in April 1918 with one squadron attached to each of 9th Cavalry Brigade's three regiments. The 2/1st Bedfordshire Yeomanry served in Essex until 1916 when its squadrons were allocated to three Home Defence divisions, then absorbed by July 1917 into the 1st Reserve Cavalry Regiment in Dublin. The 3/1st Bedfordshire Yeomanry was formed in 1915 and spent the war in Reserve Cavalry Regiments at Colchester and Dublin, providing drafts for the 1/1st. The East Anglian Divisional Engineers including the Field and Signal Companies all served with the 54th (1st East Anglian) Division in the Dardanelles and then in Egypt.

The Eastern Mounted Brigade Field Ambulances stayed in East Anglia until September 1915, with their parent Mounted Brigade which then sailed, without their horses, to Gallipoli and then on to Egypt to man the Suez Canal defences. Luton Modern School raised a cadet corps, affiliated to the East Anglian

Divisional REs. It was recognised officially only in 1918 but, like similar units across the country including the Biscot CLB, would most likely have formed long before the red tape caught up with them.

The Army in Bedfordshire 1914–18: Training and Home Defence

Home-based troops had three functions: the defence of the home-land against foreign invasion; internal security against sabotage or espionage; and training to prepare for service abroad. The threat of invasion was always tenuous but never went away; the sabotage/espionage factor was always more imagined than real; but the need to feed large numbers of troops into the maelstrom of the Western Front was permanent. As more and more trained, and then semi-trained troops were despatched overseas, then home defence came to rely largely on the older TF men who were unsuitable for frontline service, and those recruits, and after 1916, conscripts who were in training and/or too young to serve overseas anyway.

Central Force: Luton and Bedford

In August 1914, the pre-war planning of the War Office, however inadequate, was nevertheless still implemented. The British Expeditionary Force (BEF) was sent to France and Belgium, and the Territorial Force (TF) was mobilised for home defence. Given a strong expectation of an enemy invasion of East Anglia, while cyclist units and garrison troops guarded the coast, the bulk of the TF was concentrated as 'Central Force' with its HQ at Luton Hoo, in a triangle of land with Bedford, Northampton, and Cambridge at the angles. Bedford was HQ of 1st Army, which included the Highland, Welsh, and West Riding Divisions, two Mounted Brigades, and associated artillery and engineers. Luton was HQ of 3rd Army, which comprised the East Anglian, North and South Midland, and 2nd London Divisions, two Mounted Brigades, and a Cyclist Battalion. But in early summer of 1915, most of these formations would be sent to the Western Front following the almost total destruction of the BEF in the early months of the war.

The Highland Division (TF) descended on Bedford in the middle of August 1914, in eighty-seven trains from Auchterader, twelve from Stirling, fifteen from Inverness, and fifty-eight from Perth, disembarking on to hastily-erected temporary sidings alongside the Ampthill Road. These thousands of Highlanders far from home and many speaking a strange tongue were welcomed into the town and swiftly found billets, many of them in empty property but with families as well. Each of the three constituent brigades—the Argyll & Sutherland, Gordon, and Seaforth & Cameron—was allocated an area of town with battalions concentrated on blocks of streets, extending as far out as Elstow, with

Luton Hoo, HQ of 'Central Force', which consisted of TF divisions responsible for home defence, but which were soon despatched to the Western Front.

one battalion under canvas at Renhold and another, temporarily quarantined in Howbury Park, with the Hall as HQ. Divisional HQ was established at St Mary's, and the field ambulance units in various school buildings, with the artillery south of the river. It was remarkable how 15,000–20,000 men could be absorbed into the life of the town with few complaints on either side. Drills were held on the grammar school field and in Russell Park, and a cluster of huts was erected at the western end of Bedford Park. In October, King George V accompanied by Princess Louise visited Bedford to inspect the Highland Division, the 2/1st Bedfordshire Yeomanry and other locally-based units in Putnoe Park.

The Highland Division had initially been deployed to Bedford as part of Central Force, a concentration of anti-invasion TF divisions, but as it became apparent that these would be needed on the Western Front, the need for specific training was recognised and the accent changed to one of preparation for service in France. While general fitness training continued with drill and route marches, outposts defending Bromham Bridge were practised, and trenches dug on Cemetery Hill and in Clapham Park. The presence of twelve pipe-bands enlivened marches and processions and the 4th Battalion, Cameron Highlanders, was filmed marching through Bedford in 1915 wearing khaki kilt aprons, possibly *en route* for their early embarkation to join 8th Division in France. In order to bring individual battalions up to strength, both local men and Londoners who wished to serve in Scottish regiments were recruited. In the spring of 1915, additional drafts of Highland reservists and complete battalions from several English regiments were brought in to compensate for those Scottish battalions that had already left for France in November 1914 and early 1915; for the 135 deaths from unfamiliar infectious diseases; and for those Highlanders who exercised their right as territorials to opt out of serving abroad.

While Bedford was the focus for the Highlanders, the North Midland Division (TF) converged on Luton, an operation accomplished using thirty-two trains from Burton on Trent and a further forty-seven from Derby. HQ was established in Stockwood House with use of the town hall, Plait Halls, public library, Wardown House, and the recreation ground. Luton Liberal Club's lecture hall and smoke room were used as officers' quarters. The 5th Battalion, Leicestershire Regiment (TF), was one of several units under canvas. Physical drill for soldiers with 'chest management' problems was held nightly in the old skating rink in Park Street, Luton. By 1907, five years before his death, Sir Julius Wernher, the diamond magnate and Randlord, had completed improvements to the eighteenth-century mansion of Luton Hoo based on the sumptuous style of the Ritz Hotel. Its 1,500 acres (600 ha) of landscaped parkland containing two lakes surrounded the house and provided the setting for two morale-boosting events held in September 1914. The first saw over 4,000 territorial troops representing units from each of the North Midland Division's three infantry brigades, along with the division's artillery and field ambulance sections, all assembled on the polo ground for inspection by King George V. The public could purchase tickets to watch this spectacle for *3d* in advance or *6d* on the day. The second event was the inspection by Lord Kitchener of the Nottinghamshire and Derby Infantry Brigade consisting of one battalion of the Lincolnshire Regiment and three battalions of the Sherwood Foresters (Nottingham and Derby Regiment). The house had already become the Central Force HQ in August 1914, and the next year, the War Office gratefully accepted Lady Alice Wernher's offer of the parkland and lakes for military exercises and training. With the demise of Central Force, Luton Hoo would become HQ Eastern Command, removed from Horse Guards in 1916.

In February 1915, the 46th (North Midland) Division (TF) left Luton for the Western Front, and in April, the 51st (Highland) Division (TF) left Bedford. While such established formations were assembling and moving on, the efforts to reinforce regular and territorial units, and to produce the New Armies was being stepped up. Overwhelming numbers of recruits into the Bedfordshire Regiment led Lord Ampthill, cousin of the 11th duke of Bedford and commander of the 3rd (Reserve) Battalion, to establish Ampthill Park as a training depot for the regiment. By the second week of September 1914, some 800 men had enlisted at Kempston Barracks and local recruiting offices, to be despatched to Ampthill to be clothed, equipped, and receive basic instruction. In the absence of official funding, the 11th duke and Lord Ampthill met much of the expense themselves. These 6th, 7th, and 8th Battalions would shortly join their New Army divisions for service in France in 1915. In October 1914, a new battalion of the Bedfordshire Regiment was approved by the War Office to be funded by the duke of Bedford, consisting of 500 men initially but then increased up to 1,000. This would be raised as the

9th Battalion but, along with a 10th Battalion, instead of going to France, would be absorbed into the Training Reserve at Harwich. Also gathered at Ampthill were reservists, former soldiers who were returning to the colours. These were swiftly despatched to the 3rd (Reserve) Battalion at Felixstowe to become drafts for the two regular battalions. The Ampthill Park Camp initially consisted of six twenty-bed sleeping huts, cookhouse, ablutions, and recreation room, all finished to much higher standards than the normal army camp. Until a canteen was built, recruits ate at tables set out between the rows of beds. As the camp filled up, extra accommodation was built and billets were found in Ampthill itself. Nearly 2,500 recruits passed through the camp in the two years to October 1916, being sent as drafts, not only to the Bedfordshires, but to the Machine-Gun Corps and other line regiments. The camp was nominally commanded by the duke of Bedford himself, colonel of the regiment, with Bedfordshire's chief constable, a veteran of the Boer War, as his second-in-command; an experienced officer as adjutant; and around thirty NCOs. The recruits underwent drill and general infantry training, paraded in the indoor drill shed, and shot on the Millbrook full-size rifle range and the camp's own miniature range. At times, the pressure on space was such that it proved necessary to use the old militia barracks in the Bedford Arms Hotel's yard in Woburn as overspill accommodation. There, the quarters were refurbished as 'sleeping apartments' furnished with 'comfortable beds' with 'pillows and blankets', and breakfast and supper were laid on in the town hall. The introduction of conscription in 1916 put training on a very different footing and recruitment into the TF ceased entirely. The camp was far too valuable not to be used so, at the request of the adjutant-general, it became No. 9 Regimental Command Depot, responsible for getting wounded soldiers back to the front as quickly as possible. The duke continued his patronage by ensuring that trained staff would carry out the new techniques of massage, and by providing a fully equipped gymnasium. At least half of the 8,000 troops who passed through the depot were returned to service via the 3rd (Reserve) and 4th (Extra Reserve) Battalions at Felixstowe, or the 9th and 10th (Reserve) Battalions at nearby Dovercourt, all part of Harwich Garrison.

A number of other military installations were needed to service the local depots. These would include the North Midland Veterinary Hospital and Remount Depot in Stockwood Park in 1916; the Army Remount Depot on Beech Hill, Luton, in 1917; and Mobile Veterinary Sections Nos 911–1041. Troops had use of Luton Rifle Club's outdoor range in Dallow Road, and the indoor range behind the Royal Hotel in Mill Street. Along with the infantry camps, there were training units established for the artillery and the signals. Biscot Mill, Luton, was a camp for No. 6 Reserve Training Brigade, Royal Field Artillery (RFA), which was formed from the eight third-line brigade depots of the London RFA (TF). These units, which had come to Luton via High Wycombe and Kettering in January 1916, were reorganised into a HQ and four batteries armed with obsolescent 15-pounder BLC (Breech-Loading Converted) field guns. The unit's war diaries show a constant stream of comings and goings: to the first-line 47th and 56th London Divisions (TF) on the Western Front, or the second-line 60th (2/2nd London) Division (TF), prior to its being posted to Salonika in 1916, and later to home defence (HD) divisions. New recruits and 'provisionals', generally older, long-serving, men for whom foreign service was not a viable option, were posted into the unit, replacing men qualified in gun drill or riding drill who were drafted out to join units overseas, or to HD divisions. Suitable candidates were sent for training at the several RFA Officer Cadet Schools, and others were sent on gunnery courses at Woolwich and Larkhill, or telephone (signals) courses at Dunstable. Those posted to Bovington Camp or Wareham in Dorset, would be joining the newly-formed Tank Corps. In June 1916, such was the demand for infantry on the Western Front, that 100 RFA men were transferred to each of five infantry regiments, and others to the Machine-Gun Corps, with more going later in the year. In September 1916, the large numbers of men being drafted out necessitated a reduction in the organisation down to three batteries. In 1916, a number of officers were transferred to the RFC, possibly as aerial artillery spotters. As well as men, horses and mules were also being constantly drafted in from Remount Depots across the country; passed on to other units; or sent to the North Midland Veterinary Hospital or Remount Depot at Stockwood Park on London Road. As part of the anti-invasion measures, maintained throughout the war, three emergency batteries were held in readiness for swift deployment, but the camp's primary role, as the main depot for reserve brigades of the RFA, was to train recruits and to process the large numbers of drafts to frontline units. In May 1917, Field Marshal Lord French carried out a full inspection. The camp occupied an area of land bounded by Biscot Road, Leagrave Road, Holland Road, and Kennington Road, now occupied by Denbeigh Road Primary School, to the immediate north of the Skefco Works. It comprised accommodation huts for over 1,200 men; stabling for 500 horses; officers' and sergeants' messes; canteen and institute; training rooms; gun sheds; garages for ammunition limbers and general service wagons; blacksmith's forge; forage store; sick bay and veterinary surgery; and armoury. It was closed at the end of November 1919.

As well as training large numbers of infantry and artillery recruits, Bedford was the national centre for the Royal Engineers Signal Service, which had its HQ and training centre at Woburn. This was transferred to Bedford in October 1917. The constituent parts of the service were spread across the county. Bedford was the base for three of the depots: 'A' for Recruits; 'B' for signalmen and linesmen and trench work; and 'C' for telephone operators. The Signal Service Air & Permanent Line Depot was in Biggleswade, and Haynes Park was requisitioned to meet increases in training needs. Here were established the Signal Service Riding, Driving, and Saddlers Depot; the Signal Service Switchboard Operators Depot; and the Cadet Battalion. A further Signal Service Depot, including the

Motorcycle (Despatch Rider) Training School was moved from Dunstable to Wellingborough in 1918, but the central Army Signal School was established at Dunstable in April 1918.

The curriculum at Haynes Park included training in riding and driving; saddlery; line-work, and switchboard operation. The RE Signals training began with four weeks spent in the Riding School, followed by cable-laying, with practical exercises carried out around the local villages. Four or six horses pulled a wagon with a large cable-drum on the front part behind the driver. Two signallers wearing thick leather gloves paid out the cable over the back of the wagon. At road junctions, the cable would be hoisted up on to poles, which were sunk into the ground. The final part of the course was training as linesmen, rigging telephone lines on telegraph-poles, often from on horseback. In June 1916, three companies of REs from Haynes Park Camp were on exercise in Toddington, with troops billeted in Wesley Hall and the Rifle Range. The Army Signal School, Dunstable, opened in 1918 to train signals instructors under the command of the Signal Service Training Centre HQ. Other elements of the signal training service moved to Fenny Stratford (Buckinghamshire) in 1917, and to Hitchin (Hertfordshire) in 1918. Troops were billeted in Clophill and Shefford.

In Luton, which saw an average number of 25,000 soldiers in camps and billets in the town throughout the war, the Plait Halls were requisitioned: Cheapside Hall for storage and Waller Street Hall with some evening sessions allocated to the VTC (see below). It was claimed at the time that the presence of the Highland Division in Bedford offered an economic lifeline to the town and this effect was seen elsewhere in the county. The 8th (Service) Battalion, Somerset Light Infantry, had been billeted in Linslade during the winter of 1914–15, and troops billeted in Dunstable in 1914, used the town hall as their institute. The 10th Battalion, York & Lancaster Regiment, had been billeted in Leighton Buzzard up until May 1915, but in early 1916, along with Dunstable, both towns, having been soldier-less for more than six months, expressed their feeling of abandonment to the billeting authorities. Arrangements for 200 men of the 8th Battalion, Bedfordshire Regiment, to be billeted in Stotfold in January 1916 were aborted at the last minute.

As befitted their status in the community, prominent men were seen to do their duty setting an example for their tenants and employees. Herbrand Russell, 11th duke of Bedford, had been commissioned into the Grenadier Guards, fighting in the Egyptian Campaign of 1882, followed by an appointment as ADC to the Viceroy of India. He was colonel of the 3rd Volunteer Battalion, Bedfordshire Regiment, from 1897–1908 and Military ADC to both Edward VII and George V. Although in his late fifties, he continued to serve through the war as colonel of the regiment and oversaw the management of its Ampthill training camp. His cousin, the 2nd Baron Ampthill, also had a military background and commanded the 3rd (Reserve) Battalion, fed by recruits from the camp on his Ampthill estate. Following its transfer to the War Office as a Command Rehabilitation Centre, he went to France to command the Leicestershire Regiment's 13th (Labour) Battalion. Later, in 1917 aged forty-eight, he commanded the 8th Battalion of the Bedfordshire Regiment and was Mentioned in Despatches for his gallant leadership in action near Loos. At Luton Hoo, Lady Alice had three sons. Harold Wernher, the second son married the daughter of a Russian grand duke in the Chapel Royal, St James's Palace, in July 1917 wearing his cavalry officer's uniform, with the best man and the guard of honour drawn from the 12th (Prince of Wales's Royal) Lancers which spent the war in France with the 5th Cavalry Brigade. He would rise to the rank of major-general in the Second World War. Alexander, his younger brother, joined the Royal Buckinghamshire Hussars Yeomanry straight from Eton in March 1915, aged eighteen. Following service in East Africa, he transferred to the Welsh Guards, and was commissioned as a second-lieutenant. He was killed at Ginchy, on the Somme, in September 1916. Their older brother, Sir Derrick Julius Wernher, was commissioned into the (Royal) Army Service Corps, and their stepfather, the 2nd Baron Ludlow, served as a fifty-year-old staff captain. The celebrated Rugby player Edgar Mobbs, an Old Boy of Bedford Modern School, personally raised the Northamptonshire Regiment's 7th Battalion, and, having originally enlisted as a private in 1914, was killed in action at Passchendaele leading his battalion as a lieutenant-colonel in July 1917. His old school presented a Rugby Union Challenge Cup in his memory. Second-Lieutenant Addison Howard, the son of James Howard of the Britannia Works, was killed on the Somme aged twenty-three, leading a company of the Bedfordshires, just one of the many local men to give their lives.

Such examples were necessary as the flood of recruits, which had reached high water in the first six months of the war quickly slowed to a trickle. In January 1916, following the introduction of the Derby Scheme inviting men to attest and to be called on as needed, the *Bedfordshire Times* analysed the figures, which highlighted the large number of those who, although eligible, opted not to enlist. Given that, additionally, many of those who did attest were actually unavailable for enlistment, either medically unfit or engaged in work of national importance, this revelation underlines how necessary it was to introduce conscription in order to raise the numbers needed to make up the enormous losses being suffered on the Western Front.

Once the Highland Division had left Bedford, the 1st Battalion, Herefordshire Regiment of the Welsh Border Brigade in the 53rd (1st Welsh) Division (TF), spilt over from Northampton, but by July, the next wave of TF divisions was on the move, and the second-line 68th (2nd Welsh) Division arrived in the region. Two battalions of the Monmouthshire Regiment of the Welsh Border Brigade and three Cheshire Regiment battalions of its Cheshire Brigade spent time in Bedford prior to being moved on to Suffolk as anti-invasion troops later that year. Before the Welshmen left, Bedford GS OTC led a parade of the 68th Division inspected by Field Marshal Lord French, the new C-in-C Home Forces. Some soldiers of the Bedfordshire Regiment were billeted in the Honey Hill district, and in April 1916, 230 large houses in Bedford were being leased as billets by the military. Clearly, these were insufficient to meet the demand and the 'barracks' in the yard of the Bedford Arms in Woburn accommodated 150 soldiers from Ampthill for bed and breakfast in January 1916. There was a fire at 99 Castle Street, Luton, in premises used for storage by 2/4th Battalion, Leicestershire Regiment, which had been billeted in the town for the previous twelve months prior to a move to Ireland in the April.

As so many troops were resident in Bedford, they could not but leave their mark on the landscape. Practice trenches with traverses, T-shaped recesses projecting, and communication trenches like 'an enlarged rabbit warren' were dug on Cemetery Hill, near Clapham Park, but it was noted that mud and water had collected in them, taking life a bit closer to the reality awaiting them in France. The trenches dug in Biddenham Fields by 2/1st and 2/3rd Monmouths were considered the most perfect system yet dug. Described as stretching from the Paddling Place to the old stone barn, they were visited by the VTC, themselves engaged in trenching practice. A guardroom had been established in the Ford End Cottages and no one was allowed to approach the trench works, which now lie under terraces of houses built after the war. These and other trenches in Queens Park, Bedford, were used by the Bedford GS OTC, in the summer of 1916, while being instructed in bomb throwing by an Old Bedfordian officer. The OTC was given its annual inspection by the second-in-command of Ampthill Park Camp, in June 1916.

With such a large military population in the county, the Army Service Corps (ASC) also had a strong presence. From 1915, No. 38 Reserve Park and No. 11 Auxiliary MT Company were based in Bedford, while other ASC units serviced Biscot Camp in Luton. In November 1916, interviews were held at the Embankment Hotel in Bedford to recruit men into the Mechanical Transport (MT) Section of the ASC. In 1917, newspapers in Bedford, Peterborough, and Huntingdon carried advertisements, repeated throughout the year, to recruit drivers, fitters, mechanics, and virtually anyone with experience in the motor trade, to No. 373 MT Company, ASC, based at the London General Omnibus Garage in Bedford.

As more and more troops were posted abroad, then it became necessary to organise new formations for home defence. In November 1916, scattered battalions of mainly either younger, untrained recruits, or older home service men were collected together to form three new divisions. One, the 72nd Division (Home Forces), comprising 215th, 216th, and 217th Infantry Brigades, was based in the south Midlands. Formed in Bath, the division was then centred on Bedford as a strategic reserve for the anti-invasion formations stationed in East Anglia. Elements of two of those brigades were based in Bedford itself from January to

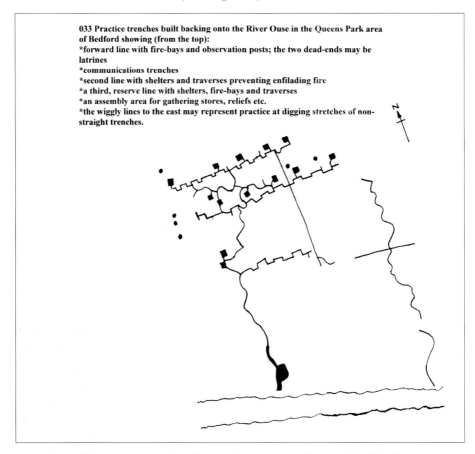

033 Practice trenches built backing onto the River Ouse in the Queens Park area of Bedford showing (from the top):
*forward line with fire-bays and observation posts; the two dead-ends may be latrines
*communications trenches
*second line with shelters and traverses preventing enfilading fire
*a third, reserve line with shelters, fire-bays and traverses
*an assembly area for gathering stores, reliefs etc.
*the wiggly lines to the east may represent practice at digging stretches of non-straight trenches.

An outline of the practice trenches dug in the Queens Park area of Bedford.

May 1917, when they were deployed to the coast of East Anglia to guard the beaches. Those billeted in Bedford included the 10th (Service) Battalion, Somerset Light Infantry; 18th Battalion, Warwickshire Regiment; 15th Battalion, Sussex Regiment (TF); 14th (Home Service) Battalion, King's Own Yorkshire Light Infantry; and 10th Battalion, Oxford, and Buckinghamshire Light Infantry (TF). No. 3 Company (HT) ASC Train was based in Bedford to service the 72nd (Home Defence) Division.

With no sign of movement on the Western Front this war of attrition revealed more and more need for logistical support of all kinds, and labour became much more regulated and organised. Ampthill became home to No. 126 Company, Canadian Forestry Corps a fifty-strong unit of lumberjacks who camped in huts in Ampthill Park from 1917. Their officers' mess was built in the guise of a log cabin. There were also detachments at Maulden and Flitwick. The main task of this unit was to produce pit-props for use in the many underground works in France ranging from dug-outs to hospitals to mines being dug under the enemy's frontline. From 1917, home-grown

Labour Battalions were also deployed locally, working in agriculture, transport, and munitions. With many women already working in the munitions industry, others carried out tasks for the military. By 1918, it was decided to formalise existing arrangements and to expand the service by setting up a Women's Auxiliary Army Corps (WAAC). Enlistment of cooks had begun in Bedford in December 1917, and a recruitment march was staged in the new year to find a further 100 women willing to serve under military discipline and control as cooks for the army.

The civilian's role in preparing to resist the expected invasion was clearly defined by the authorities in Instructions for the Civilian Population issued in late 1914. People were ordered to stay indoors and to keep off the roads, which should be kept available for troop movements. Instructions would be issued locally to inform people of the assembly points to which all vehicles, motorcycles, and bicycles should be taken in order to both requisition them for the use of defending troops and to deny them to the enemy. Similarly, assembly points to which should be delivered all tools such as spades and pickaxes would be notified. Lastly, nothing should be destroyed without orders from the military. In the meantime, people were instructed to keep their eyes open and to report anything suspicious. Sometimes local watchers could be overzealous. A minor spy scare erupted when three Peterborough men, driving near Bedford, were arrested and taken to Kempston Barracks where they were released following questioning. One factor that alarmed the chattering classes was the threats to the morality of young women. The number of soldiers around; large numbers of young women, some of them far from home and earning high wages as munitions workers; and the absence of traditional chaperonage, all contributed to public unease. Bedford was one of several towns that instituted voluntary women's police patrols, originally instigated by the National Union of Women Workers, in an attempt at damage limitation in the context of the social problems inherent in the new order of things.

The Air War in Bedfordshire

For the first eighteen months of the war, the aerial defence of Great Britain, including both aircraft and anti-aircraft (AA) artillery was the responsibility of the Royal Naval Air Service (RNAS). It was quickly realised that the Navy's aircraft, many of them seaplanes, were entirely unsuitable for intercepting either the Zeppelin airships or the later bombers. By the end of 1915, the Royal Flying Corps (RFC) whose role hitherto had been offensive warfare in foreign skies, its squadrons either supporting the BEF or deployed to the Middle East, had been tasked with home defence. Within a year, squadrons had been designated for Home Defence but were still functioning as training units, losing aircrew to frontline squadrons just as they were approaching competency. By the end of 1916 there were eleven HD squadrons. Each was assigned a permanent aerodrome with hangars and hutted accommodation; repair facilities; administration and flying control buildings; and messes, canteens, and institutes for the flying and ground staff. Each base aerodrome had several landing grounds (LG) for emergency use, or for convenient refuelling to prevent time being wasted returning to base. These might have a canvas Bessoneau hangar and a hut for the ground crew. A night-LG might have no more than a fuel tank and braziers to provide an aiming point in an otherwise anonymous and invisible field.

Goldington, on a site near the present Avon Drive, off the Kimbolton Road, became the HQ for No. 75 (HD) Squadron, which moved in from Tadcaster (Yorkshire) in October 1916 with B.E.2c fighters, later receiving B.E.2es. Goldington Manor housed the Squadron HQ with its three flights based at Therfield in Hertfordshire, and Yelling and Old Weston in Huntingdonshire. Several local sites were chosen as landing grounds (LG). These included one now under the Maulden Road Industrial Estate in Flitwick, with others at Elms Farm, Putnoe, and Biggleswade, this last operating only between July and September 1917. Goldington itself was equipped for both night and daytime operations with its landing strip where Roundmead is now. A fourth LG was proposed for Leagrave but never taken up, and No. 75 Squadron was moved to a new airfield at Lea Farm, Elmswell in Suffolk, in September 1917. Prior to the formation of the RAF, through the amalgamation of the RFC and the RNAS in April 1918, the squadron had been re-equipped with Avro 504K two-seater trainers and then, just before the war ended, Sopwith Pups. Elmswell was clearly better situated for the interception of incoming bombers and the squadron had recorded sixteen such sorties before the end of the war. Under No. 75 Squadron's local command were twenty-five searchlight sites, spread across a wide area but roughly in line with the Great North Road. At least three, at Arlesey, Everton, and Wrestlingworth lay within the county borders.

Aircraft Production

Apart from this defensive activity, Bedfordshire's contribution to the air war lay in support operations and the production of aircraft. Henlow, conveniently situated on flat, open land beside a railway line, was identified as the ideal location for Eastern Command's Engine and Aircraft Repair Depots and constructed by McAlpine over the winter of 1917–18. It opened in February 1918 when a party of forty mechanics and riggers from No. 1 (Southern) Aircraft Repair Depot (ARD) at Farnborough arrived to establish the satellite No. 5 (Eastern Area) ARD & Engine Repair Depot (ERD). The depots' tasks were to rebuild damaged aircraft and aero-engines and return them to service. By the end of the war, over 3,000 people, including 300 WAAFs and 100 American airmen for a short while, were working on mainly Bristol Fighters and de Havilland aircraft. A large estate of workshops and accommodation huts was built to standardised designs issued by the Air Ministry or to alternatives drawn up locally. The AM designs were numbered sequentially and dated. Thus the centrepiece of Henlow's buildings was the extant line of four coupled General Service (GS) hangars. Three pairs with timber Belfast truss roofs were to the 172nd and 279th designs to be issued in 1917 (172 & 279/17), and one with steel trusses (279/17 & 2102/18). A further double aircraft shed built to a combination of AM and local designs (2010/18 & HO1211) with pitched roof also survives, but the enormous, 544-foot-long (167-metre-long) Aircraft Storage Shed (1397/18), often referred to as the 'Pickle Factory', and designed to hold twelve Handley-Page 0/400 bombers, was demolished around 1990. Other surviving structures from this first building period include the HQ Offices (245/17); a large hangar-like shed for revision and lecture rooms (HO1214); and the MT Repair shed and offices (HO835). The very last two timber huts were demolished only in 1988.

Although they had begun by constructing balloons for military applications, Short Brothers of Rochester were designing successful twin-engined aircraft by 1911, training naval flyers, and developing floatplanes, predominantly on the Kent coast. But it was the lighter-than-air market that brought them to Cardington with an Admiralty contract for two airships: the *R-31* and *R-32*. The site had been chosen in 1915 for its proximity to a workforce in Bedford, open land, and transport links. The Admiralty advanced the money to develop the site with a 700-foot-long (215-metres-long) airship shed; a HQ building; engine-test facilities; workshops; and accommodation. The company then concentrated all its balloon and airship development and construction at Cardington, employing 800 people. In 1919, this element of the firm's work was nationalised as the Royal Airship Works. Across the road from the operational site was Shortstown, begun in 1917 as a garden-village type development in the Arts & Crafts style with terraces of workers' cottages, semi-detached houses for technical staff and grander houses with loggias for the managers.

With their origins in a skating-rink in Battersea, the Omnia Works of Hewlett and Blondeau had moved to Leagrave, on the north-western edge of Luton, in 1914. In London, they had contracts to build Farman aircraft for the RFC but actually delivered their aircraft to the RNAS, and then were awarded a contract to supply twelve B.E.2c aircraft. This pushed them into a move to larger premises. Although they designed their own aircraft, nothing would come of them, and they reverted to building other firms' designs. The works expanded to employ 700 people, producing some 800 aircraft, including 350 of the two-seater Armstrong Whitworth F.K.3 biplane with its 90-hp Renault-derived engine. These aircraft, quickly superseded by more advanced aircraft were used for training in the UK, the factory moving on to build Avro 504s. Despite a successful switch to producing agricultural machinery at the end of the war, the factory closed and was sold to Electrolux in 1919. The only structure remaining from the aircraft works is the segregated 450-seat canteen whose construction was given the go-ahead by the Ministry of Munitions in 1918.

In Bedford, W. H. Allen's Queen's Engineering Works turned out French-designed Rhône aero-engines at the rate of 200 per week in areas of the old

RAF Henlow, the First World War RFC Depot HQ and Offices.

RAF Henlow, coupled First World War aircraft sheds.

RAF Henlow, one of the four pairs of General Service (Belfast Truss) hangars, dating from 1917.

RAF Cardington, the HQ building of 1917, recently refurbished.

RAF Cardington, the Transformer building of 1917, now demolished.

Shortstown was built in Arts & Crafts style for workers at the Short Bros airship factory; the Crescent housed managers.

Shortstown also had terraces and semi-detached housing for Shorts workers.

Luton, the canteen of Hewlett & Blondeau's aircraft factory, now Electrolux.

factory reorganised as clean rooms. The long-established London-based carriage builders Morgan & Co. moved to Linslade in 1914 to manufacture aircraft. Vickers Vimy twin-engined bombers were brought here for assembly, and Sopwith 1½ Strutters, Airco DH6s, and Avro 504s were all built here from scratch. J. P. Whites, Carpenters & Joiners of Bromham Road, Bedford, made wooden propellers for aircraft

Air Defence

Bedfordshire's main effort in the area of air defence lay in the provision of adequate air-raid warnings. As the Zeppelin raids intensified, the railway companies instituted a system whereby incoming airships were spotted, generally on the Norfolk coast, and once their intended destination was inferred, warnings were given down the line by electric telegraph. The county lay in No. 43 Air-raid Warning District, and would receive timely warning of an attack, which enabled work to continue until the enemy was almost overhead, thus losing less production, without incurring undue risk. On 19 October 1917, the Zeppelin that dropped a bomb near an engineering works in Bull Pond Lane, Dunstable, was shot down over France the next day. A single bomb was dropped in the grounds of Luton Hoo in September 1916. To warn of imminent Zeppelin attacks, Luton installed electrically operated "squawkers" in the police station, but there were concerns that such warnings brought people out on to the streets as had happened when hooters were sounded as an air-raid warning previously in Leighton Buzzard. The public were told to stay indoors and to extinguish lights when they heard the warnings, and in Dunstable, in February 1916, the Emergency Committee decided that air-raid warnings would be delivered by three thirty-second blasts on the hooter at Waterlow's printing works. Greater damage was actually done by accidental fires than by enemy action though. In Luton, there were serious blazes at the Diamond Foundry in Dallow Road, the Brown & Green Foundry in Windsor Street, and at Lye's Dye-works in Old Bedford Road when large quantities of precious chemicals and machinery were lost.

By the middle of 1917, more dedicated AA artillery was becoming available to defend against aerial bombing attacks. In June, Bedford was provided with two AA sites: Fenlake and Manor Farm. Each site was given an 18-pounder gun, sleeved to fire 13-pounder projectiles but retaining the bigger charge to achieve a higher ceiling of 19,000 feet (5,800 metres). This gun was otherwise essentially the standard field gun of the RFA but was given a static high-angle mounting. Fenlake site could have been near the present Jubilee Park, and there is a manor farm at Harrowden, across the present A421/A600 interchange. These two, maybe linked, positions might have protected the town and the Cardington works against aircraft that would have used reflections off the river as an aid to navigation.

The Volunteer Training Corps (VTC) in Bedfordshire

Within days of war breaking out on 4 August 1914, interest was being raised in countrywide projects to set up local defence forces in case the anticipated German invasion materialised. The War Office considered this to be both unnecessary and undesirable as it would take recruits away from the proper army. However, a Central Association of Volunteer Training Corps (CAVTC) was formed and the War Office agreed to the establishment of VTC so long as no men eligible for service in the Army (under thirty-eight years of age or not employed in essential war work) were enrolled. This was often in competition with the special constabulary, which, being under civilian control, was the government's preferred option. The stated aims of the VTC were to promote recruitment to the Army; to carry out duties to release troops for the Western Front; to train over-age men and men in reserved occupations for home defence; and to prepare youngsters or those men awaiting their call-up for service in the Army. In Bedford, interested parties met at the Midland Hotel and decided to travel to London to talk to the CAVTC. The upshot of this was that the mayor, on 22 December 1914, convened a public meeting at Bedford Corn Exchange to launch a VTC, rapidly attracting 150 recruits. The council chamber of the town hall was made available for enrolments and the skating rink on the embankment was given over as a drill hall. The CTA also offered the use of its recently-opened drill hall on Ashburnham Road. Given the War Office's refusal to allow VTC to be armed at this point, the question of procuring dummy rifles for drill purposes was raised. Since no public money could be spent on the VTC, the topic of fundraising and the setting of a subscription were also discussed. That same month, a Luton VTC was launched and some 200 men had enrolled by the end of the year. Beginning on New Year's Day 1915, Luton Corn Exchange became the assembly point for drills in Stockwood Park, and a HQ was set up in Park Street. Ten former NCOs offered their services as instructors, and Lord Scott of 23rd Battalion, London Regiment, in the 2nd London Division (TF), loaned his sergeant-instructor while his unit remained in town. Also that month, the mayor of Dunstable called a public meeting to recruit a VTC, forming a platoon of the Luton corps. On Christmas Day, the *Biggleswade Chronicle* announced the inauguration of a local corps, shortly followed by corps in Ampthill, Aspley Guise and Woburn Sands, with thirty Volunteers forming a platoon at Wilstead. By January 1915, the Bedford corps had grown to upwards of 250 members, had established a HQ at the TF offices at Gwyn Street, and was drilling on two weekday evenings.

Percy Harris, MP, of the CAVTC had visited Luton and other efforts at recruitment included a series of tell-it-how-it-is articles published in the *Bedfordshire Times* and written by a correspondent explaining what was expected of a volunteer. A drumhead service was held at Elstow School where the Bedford VTC paraded alongside the 2/5th Battalion, Bedfordshire Regiment (TF), and the

Bedford Town Hall, the recruiting office for the Volunteer Training Corps.

school OTC. Luton raised a drum and fife band to accompany processions. In March, the lord lieutenant chaired a meeting with the county's War Emergency Committees, the VTC, and the chief constable, to resolve a number of issues. It was agreed that special constables would be permitted to enrol in the VTC but, in the event of an invasion or other emergency, the chief constable would have first call on them for maintaining public order and conducting orderly evacuations if appropriate. In 1916, when the Volunteers' conditions of service were changed, dual membership would no longer be permitted.

By June 1915, the Bedford VTC was preparing for an inspection by the CAVTC to be accepted for affiliation, and the resultant parade the next month attracted 2,000 spectators. Such public events and appeals continued to be effective in recruiting Volunteers. The local press helped by publishing timetables of weekly drills and results of shooting competitions. They also printed Volunteers' classification of shooting competence, later to be one of the main criteria for assessing a corps' efficiency, and hence its grant entitlement. At the end of December 1916, the *Bedfordshire Times* would introduce 'Volunteer Notes' as a new weekly feature.

Once established, VTC were frustrated that the War Office would still not allow Volunteers to wear uniforms or carry arms and had to wear an armband or brassard of red cloth with 'GR' in black letters. It was determined that the VTC would raise the money and canvass support to provide weapons and uniforms. Lady Wernher at Luton Hoo provided first fifty, then a further 200 sets of personal equipment. In April 1915, the Bedford corps placed an order for uniforms. Soon, the more clearly military activities would become more prominent. In April, 150 Volunteers attended a field day at Luton Hoo, and in May, the Luton corps assembled at the Old Volunteer Club wearing uniforms and carrying rifles, for a march to Luton Hoo where they were inspected by Col. Goodwin. Shooting practice started at the miniature range at Biddenham, at the indoor range at Toddington, and on the Skefco factory's range in Luton, and all would shortly be hosting shooting matches: Bedford triumphing over Thetford (Norfolk); and Aspley Guise *v.* Woburn Sands where a 'decider' was deemed necessary. Bedford GS OTC came to an arrangement with the VTC to share the use of the school's rifles. In February, eighty Luton Volunteers turned out for a route march, and in June, the Bedford corps organised a recruitment march for the 5th Battalion. Bi-weekly drills were duplicated as increased numbers needed to attend for instruction. In Bedford, four platoons were in training and a typical weekly schedule included a parade for the whole company on one day, with two platoons attending for drill on the following night from 8 to 10 p.m., and the other two on the next night. These sessions would run alongside time on the indoor and outdoor ranges, special events, and night-time guard duties, putting enormous pressure on men who were often of mature years and already working long hours in their daytime occupations. As Luton Hoo was such an important hub for home defence units, the War Office banned Volunteer camps in the area for the whole of August in 1915. Despite this, Luton VTC managed to camp over August Bank Holiday weekend but the Bedford VTC preferred to accept an invitation from the Hove VTC to join them in a camp at Lewes in Sussex in the July.

As the peak of voluntary enlistment fell away, in an attempt to gauge the nation's future potential for recruitment to the regular forces, Lord Derby issued attestation forms with a view to securing future commitment. Volunteers were involved in the distribution and collection of these forms and subsequently in following up those who had expressed an intention to enlist but had not hitherto appeared. In October 1915, Volunteers from Luton were recorded interviewing attestees in Flitwick, and three carloads of Volunteers carried out a sweep of Woburn Sands, on similar follow-up visits. VTC were also supplying men from their own ranks to the regular forces. The Aspley Guise corps provided a recruit to the RE, and Ampthill's instructor was awarded a commission in the Army Service Corps. Attestees would join VTC to receive some preliminary training prior to enlisting and seventeen-year-olds joined to get some idea of what the Army might expect of them. This constant turnover of members meant that training was therefore continuous. In April 1917, Regular Army instructors were putting on evening musketry training sessions and first-aid instruction at the Park Street armoury in Luton, and demonstration sessions were put on for potential recruits at the Palace Theatre.

One of the primary functions of VTC was providing security for communications and public utilities, and Volunteers across the county formed guard parties putting in four-hour shifts guarding railway bridges and Vulnerable Points (VP) such as the Clapham Road pumping station. In order to provide full, night-time cover, a total of 170 men were needed at each location, each Volunteer doing just one night a week, as more would make him ineffective in his essential day-job. As Bedford local council increased its demands for guard details, particularly at the Waterworks and Reservoir, the VTC increased its appeals for its financial support. Unforeseen events such as the landing of a military balloon near Steppingley Hospital, or the aeroplane forced down with engine trouble at Southcott near Linslade, would also prompt demands for the VTC and special constables to mount an overnight guard.

Premises were always a problem as an increasingly professional organisation needed administrative facilities; secure storage for weapons and equipment; training spaces; and social amenities. In Bedford, the town hall in St Paul's Square and the TF orderly room in Gwyn Street provided the administrative space; training took place in the Skating Rink and in Horne Lane; and the Ashburnham Road TF drill hall offered secure storage. In Luton, the Corn Exchange, Stockwood Park, and Luton Hoo provided training facilities with an office in Park Street, and the Ambulance Section meeting at the public library. Free use of the Waller Street Plait Hall in Luton was offered for two hours on three nights a week early in 1916. Dunstable's Tavistock Hall, the Yeomanry drill hall, was made available for use by the Volunteers. The fifty-strong Ampthill corps was provided with a drill room and clubroom complete with billiards table behind Mr Rushbrooke's drapers shop in Church Street.

By 1916, conscription was brought in to compensate for the marked decline in volunteering, and the War Office was beginning to see the value of the VTC. New Volunteer legislation in parliament permitted the establishment of an official Volunteer Force (VF), and exemption from military service was often accompanied by enforced VF membership and a legal obligation to attend a specified minimum number of drills. Existing Volunteers could transfer into the new VF but were required to commit themselves to serve until the war's end and to mobilise in the event of an invasion, taking an oath to that effect. The Bedford VTC's annual meeting in March 1916 reported that 490 men had served up to the end of 1915 but 190 had left. Some of these would have been youngsters, attestees, or men who had lost their exemption, to join up. Others would have been older men leaving on health grounds. On the money side, £449 (£44,900) had been received from the voluntary subscription of 6/- (£30) but £538 (£53,800) had been spent on uniforms and £62 (£6,200) on rifles, costing around £2.10/- (£25) each. The balance had come from private donations and public subsidy. Although Bedford had been expected to raise a full battalion of 1,000 men, and Luton to raise another, their maximum strengths of respectively, 550 and 660 had raised

Ampthill, Church Street, Mr Rushbrooke's draper's shop whose back room became a base for the local Volunteers.

the possibility of a merger. In the event, the two battalions remained separate and, marking their belated acceptance by the Army Council, became the 1st and 2nd Volunteer Battalions of the Bedfordshire Regiment in October 1916. Apart from the long-awaited recognition of the VF, a further welcome result was that the CTA would henceforth assume the responsibility for uniform, equipment, weapons, and formal training.

With these changes, Volunteers resigning or leaving for the forces, the recruitment of new Volunteers remained a priority. In October 1916, there was a meeting in the Bedford Corn Exchange, addressed by Lord Desborough, chairman of the CAVTC, to discuss recruitment and to advance his hopes for a second Bedford Battalion. This meeting was attended by the headmasters of Bedford Modern School and Bedford GS as the War Office had formally sanctioned the recruitment of seventeen-year-olds to the VF, a practice that had been under way for some time unofficially. In November 1917, the Bedfordshire Regiment's two Volunteer Battalions were due to march from the drill hall in Ashburnham Road to Russell Park on the embankment for inspection by the lord lieutenant. Unfortunately there were no trains so the Luton battalion could not attend. Partly as a result of exempted men being combed out and taken into the Army, attempts to recruit continued, and in January 1918, a gymnastic display and musical concert were put on in Houghton Regis and an advertisement appeared seeking 500 Volunteers for the Bedford battalion. In March, Lord French inspected over 4,000 Volunteers on the grammar school field. These were the two Bedfordshire battalions, two from Northamptonshire, and one each from Hertfordshire and Huntingdonshire.

Although there had been VTC transport sections and large numbers of volunteer drivers using their own vehicles to ferry patients between railway stations and hospitals, the official Bedfordshire Motor Volunteer Corps was formed in early 1918. There were local sections in Bedford, Luton, Biggleswade and Sandy, and Dunstable and Leighton Buzzard. The first full parade was held in April 1918. The Biggleswade and Sandy section had forty-five members, and the Leighton Buzzard sub-section hoped to recruit fifteen to twenty drivers with cars or motorcycles in the June. Volunteers were given training in map-reading and motor mechanics.

The German offensive of Easter 1918 created panic and invasion fears resurfaced with Volunteers poised to defend their country, and even instructors being sent to the front. A number of schemes planned to integrate the VF into the Home Defence forces. That of early 1917 envisaged groups of VF battalions being allocated to brigades based on East Anglian towns with a Reserve of six battalions being held in Bedford. This Reserve included the two Bedfordshire battalions along with one from each of Huntingdonshire, Northamptonshire, Cambridgeshire, and Hertfordshire. In the event, a different scheme was implemented whereby, on mobilisation in the event of an invasion, the Bedford battalion would join 215 Infantry Brigade at Ipswich, and the Luton battalion would join a Composite Brigade based in Northampton. The VF wound down from the time of the Armistice in November and would finally be disbanded early in 1920. However, the government held back the Motor Volunteer Corps until the next year in case it was needed for strike-breaking in the event of industrial unrest.

Munitions Production

Firms manufacturing staples, which were necessary to most industrial production, would obviously continue their peacetime work into the wartime economy. Others would be required to adapt their normal working to the demands of war. Luton's Skefco works had manufactured ball-bearings since 1911, when the firm had been established at, Leagrave Road, with Britannia House, its Beaux Arts-style offices, added in 1916–17. George Kent Ltd had been manufacturing meters on Biscot Road since 1908. In 1914, the factory took on a War Office contract to produce detonators and fuses, adding an extension to the existing premises. With this hurriedly-erected facility, Kent's would ultimately employ 5,000 workers. The War Office then asked them to expand their business to include filling the detonators and fuses with high explosive in a separate National Filling Factory.

Under pressure from the War Office, in January 1915, Luton Council was forced to approve immediate plans for Kent's new fuse-filling factory, which would be built at the Chaul End crossing of the Great Northern Railway. It would need an adequate and dependable electricity supply, and Kent's was being given only three months to be up and running. Complicating matters further, the director of Army Contracts at the War Office was complaining that delivery of a contract awarded to the Thermo Electric Ore Reduction Corporation Ltd was already late due to problems with electricity supply. The council was awaiting parts for its generating station and was unable to proceed without them, and was already trying to meet increased demand for power from Vauxhall Motors, Skefco, and all the other firms with War Office contracts. Once this problem of electricity supply had been resolved, production commenced. This highly dangerous work was carried out by a workforce of 3,000, over three-quarters of whom were women. The two sites produced 140,000 filled fuses a week, of twelve different types, for artillery shells. Hostels, including the top floor of Blundell's Department Store and rented private houses, were organised in Luton for those workers from afar. On site, a canteen and sickbay were provided and, given the dangerous nature of the work that caused fatal accidents, also an ambulance and fire engine. Four girls were killed in an explosion in March 1918, while many others received injuries. A foundry was added in 1916 to recycle vital metals, such as brass, which were in short supply. After the war, the Chaul End buildings became a dye works. Hayward Tyler of Luton supplied marine salvage pumps for the Admiralty.

Moving out of London in 1905, the Vauxhall & West Hydraulic Engineering Company established a vehicle plant in Kimpton Road in 1907. Their original offices were extended in 1915 and again in 1919. Their D-type Tourer of 1912 was accepted by the War Office as a staff car, and 2,000 were built. A new factory in Pondwicks Road, Luton, was built in 1916, for Balmforth's, the boiler makers, who made bomb casings. In Bedford, W. H. Allen's Queen's Engineering Works built steam turbines for the Royal Navy and set up a new dynamo shop, while the iron foundry continued to produce high quality castings. New work included condensing sets and pumping machinery. When the old factory was converted into clean rooms for building aero engines, the dirtier processes were diverted to a new factory in Ford End Road, Biddenham, with new offices in Hurst Grove. The Britannia Works occupied 20 acres (8 ha) in 1908 producing the 2-foot (61-cm) narrow-gauge Howard Light Railway, as well as steam ploughs and steam wagons. The Vulcan Works built diesel locomotives for use on industrial light railways. The Motor Rail and Tramcar Company, which had moved to a new works in Houghton Road (or Elstow Road in some accounts), Bedford, in 1916, built 20-hp 'Simplex' light, four-wheeled petrol locomotives for use on 60-cm (1-foot, 11⅝-inch) narrow-gauge railways in France. In 1917, a new 40-hp version, of which 300 were produced, came with two variants: one was protected against shrapnel with steel doors, and the other was a completely enclosed and

Above: Luton, the Skefco ball-bearing factory on Leagrave Road.

Left: Luton, Vauxhall's offices on Kimpton Road, begun in 1907.

fully-armoured version for operation in the front line. While they were not used at home during the war, one ended up at the 'Stonehenge' brickworks in Leighton Buzzard where it ran until 1955. An example of the protected model survives at Beamish Museum, County Durham. The company produced some inspection cars for the Ministry of Munitions in 1919, testing them on the Bedford–Hitchin line. Igranic in Elstow Road were involved in developing controls for electric motors and moved into batteries and battery-charging equipment. Gossards in Billington Road, Leighton Buzzard, was started up by the government to manufacture anti-submarine netting to be strung along the sides of larger warships in such anchorages as Rosyth and Scapa Flow where the Grand Fleet was based. Its neighbours, Bullivant & Co.'s wire works in Grovebury Road, produced barbed-wire for use on the Western Front.

It was not only commercial concerns that were sucked into meeting the needs of the munitions industry. The Ministry of Munitions contracted Bedford School to manufacture high-pressure valve bodies for use in submarines for Yarrow's, the shipbuilders; and 13-pounder shells for the South East Midlands Munitions Board. Fifty volunteers in three shifts worked for three and a half hours every other day, with additional shifts of similar duration at the weekends worked by extra volunteers. To keep up morale, in November 1917, King George V came to Luton to pay a visit to Kent's in Biscot Road and the Thermo works off the Hitchin Road, and early in 1918 he visited W. H. Allen's 'Queens' Works in Bedford.

Leighton Buzzard, the Admiralty's Gossard factory in Billington Road.

Military Hospitals and Welfare

No one could have anticipated the enormous efforts that would be required to care for the vast numbers of sick and wounded generated by the war. There were only tiny numbers of military nurses and organisations such as the British Red Cross and the Order of St John of Jerusalem combined to organise trained groups of mainly female volunteer nurses, and mainly male nursing orderlies, as Voluntary Aid Detachments. The 46th North Midland Division (TF) arrived in Luton in August 1914, taking over Wardown House in the October as its sickbay until the division was deployed to the Western Front in 1915. It was passed to Nos. 12 and 14 British Red Cross VADs. The military had added a wooden annexe, which, along with three wards downstairs and three smaller ones on the first floor, could accommodate a total of sixty-five beds. There was an operating theatre, a recreation room, and a pack store enabling soldiers to return to duty with their kit. Staff quarters and offices occupied the remainder of the upper floor. Both wounded soldiers from the front via the 1st Eastern General Hospital (TF) in Cambridge, and sick ones from the Artillery Camp at Biscot Mill or billeted in the town could be accepted as patients. In the thirteen months to the end of 1916, nearly 1,000 patients were admitted with no deaths. A further 950 were admitted in 1917 staying for an average of twenty days of whom only five died. A trained nurse was on duty each day and night, but the majority of nursing was carried out by the volunteers. The men of No. 1 Section, Luton Red Cross, assisted in ambulance work, portering, and stores tasks.

All over the country, houses grand and humble were being turned into VAD hospitals. Woburn Cottage Hospital, now a private house in the village, which had been founded by the Duchess Mary in 1898, became part of Woburn Military Hospital in Woburn Abbey in 1914, also set up by the Duchess Mary, with 160 beds, an X-ray room, and an operating theatre. It received its first wounded soldiers from the Western Front in November 1914. In November 1916, it was reported that staff numbers for stretcher work at Woburn were inadequate for unloading the numbers of wounded arriving and had to be supplemented by additional local volunteers. Wrest House, the very first of many such houses across the country offered as convalescent hospitals, received its first wounded in September 1914. Some wounded, such as those 160 cases from the Battle of Mons, were just passing through on the hospital train, which arrived at Bedford Midland Station in September 1914, *en route* for Leicester Military Hospital, but they still needed care and attention, however temporary, from local volunteers. Hinwick House was just one of the many auxiliary hospitals staffed by VADs. Sometimes initial enthusiasm outpaced need. Having treated 300 patients, the Leighton Buzzard Red Cross Hospital closed in December 1914 owing to the proximity of other hospitals nearby in Tring and Aylesbury. In other places, the original premises were overwhelmed by demand. The Eaton Socon Relief

Luton, Wardown House, a military hospital in the First World War.

Hinwick House was a military hospital in the First World War and an officers' mess for RAF Podington in the Second World War.

Hospital, run by No. 8 Bedfordshire VAD, closed in February 1916 but with the hope that new, more suitable, premises might be provided. Built in 1857–79, the Three Counties or Fairfield Hospital/Asylum in Kingsley Avenue, Stotfold, treated shell-shocked patients. More than thirty war hospitals are listed in Appendix XI and that list is unlikely to be complete.

As well as caring for the wounded, volunteers set up and staffed welfare facilities for the thousands of troops stationed in the county. On one hand, there were facilities catering for hundreds of troops each day, such as the Bunyan Canteen and the Central Recreation Room in Bedford Corn Exchange, Biscot Camp's YMCA hut, opened in April 1916 by Princess Victoria of Schleswig-Holstein, and the Waller Street Plait Hall used by the YMCA as a recreation centre for soldiers stationed in Luton. While on the other hand were the humbler YMCA huts for the Canadian Forestry Corps in Ampthill, Flitwick, and Maulden. REs training in Haynes Park could visit the canteen and recreation room in Clophill's parish room, and in Biddenham, a barn, now the village hall, was converted into a canteen and recreation room in December 1915. One of the dozens of voluntary welfare organisations that appeared during the war was the British Women's Temperance Association, which had branches in places with large concentrations of troops. Bedford was one of those places selected to be given a refreshment and recreation room serving cheap beverages and snacks to soldiers as an alternative to alehouses and licensed premises. The local population was also catered for. When the food shortages began to bite in 1918, Dudeney & Johnston Ltd of High Street, Bedford, set up communal feeding, an idea that would be more widely developed in the Second World War as British restaurants.

The most effective way of compensating for the loss of food-imports was to ensure that agricultural production was maximised. Bedfordshire was divided into fourteen districts by the War Agricultural Committee, which met at Shire Hall, Bedford, in February 1916. One of the Committee's early initiatives was an attempt to compete with the munitions industry by recruiting women for work on the land and by offering the appropriate training. Many of the POWs who found themselves quartered in Bedfordshire must have been very happy to be allowed to work on the land, feeling it a much safer option than fighting on the Western Front. Some POWs were kept in camps and guarded by men of the Royal Defence Corps, but the majority were organised into small work parties and based on individual farms or farming villages. In Leighton Buzzard, No. 20 Market Place is recorded as having served as POW accommodation. In December 1916, two German POWs escaped from the Woburn camp, and after a night of searches by camp guards and Special Constables, they were arrested and taken to Luton next day. Two other escapees, a year later, were recaptured the same day.

The Interwar Period, 1919–39

The reading of the King's Proclamation of Peace in Luton on Peace Day in July 1919 provided the flashpoint for large amounts of resentment among, especially, those of the town's ex-servicemen who felt let down by the borough administration and denied a chance to commemorate lost comrades. In the ensuing riot, the military from Biscot Camp were called in to control the disturbances that culminated in the burning of Luton town hall, and were able to restore order only in the small hours of the next morning when a large body of reinforcements from Bedford arrived. Whether the promise of new employment opportunities or of the provision of new estates of council housing over the following decade managed to appease the rioters is unknown.

The Army between the Wars

The 4th (Special Reserve) Battalion had been associated with Hertfordshire since the reforms of the 1870s, and the 1st and 2nd Volunteer Battalions had constituted the all-TF Hertfordshire Regiment since 1908, so the amalgamation of the two regiments was a logical development and in 1919, the Bedfordshire & Hertfordshire Regiment was born. However, it must be noted that, strangely, the Hertfordshire Regiment remained in the form of a single territorial battalion, independent of the newly combined regiment. The TF, which had ceased recruitment in 1916, was reconstituted in 1920 as the new Territorial Army (TA). The ten years following the end of the war saw a reaction against the military aspects of the nation. On 27 June 1929, the Rotary organised a river pageant and military tattoo to raise funds for the Royal National Lifeboat Institution and the Bedfordshire County Hospital. The Bedfordshire & Hertfordshire Regiment's 2nd Battalion provided its band as well as its silver drum and fife band using its newly presented silver drums. This, it was generally felt, was an entirely appropriate role for the Army.

The creation of the new TA necessitated sweeping changes, with regiments of horsed yeomanry cavalry gradually being converted to either artillery or armour. Accordingly, the Bedfordshire Yeomanry was transferred to the RFA in 1920 as the 10th (Bedford) Army Brigade, RFA, TA, and after several more changes of title, in 1938, it became the 105th (Bedfordshire Yeomanry) Army Field Regiment RA (TA) comprising Nos 417–420 Batteries. As a consequence of the uncertainties surrounding the Munich Agreement, rearmament accelerated, and during 1938–9, all TA regiments were required to duplicate themselves. This was achieved by selecting a cadre of officers and NCOs around which new units might be built. In the case of the Yeomanry, duplication left 417 and 418 Batteries with the parent 105th Regiment, while 148th (Bedfordshire Yeomanry) Army Field Regiment RA, TA, its duplicate, was built around 419 and 420 Batteries. In the infantry, the nucleus of a new 6th Battalion was formed from a cadre drawn from the 5th Battalion, Bedfordshire and Hertfordshire Regiment (TA). The Hertfordshire Regiment also cloned a second TA battalion at this time.

Just as the creation of the TF in 1908 had demonstrated a need for new premises, so did the new TA in the period after 1920. In Bedford, the infantry were given a new drill hall in Ashburnham Road, opposite that of the Yeomanry, and designed by the same architect in a similar neo-Georgian style. It was opened on 16 December 1922, by General Lord Horne, C-in-C Eastern Command. A large two-storey, brick and stone T-shaped administration block with the Bedfordshire Regiment's crest on the gable, contained offices, recreation rooms, and accommodation for the resident RSM. The drill hall measured 70 by 45 feet (21 by 13 metres), with a 30-yard-long (27-metre-long) indoor miniature battle range with scenic effects adjoining it. Ranged around the large parade-ground were the armoury, stores, and workshops. It is now well-maintained as a religious and social centre. In Ampthill, the premises in the old wrinkly tin gymnasium were described as barn-like with everything within quickly becoming covered in mould. The establishment of a new drill hall in Woburn Street was reported in the *Bedfordshire Times* on 20 October 1922. This converted house included a hall, indoor miniature range, clubroom, orderly room, and residence for the sergeant-major. The Victoria Street drill hall in Dunstable and the Bossard Hall in Leighton Buzzard both appear to have been built in the early 1930s to a similar plan. A two-storey block at each end, one of which containing a dwelling for the resident instructor, and the other the orderly room and mess, bracket a hall parallel to the street frontage. The Dunstable and Leighton Buzzard halls were both in use by 1933. A much earlier hall at Biggleswade remained but was provided with a new administration block in the 1930s. In October 1918, the armoury, stores, and offices of the Luton companies of the 5th Battalion were passed to the Luton branch of the Discharged Sailors and Soldiers Federation, so a temporary HQ was established in Castle Street in 1920. The new drill hall on the Old Bedford Road was promised in 1922, and appeared in the 1924 Kelly's Directory entry as home to Luton's infantry, artillery and RE units. In Ampthill, the stopgap conversion lasted only fifteen years, as an entirely new drill hall, on a new site, further along Woburn Street, was designed in 1937, by architect Ivan Daughtry. The two-storey, five-bay front block in typical neo-Georgian style is in brick with stone dressings. In line behind it are the hall, garages, armoury, and stores, still in use by the ACF. Interestingly, the 1927 survey of the Bedford Arms Hotel in Woburn carried out for the 1925 Rating and Valuation Act, records that its courtyard contained the 'drill hall occupied by the 5th Battalion of the Bedfordshire & Hertfordshire Regiment', suggesting it was still in active use as a drill station.

Bedford, Ashburnham Road, the new drill hall for the Bedfordshire and Hertfordshire Regiment's TA battalion.

Ampthill, Woburn Street, the house converted as a drill hall in 1922.

Dunstable, Victoria Street, the new drill hall in use by 1933.

Leighton Buzzard, the Bossard Hall, opened as a drill hall by 1933, it is now used by the Royal British Legion.

Biggleswade, Shortmead Street, the new front block added to the Yeomanry's earlier hall.

Luton, Old Bedford Road, the drill hall started in 1922.

Ampthill, Woburn Street, the new purpose-built drill hall of 1937, still in use by the ACF.

Woburn, Bedford Arms Hotel, the stable yard contained buildings, which operated as a TA drill hall into the 1920s.

The RAF and the Aircraft Industry

After the end of the war, the newly-formed RAF was fighting for its very survival. Few of its wartime bases survived but those that did included two in Bedfordshire: Cardington and Henlow. At Cardington, Short Brothers' airship factory had been nationalised in 1919 as the Royal Airship Works. An airship hangar (No. 1 Hangar) had been constructed in 1916–17 by Main of Glasgow, but with the contract to build the *R-101*, it became necessary to extend this structure, its final dimensions being 812 by 275 by 180 feet (247 by 83 by 55 metres). No. 2 Hangar, of similar size when extended, was brought from the Admiralty's airship research station at Pulham in Norfolk in 1927 to house the *R-100*. The Cardington-built *R-38* had crashed in 1921 with a high loss of life. The *R-101* was lost in France on its maiden flight in 1930, with a slightly greater number of deaths. On board were Air Vice-Marshal Sir Sefton Brancker, an Old Bedfordian who had been prominent in the development of the RFC and the RAF, and Baron Thomson of Cardington, the air minister. Despite the successful transatlantic flight of the *R-100*, the decision of the Inspectorate of Airship Development was to scrap it and to abandon the whole programme. Balloon development continued throughout and the hangars were used for aircraft storage from 1933 when No. 2 ASU was established at Cardington. While it is the pair of monumental hangars that continue to dominate the site, they were accompanied by a large number of workshops, power plants, and gasholders, all covering a large area between the A600 road and the Bedford–Hitchin railway line. The very grand HQ building, recently beautifully restored to something eclipsing its former glory faced the Crescent in Shortstown. The updated 1925 Air Ministry plan records the insertion of No. 2 Hangar and the building of the hutted camp by 1937. About 70 yards (65 metres) south-east of the hangars was the Mooring Tower. This was a 200-foot-high (61-metre-high) mast with eight supporting columns set within a ring of twenty-four Snatch Block Anchorages. At a height of 170 feet (52 metres) was a circular platform, 40 feet (12 metres) in diameter on to which passengers would disembark. At the base of the mast was a machinery house for three steam winches operated from the upper platform. Pumps were installed for raising ballast water to the airship, along with a 12-inch (30-cm) gas main, and a 10,000-gallon-capacity (45,700-litre-capacity) petrol tank. Hydrogen gas was produced on site by passing steam over red-hot iron ore. In 1932, RAF Cardington had been removed from direct Air Ministry control, administered by the Directorate of Airship Development, and then in 1938, airships having totally disappeared from the military flying agenda, the Balloon Development Establishment (later Unit). A new process for producing gas was developed by ICI who installed a compressor and a bottling plant for supplying the barrage balloon stations equipped with the Cardington-developed high- and low-altitude balloons. Members of the new RAF Balloon Command, including large numbers of WRAF personnel, were trained in their use at Cardington.

Cardington, the two vast airship hangars; Hangar 1, on the left was built in 1917 and extended in time to house the *R-101*; Hangar 2 was imported from Norfolk and extended for the *R-100*.

Henlow had finished the war as No. 5 Eastern Area Aircraft Depot, but was then renamed as the Inland Area Aircraft Depot in 1920, and as the Home Aircraft Depot and Parachute Test Unit, in 1926. In 1924, the Officers' Engineering School had moved in from RAE Farnborough, and Frank Whittle would join the course there in 1932. There were also four operational RAF Squadrons based there, flying Snipes and Gamecocks. The performance of parachutes was tested by airmen dropping off the struts of a Vickers Vimy bomber. In 1936, the engineering school became the RAF School of Aeronautical Engineering with three training wings, plus a MT Training School and the Pilot-less Aircraft Section (PAS) from Farnborough. In 1937, the RAF Initial Training Unit arrived as an offshoot from Uxbridge but soon moved on to Cardington. Henlow also acquired an extensive hutted camp to absorb the 5,000 trainees and resident staff, some of whom had previously been accommodated in tents. Within a short time, the approach of war saw some of the training functions dispersed and the primary repair and maintenance functions reinstated.

Only in 1932 was the government's ten-year rule abandoned. This policy had blocked military growth by restricting the Defence Budget on the grounds that, after 1918, it would take ten years for potential enemies to rearm. By 1930, however, a tentative start had been made on rearmament with the reorientation of the RAF to face Germany rather than France, and an ambitious expansion programme. The programme's main thrust was the provision of fighter stations in a defensive ring around London, and of bomber stations down the eastern side of the country. Cranfield was chosen as the site of a bomber station and it opened in July 1937 with three dozen Hinds from Abingdon, Andover and Farnborough, soon to be replaced by Blenheim 1s. Cranfield was built to the highest standard for a permanent peacetime RAF station using the Air Ministry's plans, from the guardroom (4-7/35) to the water tower (5992/36), drawn by the staff architect Mr A. Bullock FRIBA and approved by the Royal Fine Arts Commission and the Council for the Preservation of Rural England (CPRE). The nucleus of the airfield was an arc of three C-type hangars (2042-3/34) with a fourth (1583/35) to their rear. Each hangar is 300 feet (92 metres) long, 150 feet (46 metres) wide, and with sliding doors 35 feet (11 metres) high, sufficient to house a squadron. Technical and domestic buildings were all built in the same neo-Georgian style, designed to impart gravitas to what was still seen as an upstart service. Around the hangars were the standard 'Fort'-type watch office of the time (1959/34); fuel-tanker garages, fire-engine shed; stores and workshops. The armoury, Photographic Section, and MT Section completed the technical site. Behind this complex were the H-shaped barrack blocks, institute or canteen, sergeants' mess, sickbay, and decontamination centre. A little further away to the west was the officers' mess, now Lanchester Hall. An estate of housing was built for the airfield's personnel with differentiated types of housing for grades and ranks, still visible around what amounts to a village green.

Improvements and additions to Henlow included a guardhouse (1006-7/33), which was a composite of a 1924 design with additional fire party, ambulance garage, and post office. Whereas many of the First World War-era buildings were to local, one-off designs with 'HO' drawing numbers, many of those original buildings would now be replaced by standard Expansion Period buildings. These included the institute, sergeants' and officers' messes, barrack blocks, Station HQ, and married quarters.

In contrast to the curbs on the RAF's development into the 1930s, private flying was becoming a popular pastime. Both the AA and the RAC sponsored landing grounds where aircraft could land, refuel, and proceed on their journeys. The AA established such LGs at Marsh Leys Farm, Bedford; and at Dunstable, now under Lewsey Farm housing. The RAC's field was an 1800s racecourse at Racc Mcadows Way, Elstow.

The Percival aircraft company moved to Luton in 1936, establishing a factory for the Gull, with an adjacent flying field. Very soon afterwards, the Air Ministry, finally realised that more pilots would need to be trained for the expanding RAF, and set up a flying-school, contracted out to Marshalls of Cambridge. No. 29 E&RFTS opened in Luton in August 1938, a month after Luton Corporation, emulating other ambitious towns, had opened a municipal airport. Pilots were trained on Hawker Harts. Percival's military version of the Gull, the Proctor, first flew from Luton in October 1939. Airfield buildings were rudimentary with an improvised control tower, a hangar, a flying clubhouse, and some hutted workshops. Donald Marendaz was a former RFC pilot and racing driver who

RAF Cranfield, a C-type hangar, one of four constructed in the 1930s.

RAF Cranfield, the water tower, centrepiece of the airfield's works department.

RAF Cranfield, the officers' mess, now Lanchester Hall.

RAF Cranfield, the airmen's dining room, with details like an Art Deco cinema, and now Sir Stafford Cripps Hall.

RAF Cranfield, a Q-type airmen's barrack block.

RAF Henlow, the guardroom.

RAF Henlow, the sergeants' mess.

designed both cars and aircraft. An airfield had been established at Barton-le-Clay in 1935 as a home for Luton Aircraft Limited, one of several small companies building light aircraft and gliders, including the unsuccessful Marendaz Aircraft Co., which had been set up to build biplanes to the owner's design. However, at the request of the Air Ministry, Marendaz was licensed to set up the Bedford School of Flying in 1938 training up to 500 pilots in the two years it operated, flying a de Havilland Moth and an Avro 594 Avian. Marendaz also acquired a second airfield of 87 acres (35 ha), possibly at Mead Farm, Eaton Bray, in 1939, partly due to complaints about the noise in Barton-le-Clay. Apparently the two airfields were run jointly until war broke out when training would be concentrated on the Barton site. Although it has been suggested that a hangar had been built pre-war, no such structure appears on a 1939 map. Marendaz had grand plans to open a 'first-class flying ground' at Mead Farm, on 1 September 1939, but events intervened and, in any case, Leighton Buzzard Urban District Council was not interested in a civil aerodrome. Marendaz was, incredibly, accused of spying in June 1940, when he, allegedly, photographed an Oxford crash-landing on his Eaton Bray field, and then, as an associate of Oswald Mosley, he was briefly interned in 1940.

After 300 years in the ownership of the Osborne family, Chicksands Priory (or as it is rendered in a Ministry of Transport schedule of private wartime railway sidings, 'Creaklands Priory') was bought by the Crown Commissioners and let out to tenants in 1936. It would be requisitioned by the Royal Navy early in the war as a 'Y' Station, intercepting enemy wireless transmissions, and then transferred to the RAF in 1940. As the result of the experimentation into the reception of radio transmissions, it transpired that Leighton Buzzard enjoyed the circumstances that would prove ideal for global radio communications. Proximity to the country's central spine of Post Office Telephone cables added a further benefit. RAF Leighton Buzzard (later RAF Stanbridge) was set up as the RAF's central communications station, known as 'Q Central'. In view of the urgency, contingency plans were put in hand to establish facilities in existing buildings in the town for use until the final structure was completed.

Air Defence and Air Raid Precautions (ARP)

One of the successes of the First World War was the London Air Defence Area (LADA), which ultimately involved a co-ordinated system of spotters, AA guns, and fighter interception. The spotter element was worked up and rolled out across the country as the Observer Corps. With its HQ in Bedford, No. 12 Group formed in 1935, with a control room in the telephone exchange and an emergency centre in the Montrose Hall in Harpur Street. No. 12 Group's network of aircraft-spotting posts was established with the first two opening in Buckinghamshire in 1936, joined by two more there, plus eight posts in Bedfordshire in 1937 and six in Northamptonshire in 1938–9. The Shefford post was added in 1939. The Bedford centre was linked to Fighter Command at Uxbridge, which controlled fighter stations at Duxford, Wittering, and Northolt. Tests to develop acoustic systems that amplified aircraft noise proved unsuccessful so observers were confined to visual sightings, reliant on familiarity with aircraft recognition charts. Observers were also required to report on the fall of bombs in order to identify either delayed action or unexploded bombs, and crashed aircraft. Tall structures such as windmills and church towers were adopted as elevated spotting platforms and some wooden sheds referred to as rabbit hutches were erected to accommodate observers but with a minimal degree of protection from the elements. Communication was by public telephone. Fortunately, radio direction finding, later known as radar, was developing fast and would prove decisive in air defence. The responsibility for AA defence had been delegated to the TA in the mid-1920s, but it would be another ten years before any significant steps were taken to implement this policy, and no Bedfordshire TA unit was involved.

The Home Office formed a dedicated Air Raid Precautions (ARP) Department in 1935 and began to issue advice to local authorities on Civil Defence, particularly the provision of shelters for the civilian population and especially in densely populated areas, with an emphasis on defence against gas. The British Red Cross and the St John Ambulance Brigade became involved in preparations for treating the casualties of aerial bombing. Although many still proved reluctant to accept

Bedford, the telephone exchange in Harpur Street, which became the first HQ of the (Royal) Observer Corps.

the possibility of war, Chamberlain's dire warnings about the bomber always getting through prompted some albeit desultory preparation. In Dunstable, air-raid trench shelters were dug in Grove House Gardens which were owned by the corporation, in 1938, and an ARP exercise was held the next year, just prior to war being declared. A Consortium arrangement with Northamptonshire for ARP labour and equipment included Bedford, Luton, Leighton Buzzard, Biggleswade, Sandy, Ampthill, and Dunstable. A County Emergency Committee was set up with South Bedfordshire Control, in the council offices in Dunstable. In 1938, the RAF Civil Camouflage Section based at Adastral House, Holborn, in central London, selected Vauxhall Motors as one of the first industrial locations to be examined for the production of camouflage schemes. Hayward Tyler's factory in Luton was also camouflaged; given protective wire guards over windows both to protect against flying glass from bomb-blast and to retain a barrier against gas; and recruited a works fire brigade. It was also one of the few firms that followed the Home Office guidance and dug trench shelters early in 1939. These trench shelters were simple cut-and-cover affairs with shelter bays linked by narrow passages and with as few exits as possible, protected by gas curtains. This advice to factories was followed by the issue of similar advice to local authorities in 1938 and, by the end of the year, to householders. Suggestions for domestic shelters ranged from radical and expensive structural alterations to houses, to structures marketed by private industry offering minimal protection but exploiting a commercial opportunity. Across the country, few local authorities did very much as they were only required to provide public shelters for 10 per cent of the population as the majority, so the official line went, would be sheltered at work or at home. In Luton, however, the borough council decided to make elaborate and costly provision. From May 1939, work was begun on digging deep tunnel systems in four locations: Upper George Street where basements opposite the town hall were extended under the road; Beech Hill; and Albert and Midland Roads in High Town. In Beech Hill, according to a guided tour on YouTube, the 6-foot 6-inch-wide (2-metre-wide), brick-vaulted tunnels reach a depth of 80 feet (25 metres) and extend for 250 yards (230 metres). Both entrances are accessed by several flights of concrete steps but an emergency exit uses fixed vertical ladders to reach street-level manholes. Incorporated in the tunnels are doglegs designed to minimise the effects of blast, a lesson learnt in the trenches of the First World War, but not applied everywhere. The Beech Hill tunnel would accommodate 1,411 people. The four tunnel systems, together with thirty additional cut-and-cover tunnels could absorb a total of 8,100 people representing something over the requisite 10 per cent of Luton's pre-war population. By the summer of 1939, these communal arrangements had been accompanied by the official trio of personal air-raid precautions: stirrup-pumps, Anderson shelters, and gasmasks, which had all been launched on an apprehensive public.

Munitions

The Britannia Works in Bedford had closed down by 1932 but, fortunately, other industrial concerns were expanding. Vauxhall Motors in Kimpton Road, Luton, put up a new assembly building in 1935, opposite their offices. That year, the Bedford Truck Division of Vauxhall Motors submitted prototypes of a modified 2-ton lorry built to War Office specifications. By 1938, further trials had produced the 15-cwt GS 4×2 Truck. An initial order for 2,000 was placed in 1939 with the first fifty in the shape of the *portee* designed to carry the 2-pounder A/T gun. They were also issued to the TA for use with the far less effective 25-mm Hotchkiss A/T gun. By the end of the war, a quarter of a million trucks would be produced for use primarily by the Army but also by the Royal Navy and the RAF. In 1938, Hayward Tyler of Luton extended their factory in Luton with new buildings. Igranic in Bedford were producing batteries and radio components for receivers and transmitters. AC Sphinx moved into a brand-new factory manufacturing spark plugs, fronting on to the A5 in Dunstable, in 1934. It would become AC-Delco after the war, the name by which it is remembered.

Luton, Vauxhall's extended motor works in Kimpton Road.

As war approached, many of the ruling class had been seduced by the perceived benefits of fascism. Hastings Russell, 12th duke of Bedford, was closely associated with fascist groups but, as a pacifist, campaigned for appeasement and the avoidance of war. As a major sponsor of the British People's Party and having affinities with The Link and other extreme right-wing parties, he narrowly avoided being interned. It was believed by some in MI5 that he had been earmarked by the Nazi leadership for a prominent role in government were there to be a successful invasion of Britain in 1940/1. In 1945, he relaunched the British People's Party and wrote widely as a Holocaust denier. John (Ian) Russell, however, 13th duke of Bedford, fought in the early years of the war in the Coldstream Guards.

5

Bedfordshire in the Second World War, 1939– 45

During the Second World War, Bedfordshire was at the heart of a number of secret or covert operations. Known as 'Q Central' and operated by RAF No. 26 (Signals) Group, Leighton Buzzard was the hub of Britain's defence telecommunications system, using both landline and radio to provide Command and Control channels for the entire network of radar stations and for RAF Fighter and Bomber Commands. Woburn Abbey was the centre for political warfare, using surrounding villages for billets and out-stations. RAF Tempsford was the departure point for SOE missions into Occupied Europe. The 'Y-station' at Chicksands Priory intercepted radio traffic for deciphering at Bletchley Park, over the border in Buckinghamshire. The various components of this clandestine web made up the 'Bedford Triangle' predominantly based in this county but also spilling over into neighbouring ones. However important and distinctive these secret elements were, they represented only several among the many that made up the military landscape, with depots, airfields, training camps, and significant industrial output, all contributing to the whole picture.

Deployment of Local Units World War II

Units originating in Bedfordshire fought in all the main theatres of operation during the war: in the Middle East, at home, in the Far East, in North Africa, and in most parts of continental Europe. To avoid problems caused by territorials opting for home service in the First World War, the TA was immediately put on the same legal basis as the regulars from the very start.

The Bedfordshire & Hertfordshire Regiment

The 1st Battalion was stationed in Jerusalem, in Palestine, on the outbreak of war and stayed in the Middle East as part of the 14th Infantry Brigade, serving in Egypt, Syria, Crete, and the Western Desert, being present at the siege of Tobruk. It was then redeployed to India in March 1942. In 1943, it was reorganised into Columns 16 and 61, popularly known as the 'Chindits', for long-range penetration operations in Burma. The 2nd Battalion belonged to the 10th Infantry Brigade in the 4th Division and went to France and Belgium with the BEF in September 1939. After Dunkirk, it remained in the UK until March 1943 when it landed in Algiers to take part in the Tunisian campaign, suffering heavy casualties. After a spell on the Suez Canal, it finished the war in Greece. The 3rd and 4th (Reserve and Extra Reserve) Battalions manned the depots, training recruits and providing drafts for the other battalions. The 5th Battalion sailed for India in October 1941, and was then deployed to Malaya to defend against the Japanese invasion. With the fall of Singapore, the battalion went into captivity and was not reformed. A third of those captured died in captivity. The 6th Battalion, the pre-war duplicate of the 5th Battalion, spent much of the war in the UK in 54th Infantry Division, initially in Suffolk, stationed between Aldeburgh and Bawdsey; then in Northumbria on similar anti-invasion duties; then in the Cotswolds as part of GHQ Reserve; and then back in Suffolk. Incidentally, the 6th Battalion had the Hertfordshire Regiment's two battalions as neighbours in its first deployment to Suffolk. From 1944, it served in 21st Army Group as Line of Communications troops. In 1936, former soldiers in the forty-five to sixty age range had been recruited into the National Defence Companies (NDC), and in 1939, these were absorbed into Home Service battalions. When the 7th Battalion, Bedfordshire & Hertfordshire Regiment, was raised in 1939 it took in the Bedfordshire NDC as its 'A' Company. The 7th, 2/7th, 10th, 70th, and 71st Battalions were all formed to provide drafts for the frontline battalions, and thus, as units, remained in the UK. Going on to join 203rd Infantry Brigade in Devon and Cornwall, the 8th Battalion had formed in October 1940 at No. 3 Infantry Training Group in Bury St Edmunds (Suffolk). From July 1941, it joined 73rd Independent Infantry Brigade until the end of 1942, and then remained in Cornwall on coast defence duties. The 9th Battalion also served at home, first in Norfolk and then in London in Home Defence divisions. The 30th Battalion was posted to North Africa in December 1943 to masquerade as two complete infantry brigades, the 172nd and 173rd, in the notional 57th Infantry Division, as part of a deception operation to create uncertainty over the landings in Italy. A year later, it was serving as 8th Army Troops in Italy and the Balkans through to May 1945.

The Bedfordshire Yeomanry Artillery Regiments

In November 1939, the 105th (Bedfordshire Yeomanry) Army Field Regiment became the 52nd (Bedfordshire Yeomanry) Heavy Regiment, RA (TA), accompanying the BEF to France but being disbanded after Dunkirk. Reformed in 1943, it fought in north-west Europe until the end of the war when it was disbanded once again, in Germany. The 148th (Bedfordshire Yeomanry) Army Field Regiment, having gained a third battery, (512 Battery), joined the 18th Division and fought in the Malayan campaign, being captured after the fall of Singapore, never to be reformed.

Cadets

In 1942, Miss Olive Brown of Dunstable formed No. 186 Company of the Girls' Training Corps, aimed at providing sixteen to eighteen-year-old girls with pre-service training. Two years later, she formed No. 15 Girls' Nautical Training Corps, with TS *Preston* as its HQ in the Old Mill in West Street. While the Sea Cadets had been in existence for many years, the Dunstable unit (No. 15) received recognition from the Admiralty only in 1942. A number of army cadet units had also been around since the 1890s, but the ATC and ACF both officially began in their present form in 1941, promoting military life. Along with the Junior OTC at Bedford GS, Bedford Modern School, and the Ashton GS, Dunstable, these organisations prepared their members for conscription into the forces, as did service in the Home Guard for youngsters awaiting call-up.

The Army in Bedfordshire: Command Centres, Camps, Barracks, and Billets

During the First World War, rather than facilitating liaison, the juxtaposition of so many HQs at Horse Guards in Whitehall caused confusion and duplication, with the result that HQ Eastern Command was moved to offices in Pall Mall in 1916. By 1939, it had settled at Hownslow Barracks, but in 1941, an Advance HQ was established in Luton Hoo. In Dunstable, Bennetts Brewery, located on the corner of Chiltern Road, and the Tavistock Hall, the old yeomanry drill hall, together housed the HQ of Eastern Command's East Central Area; with Bedford sub-Area's HQ, at 27 The Embankment.

Kempston Barracks had served as the barracks and depot of the Bedfordshire and Hertfordshire Regiment up to the start of the Second World War, but a rationalisation of infantry training placed the region's training at No. 3 ITC, Bury St Edmunds, the Suffolk Regiment's Depot, which appears, nevertheless, to have retained an annexe at Kempston. Throughout the war, Kempston's major role was the convalescence and rehabilitation of wounded soldiers. Ampthill Park was once again occupied by the Army and Colmworth was home to a Pioneer Corps Camp, probably providing guards for the neighbouring POW Camp. The Vauxhall Motors car showroom in Kimpton Road, Luton, was used as a temporary barracks in 1940, and a RASC (TA) unit was housed in a former hat factory in Old Bedford Road. Luton, also home to a RASC training unit and an ATS HQ, later became a major base for the newly-created REME in 1941. Hasells Hall, Sandy, was requisitioned in January 1941 with, as its first tenant, 117 Field Regiment, RA that, though on the books of the 2nd London Division, had spent much of 1940 on the Suffolk invasion coast with the 6th Bedfordshires, probably manning static obsolete naval guns. They had been under canvas there so the hall would have offered some welcome luxury. It next became the Junior Leaders' School for II Corps. Also near Sandy, Woodbury Hall was used as billets for troops prior to its use by SOE. Milton Ernest hosted a detachment of the Army Veterinary Corps and later on, US Military Police, the 'Snowdrops', on their Harley-Davidsons, would occupy premises in Dunstable's High Street North, later a launderette. The Luton Corn Exchange and Electricity Showrooms served as canteens for troops. Not all troops spending time in the county were fortunate enough to have the luxury of a proper roof over their heads. In the fields north of Stopsley's Venetia Road, a tented encampment housed first, TA units, then REs, and then infantry of the South Staffordshire Regiment, who may possibly have been reforming following their evacuation from Dunkirk. Stockgrove Park in Leighton Buzzard was occupied by a Casualty Clearing Station of the RAMC (TA), which then went to France with the BEF and was believed overrun by the advancing German army. Other RAMC units remained at Stockgrove Park until 1941, when their place was taken by a commando unit that camped in the park and trained in neighbouring quarries. They were followed by 66 (Lowland) Medium Regiment, RA (TA) prior to its move to North Africa. As well as the bigger houses, many smaller buildings were requisitioned by the military in competition with many other agencies. In Sandy, the small hall at the Baptist Schoolroom was home to 'six sections of troops' until May 1941, when it became a Civil Defence Rescue Party Depot. Also taken over in September 1940 by the War Department was the Sandy Public Elementary (Church of England) School. This was then handed over to the Civil Defence Committee by the Ministry of Health in May 1941 as a Mobile Unit Depot and Rest Centre.

Bedford, 27 The Embankment, Eastern Command's Bedford sub-Area HQ.

Hazell's Hall, Everton, was used by the army before Special Operations Executive took it over.

Harlington was the venue in March 1944 for troops of the 5/7th Gordon Highlanders of 51st Highland Division who had returned to Britain from North Africa to prepare for the invasion of Normandy.

The Secret War

In what proved to be a foretaste for the developments in communications technology that would characterise the area, the Cardington hangars had been used as stores for equipment, which included the ultra-shortwave radio station, built at Lympne in Kent, as part of an Anglo-French telephone link. Many of these components would soon be cannibalised in the radar research programme which had been moved from Suffolk to Dorset in 1940, before ending up at Malvern in Worcestershire.

Communications Facilities and Operations

RAF Leighton Buzzard (later RAF Stanbridge), run by RAF No. 26 (Signals) Group, and operating as 'Q Central', controlled a significant part of the country's military speech telephone network and nearly all the landline teleprinter communications system, and soon attracted users from all the armed services and security agencies. It covered an area, formerly occupied by the Marley Tile Works, of mainly sand and clay pits, generally flat with a highest point of 375 feet (115 metres), and extending to 109 acres (44 ha). This terrain proved ideal for the excavation of dozens of underground bunkers housing not only communications equipment but, on the advice of the GPO, a RAF Fighter Command standby emergency operations room for use in the event that Bentley Priory were to be knocked out. The site initially chosen for this standby operations room had been Liscombe Park, a manor dating from the seventeenth and eighteenth centuries, over the Buckinghamshire border, 2 miles to the west of Leighton Buzzard. Both this and the Leighton Buzzard facility were used for the training of WAAF plotters, the latter contingent being housed in the old workhouse in Grovebury Road. Until the new underground facilities had been completed, the basement of the Lake Street Corn Exchange (now demolished) housed hundreds of teleprinters. RAF 60 (Signals) Group, Fighter Command, responsible for the management of the RAF's radar stations, formed in March 1940. It, too, established its HQ in Leighton Buzzard, initially in Carlton Lodge and then in Oxendon House, Plantation Road. The two major factors which brought 60 Group to the town were its relative proximity to the central fighter-control system at Stanmore, and the presence of 'Q Central', given that the maintenance of guaranteed secure communications between the filter rooms, the fighter airfields and the radar stations, was of paramount importance to the Air Defence of Great Britain. These communications operations made use of the radio masts of RAF Edlesborough (formerly RAF Dagnall) on the Dunstable–Tring road. Many buildings in the town were requisitioned as billets and ultimately a camp housing over 1,500 RAF personnel would occupy a large part of the Marley site. The complex was guarded by a detachment of troops from the KRRC billeted in Church Road and, after its formation in 1942, a 250-strong squadron of the RAF Regiment, quartered in the new camp. Sandwiched between the old telephone exchange and the former Midland Bank (now HSBC) in Leighton Buzzard High Street, a 'Q Central Reserve' was built. Having gained some windows, the building is now a Kingdom Hall.

The RAF Communications School was housed at RAF Henlow. RAF Tempsford and Old Woodbury from January 1942 provided the HQ of the Wireless Intelligence Development Unit and the operational base for the Wireless Development flights, which were testing the suitability of various aircraft for carrying radio navigation aids such as Oboe and GEE. Milton Ernest Hall was home to the communications section of the 8th USAAF HQ, providing navigational assistance and radio countermeasures support for operations. As well as occupying the hall itself, accommodation spilled over into Nissen huts in the grounds.

The BBC conducted a number of operations in the county. Radio transmissions to the populace were vital for the spread of information and for maintaining morale but could unwittingly provide enemy pilots with a useful radio direction finding service. Fighter Command would therefore take the BBC off the air when bombing raids were imminent. The BBC set up an alternative network of Group 'H' transmitters, sixty-one in all, located near large towns, and close to a tall structure that could hold the aerial thus obviating the need for a tower. One of these was located to the east of Biggleswade, on the road between Wrestlingworth

Leighton Buzzard High Street, between the former Midland Bank (now HSBC) and the old telephone exchange was 'Q Central Reserve', now a Kingdom Hall.

Milton Ernest Hall housed the Communications Section of the 8th USAAF HQ.

and Tadlow, possibly on a site now marked as a telephone exchange. Owing to the effects of bombing the BBC evacuated many of its departments out of London, moving much of its music output to Bedford. It established three studios and a control-room in the Bunyan Hall schoolrooms with three further studios nearby. The BBC Symphony Orchestra broadcast concerts from the Corn Exchange and the Great Hall of Bedford GS, housing its administration in the Bunyan Meeting House. Concerts were recorded in Bedford and sent to London by train for broadcasting. Around 500 BBC staff and radio *artistes* were billeted in Bedford. Hotels in Bushmead Avenue and 52 de Parys Avenue were among the buildings used by the BBC. Religious Broadcasts were also relocated to Bedford, centred on the Trinity Chapel of St Paul's Church, which hosted over 1,000 broadcasts of *The Daily Service*. It was also the venue for the Day of Prayer in September 1941 when Dr Cosmo Lang, the archbishop of Canterbury, and Dr William Temple, archbishop of York, led the service. The BBC lodged strong objections to the *Soldatensender* transmissions of the PWE (see below) on the grounds that they would be quickly recognised as black propaganda and would undermine the BBC's reputation for honesty. The PWE's operations were perceived as being so successful that the BBC's objections were overruled by the Ministry of Information. The BBC was more comfortable transmitting messages to the Resistance from places like Chicksands Priory, rather than being associated with questionably useful black (or, even worse, grey) propaganda.

Bedford, 52 de Parys Avenue was used by the BBC and the Government Code & Cipher School.

Bedford, the Bunyan Meeting House was the BBC's administrative centre; behind the cars, a doorway leads to an Air Raid Precautions warden's post.

Bedford Corn Exchange hosted meetings of the Volunteer Training Corps in 1916 and concerts and social events for the services throughout both world wars.

In the period leading up to the invasion of Normandy, the BBC and the US Armed Forces Network combined to provide entertainment. The Glenn Miller Band was based in Bedford using the Co-Partners Hall, the former Gas Works social club off Ford End Road, as a recording studio and radio station. Two houses in Ashburnham Road provided digs for Miller and his musicians. His last flight was made from Twinwood Farm on 15 December 1944 following a concert on the airfield.

The 'Y' Service and GC&CS

During the First World War, the 'Y' Service had been developed to eavesdrop on enemy radio transmissions, and this practice would provide the basis for the GC&CS (Government Code and Cipher School), which was set up at Bletchley Park, over the border in Buckinghamshire. In 1936, Chicksands Priory had been acquired by the Crown Commissioners and leased to a private tenant. In 1940, it was requisitioned by the Royal Navy and then passed to the RAF for use as a 'Y'-Station, supplying coded ULTRA signals to Bletchley Park. The Priory building itself served as the Operations Centre until 1945. Intercepted signals were despatched every evening by motorcycle to Bletchley Park for decoding. The Meteorological Office at Dunstable functioned as a 'Y' Service intercept site linked to GC&CS from 1941. Not only did it collect radio traffic for onward delivery to Bletchley Park but it also benefited from those decoded weather reports it received back, ready for dissemination. Wrest Park at Silsoe provided 'Y' Service personnel from Chicksands with overspill accommodation. There

Chicksands Priory, the old building, an Auxiliary Hospital in the First World War, became the Operations Centre of a 'Y' Station, intercepting German radio traffic for decoding at Bletchley Park in the Second World War; it is now the Intelligence Corps' officers' mess.

Chicksands Priory, a former transmitter or receiver building.

Bedford, Ardor House on the corner of Broadway, was a code-breaking school for MI18, then a Japanese language school serving the Government Code & Cipher School.

Bedford, this Arabic
language school for
the Government Code
& Cipher School was
located on the corner of
Albany Road and The
Embankment.

were billets for WRNS (Wrens), on the books of HMS *Pembroke V*, and WAAF
personnel from Bletchley Park at Woburn Abbey.

In Bedford, Ardor House on the corner of Broadway, began life as a code-
breaking school for MI18. It later housed a Japanese language school serving
GC&CS, which moved to 7 St Andrews Road in June 1942, and the next year, to
52 de Parys Avenue. An Arabic language school for GC&CS was located on the
corner of Albany Road and the Embankment.

Political Warfare Executive (PWE) and the Political Intelligence Department (PID)

The Political Intelligence Department was based at Foxgrove/Froxfield, a villa
on the Woburn estate, but soon moved to the larger Marylands. After a move
back to London, the organisation was wound up, its functions being transferred
to the Foreign Office Research Department based at Balliol College, Oxford.
However, the PID label remained as a cover for the PWE, which was initially
supervised by Hugh Dalton. When Dalton was moved on to lead the SOE, his

secretary, Hugh Gaitskell, took over, living at 6 Leighton Street, Woburn. The psychological warfare units of the PWE were housed in the Riding School and Stables of Woburn Abbey, as well as in the half-timbered Paris House, which had been brought over from the Paris Exhibition of 1878 and reassembled in the park. Recreational facilities included a cinema, and billiards tables and a dance floor were installed in the stables for the use of the large number of staff based in the abbey. The duke's only stipulation being that he must not be able to set eyes on any of these people. The PID's printing workshop was housed in the hangar that the Flying Duchess had used until her disappearance in 1937 and then moved from there into Marylands, originally the estate workers' model hospital. When the volume of printing became too large to handle, a Home Counties Newspapers title with offices in Manchester Street, Luton, was brought in to the operation. The PWE, by now run by the journalist Sefton Delmer, was dedicated to producing black propaganda and a radio station was set up in secure buildings on the edge of the Woburn Estate at Milton Bryan. Radio programmes under the signature *Soldatensender Calais* were broadcast live at the time of the invasion of France, purporting to be a German station but actually coming from the extremely powerful Aspidistra transmitter at Crowborough in Sussex. These transmissions would reach German troops in Europe and Scandinavia, and even U-boats in the Atlantic. Music and sports reports were interspersed with a mixture of genuine news and morale-sapping inventions. The content was then reprised in the *Nachrichten Fur Die Truppe* newspaper produced by the *Luton News* and air-dropped over the German lines the next day. During the Normandy landings, listening German intelligence officers were tricked into thinking that the landing beaches covered a more extensive area than they actually did.

As well as Woburn, PWE operatives worked out of Aspley Guise with French and German sections in village houses along with a recording studio. Delmer lived in the Rookery at Aspley Guise, and rectories at Broughton, Eversholt, Toddington, Tingrith, and Holcot were requisitioned. Leys Farm, Milton Bryan, was the Research Unit for Central and Eastern European operations; Scandinavian efforts were centred on Woburn Park Farm; Polish and Czech on the Holt at Woburn; and Italy and Southeast Europe on the Grange at Newton Longville. PWE also maintained a transmitting station at Potsgrove, where two transmitters, Poppy and Pansy put out material from its sixteen scattered studios. One of the transmitter buildings, Pansy, and a generator house survive. All this output had been co-ordinated from Milton Bryan where impressive remains of the central transmitting station, standing in a compound of 5 acres (2 ha), and surrounded by huts, generator building, air-raid shelter, and guardroom, survive. There are tentative plans (2018) to establish an Intelligence Services Museum there.

Woburn, Paris House was used by the psychological warfare units of the Political Warfare Executive.

Woburn's Park Farm housed Political Warfare Executive's Research Unit for Scandinavian affairs, and some of the Air Transport Auxiliary's administrative and maintenance operations relating to the Satellite Landing Ground.

Milton Bryan, the recording studios built for the production of black propaganda by the Political Warfare Executive.

Potsgrove, the building housing the Political Warfare Executive's Pansy transmitter survives with a smaller generator building alongside, but Poppy has gone.

The Meteorological Office's Forecasting Division at Dunstable (ETA)

Leaving a small HQ office in London, the Meteorological Office's Forecasting Division was moved via Birmingham to Green Lane, Dunstable, in February 1940. An initial staff of 700 had increased to 6,000 by the war's end. Duties ranged from being ready to offer advice on the effects of gas attacks to forecasting the weather for naval and air operations. Data was received from over 500 reporting stations, often on airfields, and nearly 300 ships. Information from foreign sources diminished throughout the war continuing to be received only from Portugal, Iceland, the USA, and Canada. Reports did get through from clandestine sources in occupied Europe, particularly from Poland, but from April 1940, the contents of German radio transmissions were deciphered at Bletchley Park and forwarded to Dunstable. Despatch riders from Dunstable shuttled up to four times a day between London HQ and Bletchley Park. Direction finding methods were employed at Dunstable by triangulating with St Eval in Cornwall and Leuchars in Fife by telephone in real time to observe atmospherics. This would help to inform Bomber Command's day-to-day planning in respect of the upper atmospheric conditions which would impact dramatically on bomber operations. By 1945, the office had established a dedicated radar research station on Dunstable's East Hill equipped with a 10-cm radar.

Special Operations Executive (SOE) and Office of Strategic Services (OSS)

SOE began life in June 1940 when three existing organisations combined to 'set Europe ablaze' by carrying out sabotage and subversion, and by encouraging and providing material support for resistance groups in Occupied Europe. Its primary means of achieving this was by inserting agents and radio-operators by air. Agents were trained and their equipment developed all over Britain, but it all came together at places like RAF Tempsford from which agents were flown to their different areas of operation. Agents and aircrew were briefed and issued with their specialist equipment at Gibraltar Farm on the eastern edge of the airfield. Here, one of the barns still stands as a memorial to all those involved, especially the men and women who would never return. Waterloo Farm, Hasells Hall, Tetworth Hall, and Tempsford Hall all served as secure accommodation for SOE personnel while they awaited their flights. By 1945, RAF No. 138 Squadron had delivered almost 1,000 agents, nearly 30,000 containers, and 10,000 packages in the course of nearly 2,500 sorties, losing seventy aircraft in the process. Tempsford, with its rigorous security, was also made use of as the home of the Royal evacuation flight, where a twin-engined Hudson was on permanent standby.

Tempsford, the barn at Waterloo Farm used for briefing flight crews and Special Operations Executive agents, and permanently maintained as a memorial to them.

Tempsford Hall, used as accommodation for those transiting the airfield.

Henlow had been the RAF Parachute Test Unit from 1923 and assumed the role of testing supply drops for SOE from 1940. RAF Cardington provided parachute training facilities for SOE. Woodbury Hall near Everton was used for training SOE operators in the use of radios. Howbury Hall, Renhold was SOE Special Training School (STS) No. 40, training operators on air-landing communications, particularly Eureka beacons and transmitters, and air-to-ground radar. SOE also maintained a transmitter station at Potsgrove (Poppy) alongside that run by PWE (Pansy). Under the auspices of the BBC, the transmitter at Chicksands Priory was also used by SOE and OSS to send inscrutable, but highly important, personal messages to agents or Resistance contacts. Bunkers Farm at Hockcliffe housed STS Nos 43 and 46, moved there from Surrey in 1942, and training Czech wireless operators.

Contemporary accounts of the unusually tight security at Milton Ernest Hall have been taken as evidence that clandestine activities mounted by the US Psychological Warfare organisation and/or the OSS took place there. It has further been suggested that the mysterious disappearance of Glenn Miller, who took off from here on one of his last recorded flights, may be linked to such activities. If the hall was providing support in the way of navigational assistance and radio countermeasures expertise for the units based in the area carrying out Carpetbagger-type operations, dropping leaflets, agents, and supplies, then secrecy would have been a high priority.

Woodbury Hall near Everton was used for training Special Operations Executive radio operators and later became a POW Camp.

Wartime Aviation

In the context of the air war, Bedfordshire is probably most associated with Glenn Miller, his concerts in the area and his mysterious disappearance for which there are many and varied explanations. He played his last concert at the American Red Cross Club in Bedford before leaving from Twinwood Farm on 17 December 1944, but there are many more important elements in the story of the county's contribution to the war in the air.

Airfield Construction

The new airfields needed by the RAF and then the 8th USAAF lacked the solidity and elegance of the pre-war stations such as Cranfield or Henlow, but the need for speed of construction and the scarcity of materials meant that a utilitarian approach involving structures of a temporary nature built of cheap materials became the new norm. Vulnerability to aerial bombing dictated that the close-packed order of the pre-war stations would be abandoned in favour of a dispersed approach. Aircraft would be scattered across the airfield and hidden from view where possible. At Podington, the fifty dispersals ensured that the bombers were never concentrated together. Similarly, hangars and other technical site buildings were distributed across the airfield rather than being tightly grouped together as had previously been the rule. Communal sites could be up to a mile from the airfield itself. The ATA pilots at Woburn Park were ferried to their digs by car but on most airfields it was the bicycle that was essential. In contrast to the solid C-type hangars at Cranfield, those at the new airfields had corrugated-iron sheets attached to steel frames making it possible to erect them quickly using unskilled labour with the potential to move them about. One of Podington's hangars ended up at Desborough in Northamptonshire. The earliest of these wartime hangars was the Bellman (8349/37) a surviving example of which was put up at Luton, but the most common was the T2 (3653/42) mainly allocated to bomber bases. Podington had two; Thurleigh had four; Tempsford had six; and two were erected at Luton to house the Napier aero-engine works. A quite rare T3 hangar (3505/42) was provided at Cranfield in 1944 to ease the pressure on the four main hangars. The B1 hangar (11776/42) was supplied to many bomber airfields by MAP as a civilian-manned repair facility but Bedfordshire's only survivor is at Tempsford. Luton's two T2 hangars and a Blister hangar can still be seen along with the Bellman. Twinwood Farm was provided with six Blister Hangars (FCW4571) and others were put up at Luton and Old Warden with eight of the Extra Over design (12532/41) going to Cranfield. Both Podington and Thurleigh, whose main contractor was W. & G. French, had three dozen dispersal pans and their original concrete runways all had to be extended for use by the 8th USAAF's heavier bombers. With three concrete runways and over twenty dispersals Twinwood Farm opened in April 1942, as a satellite of Cranfield. Examples of the last of the designs for semi-permanent watch offices (518/40) were built at both

Thurleigh and Tempsford, but by 1941, the majority of airfield buildings were either of 'temporary brick' (tb), single-thickness walls with buttresses, or various types of hutting. The new tb watch offices were initially purpose-built for particular usages so Twinwood Farm's was designed specifically for night-fighter stations (12096/41) and Podington's for bomber satellites (13726/41) but with reduced size windows (15683/41). In a class of its own, the watch office at Henlow is reputed to have been constructed out of the crates in which Hurricanes arrived from Canada ready for assembly. An attempt was made in 2006 to dismantle it and re-erect it at the RAF Museum, Hendon, but its decomposition had already gone too far and demolition was the only option. The non-standard watch office at Barton-le-Clay, now demolished, may have been the result of private enterprise when Marendaz was running the flying school there. A small watch office standing in front of the Gulfstream hangar at Luton probably dates from 1952 and has twice since been superseded by more modern structures.

Even in tb, some buildings are quite distinctive such as Podington's parachute store (17865/39) or operations block (228/43) or the gymnasium/chapel (14604/40) at Cranfield, but the majority of buildings, either in tb or as Nissen huts have very little to distinguish them. Tempsford's main stores (3934/43) or the flight and squadron office (15895/40) at Twinwood Farm are very typical of these standardised buildings. At Podington, the standard group of specialist buildings that adjoin contemporary watch offices remains: the night-flying equipment store (12411/41), the floodlight tractor and trailer shed (1296/40), both in tb, and the Nissen hut fire-tender shelter (12410/41).

Luton, a Bellman hangar erected as part of the Percival aircraft factory.

RAF Tempsford, a B1 hangar used by Ministry of Aircraft Production's civilian maintenance staff. (*Adrian Armishaw*)

RAF Luton, a Blister hangar for sheltering fighter aircraft.

RAF Twinwood Farm, the watch office designed for night-fighter stations.

RAF Podington, the watch office installed on bomber satellite stations.

Above: RAF Henlow watch office does not appear on the 1940 Air Ministry plan and is reputed to have been improvised using the crates in which Hurricane fighters were delivered from Canada for assembly on site to be flown off by Air Transport Auxiliary pilots.

Left: RAF Cranfield, the original 1930s 'Fort' type watch office with additions up to recent times.

RAF Tempsford, Gas Respirator Store, a typical building in temporary brick (tb).

RAF Podington, the operations block, isolated on a separate site.

The construction of these airfields was an enormous undertaking involving laying miles of concrete runways, hard standings, and perimeter tracks. At Sharnbrook, a water-pumping station was built to serve Little Staughton, Thurleigh, and Podington airfields via several miles of 7-inch-diameter (17.5-cm-diameter) cast-iron pipe. The effects of planting the equivalent of new villages could, in social terms, be overwhelming. Thurleigh and Podington were built to accommodate complements of, respectively, 2,972 and 2,894 personnel. Tempsford with its strange mix of secret and clandestine operations had 2,092 including 275 WAAFs. A large number of country houses were requisitioned for a variety of purposes. Hinwick House and Hasells Hall both served as RAF officers' messes for, respectively, Podington and Tempsford. Tempsford's WAAFs were billeted in a hutted camp, now occupied by 'The Lawns' housing opposite the Old Vicarage on Potton Road in Everton.

Flying Operations

Luton became home to a flight of Defiants from Northolt for a few months late in 1940, one of which shot down a Heinkel III over Brentwood, and Twinwood Farm saw five squadrons of Mustangs briefly in 1943, carrying out exercises in preparation for D-Day, but the main operational effort was given over to bombing and training. Podington opened in July 1942 on land at Crossways Farm owned by Colworth House. It began as a satellite of Chelveston, which had been testing gliders until the 301st Bomb Group of the 8th USAAF arrived in July 1942 and commenced bombing operations in the September. Podington became a USAAF station in April 1943 used by troop carrier, photo-reconnaissance, and anti-submarine squadrons. A brief occupation by the 100th Bomb Group was followed by the arrival of the 92nd Bomb Group, which was involved in special operations until the end of the war in Europe. Thurleigh effectively began operations in September 1942 when the 8th USAAF 306th Bomb Group consisting of three squadrons of B-17s arrived. Over the next thirty-eight months, they carried out over 9,500 sorties in 342 operations and had lost nearly 200 aircraft, creating the record for the longest posting. Thurleigh was the HQ of 40th Combat Wing, which consisted of twelve squadrons in three bomb groups spread across six airfields in four counties. Tempsford opened in the summer of 1941 under No. 3 Group RAF Bomber Command, and hosted Wellingtons of No. 11 OTU for a few months into 1942. It also flew the Wireless Development Flight's Wellingtons and carried out other tasks for the Bomber Development Unit. Its location and its appearance as a derelict farm made it suitable for clandestine work. From March 1942, the airfield's main activities involved flying Whitleys, Lysanders, Hudsons, and, eventually, Halifax and Stirling bombers, to deliver and pick up agents, and to drop supplies, weapons, and radios into Occupied Europe. This was the bread-and-butter activity, dangerous enough in itself but, additionally, there were still more dangerous one-off operations. Paratroops were dropped by Halifax into Norway to destroy the heavy water plant, and Liberators flew sorties from Brindisi into Poland to supply the Resistance. Decoy bombing raids were occasionally, carried out to divert attention from other covert operations. After VE Day, Liberator troop-carriers air-lifted troops to the Far East.

Training

The county was prominent in the pilot-training programme, which the RAF had begun in the mid-1930s and which accelerated as war drew ever nearer. From April 1937, Marshall's of Cambridge had managed a flying school based on Luton Airport taken on by the Air Ministry as No. 29 E&RFTS. Short Bros were managing a combined EFTS in Northern Ireland but were forced to find a new home in July 1940 so No. 24 EFTS moved into Luton. By the time it moved to Sealand near Chester in February 1942, there were places for ninety-nine trainee Navy pilots, flying Magisters. Barton-le-Clay was used as a relief airfield and a hangar and hutting were erected there. Even though it was inspected in 1940 and, most probably requisitioned at that time, there is no evidence that Eaton Bray was used during the war, but it was only in 1945 that it was reported as returned to private ownership. In September 1939, Cranfield began operations as a bomber training station and cohorts of aircrew began their six-week training course. Each course aimed to include thirty pilots, observers, and air gunners, being prepared for service in what would be No. 1 Group RAF Bomber Command. Wear and tear on the grass field necessitated work to lay two hard runways, a process that lasted into the spring of 1940, and which effectively confined operations to ground training. While this work was in progress, it was decided that Cranfield would continue as a training base and a number of new buildings were added including the airmen's dining room (12922/38) now the Stafford Cripps building; the new sergeants' mess (478/39) now Mitchell Hall; three further airmen's barracks (9965/38); and several instructional buildings. The station was transferred to No. 23 Group, RAF Training Command and No. 14 SFTS arrived from Scotland, flying Harvards and Oxfords. In 1941, Cranfield was transferred to Fighter Command as No. 51 Night Fighter OTU, flying Havocs, Blenheims, and Oxfords, and using Twinwood Farm as a relief landing ground. In 1942, four squadrons of USAAF night-fighter personnel arrived and were equipped with Beaufighters before moving on. Increased occupancy and developments in aircraft technology made it necessary to increase the length of both runways to 2,000 yards (1,850 metres) and to construct more hangars. From August 1943, the development of Airborne Interception (AI) radar saw Cranfield set up as the main training station for night fighter crews of Mosquitos and Beaufighters, with largely home-grown specialist simulators for instructional use. Specially adapted AI Wellingtons and Hurricanes provided a supplement to the more numerous training aircraft already present. Pressure on space continued to increase, and in late 1944, there were around 150 aircraft of over a dozen different marques on the books, with No. 3501 Storage Unit handling a further hundred or more every month. With the end of the war in Europe, No. 51 OTU disbanded in June 1945.

RAF Cardington maintained its status as the RAF's primary base for balloons. Between 1939 and 1943, some 10,000 RAF and WRAF balloon handlers had been trained as well as 12,000 balloon operators and drivers, with new Balloon Squadrons forming up until August 1944. New conscripts arrived at No. 2 Recruit Centre throughout the war, and at the end, thousands were demobilised from No. 102 Personnel Dispersal Centre. RAF Henlow continued engineering training throughout the war as No. 13, later No. 14 School of Technical Training with up to 6,000 trainees on roll at any one time. Henlow with its history of parachute development became one of the sources of instructors as the airborne forces were trained prior to operations in Italy and on D-Day. Pilots and aircrew from Tempsford practised covert flying operations at RAF Somersham near St Ives in Cambridgeshire, and learnt precision dropping of fragile loads by parachute at RAF Henlow. After the USA's entry into the war, OSS operatives were based in Tempsford to learn the elements of their role. At Thurleigh an instrument pilot training school was staffed by female WAC Link Trainer instructors seconded from the factory in California. During 1944, 1,120 combat pilots and navigators received 7,706 hours of instrument training. Traditional ways of carrying out bombing training were found to be wasteful of space and time so a number of alternative techniques were developed. One was the infrared target where an infrared beam was projected and the incoming bomber photographed it on light sensitive paper, which when examined would reveal the degree of accuracy. Projectors were installed across the country and from December 1943 many of them were in urban areas. Luton received an ex-mobile unit in December 1944 and GPO premises, probably the telephone exchange, would have been responsible for the projector's maintenance.

Aircraft Storage, Delivery, and Repair Facilities

One of the lesser-known airfields was Woburn Park. No. 34 Satellite Landing Ground (SLG) opened by July 1941 under No. 6 MU and then No. 8 MU. There is currently an airstrip to the east of Park Farm used by the 'Moth Club' and one of the two wartime airstrips ran parallel to it but extended further north across the Woburn–Froxfield road ending by the trees. Presumably, this was the airstrip that, according to the Air Ministry documents, was 1,400 yards (1,290 metres) long. However, the airstrip used by the duchess until her disappearance in 1937 had lain to the north-east but a second wartime airstrip ran parallel to it but to the eastern side of the wood, in the area now occupied by the Safari Park. Given the presence of suitable buildings at Park Farm, it is unlikely that the SLG was provided with any of the customary structures found at most other SLGs: bungalow watch office/HQ; Robins hangar for carrying out repairs under cover; oil store; and crew rooms. The ground staff at Woburn would have numbered around four RAF officers and thirty ORs. Initially Woburn held numbers of Hurricanes, Spitfires, Albacores, Masters, Tiger Moths, Magisters, Swordfish, and Battles, many of them from repair units. In June 1943, the SLG held thirty-six aircraft, scattered under cover of the surrounding trees. Those same trees would prove hazardous to pilots taxiing aircraft, especially when the larger four-engined bombers arrived. In the period leading up to D-Day, Stirlings were flown in to be fitted with glider-towing gear, with up to 200 parked there at once. As the MUs had insufficient pilots, female ATA pilots brought in most of the larger aircraft. Some of those same Stirlings would return to Woburn at the end of the war to be broken up. The ATA worked out of Luton Airport as No. 5 Ferry Pool, using Barton-le-Clay as its relief training ground. In 1943, the pool relocated to RAF Thame at Haddenham in Buckinghamshire, but continued to bus student pilots out to Barton for training until 1945. This grass field then reverted to civilian use and now lies under agriculture.

In 1939, No. 13 MU incorporating No. 6 Repairable Equipment Unit, RAF Henlow was the only designated repair facility up and running under RAF No.43 Group which soon became a civilian organisation under MAP. A number of commercial firms carried out work on damaged aircraft under the auspices of the Civilian Repair Organisation, itself a branch of MAP. At Old Warden, Shrager Bros carried out aircraft repairs in two hangars, one of which was an original Shuttleworth hangar with the Blister hangar added to its front. They overhauled Harvards, Proctors, and Magisters, and carried out modifications to Mustangs. Vickers carried out fabric repair work on poorly-finished aircraft at Tempsford. At Luton, Percivals ran a repair operation for Vega Gulls, alongside No. 8 MU's Purgatory Site where aircraft were stored in bits, prior to being assembled as required.

For much of the war, No. 3501 Servicing Unit operated alongside the Fighter Command OTU at Cranfield, occupying valuable hangar space. From the middle

Old Warden, the Blister hangar and other early buildings.

of 1943, their work expanded, and by the end of 1944, hundreds of Spitfires, Tempests, Hurricanes, Typhoons, and Mustangs had been fitted with new engines or received modifications to their existing ones. So great was the pressure on space that No. 3501 SU was moved out of Cranfield to be relocated at Middle Wallop in Hampshire.

Depots

The infrastructure to support airfields included the repair and maintenance of aircraft; the supply of fuel to the airfields; and the storage and distribution of ordnance and vehicles. Milton Ernest Hall housed the Advanced Air Service HQ, later HQ Strategic Air Depot Area administering the four Strategic US Air Depots at Watton (Norfolk), Little Staughton straddling the Bedfordshire–Cambridgeshire border; and Honington and Wattisham in Suffolk, depots responsible for servicing and repairing the aircraft of the 8th USAAF. It had an airstrip made of Pierced Steel Planking (PSP) for use by senior officers and liaison aircraft. Around the hall were accommodation huts, an officers' club, and a large recreation hut with a dance floor.

From 1941, the government began to develop fuel supply based on a network of pipelines beginning at Avonmouth near Bristol and travelling east along the Thames Valley to the Air Ministry Aviation Fuel Reserve Depot (AFRD) at Aldermaston near Reading, with a spur down to Southampton. A further pipeline went north from Avonmouth to Stanlow on the Mersey and from there, across the Pennines to Nottinghamshire where an AFRD was built at Misterton. It was then decided to extend the pipeline from Aldermaston north-east as far as Sandy. The basic ring was then completed when the pipeline from Misterton down to Sandy was laid. Sandy thus became a key point on this ring as it was both the junction point of the main ring and the jumping-off point for the extension to Saffron Walden, which would feed all the East Anglian airfields. An AFRD was established here with twenty 4,000-ton C2 tanks each holding 5 million litres, but just one bomber raid on Germany could consume 12,000 tons or 3 million litres. Sandy is located 70 miles (112 km) from Aldermaston and the same from Misterton, while Saffron Walden lies 23 miles (37 km) to the east. A short spur off the main pipeline, to the south of Sandy, ran to the Crawley Crossing Aviation Fuel Distribution Depot (AFDD) with four 500-ton D1 tanks (625,000 litres). This lay next to the railway at Ridgmont and thus decanted oil into both rail and road tankers for onward delivery. One of the tanks is still used to fill up HGVs off the M1, while another survives but is unused. The Sandy depot is still operating and can be seen between the road to Potton and the track of the former railway that served it. One of the characteristic white stiles that mark the course of the pipeline may be seen on the approach to Warren Farm.

A programme of mustard gas production had been started in 1937 with an increase from the outbreak of war. This was centred on the Runcorn area of

Above: Crawley Crossing, fittings still in use today on one of the original aviation fuel tanks.

Right: Sandy, a regulation white stile marking the spot where the pipeline crossed the former railway line, now marked by the track to Warren Farm.

Cheshire at a factory named Randle. The product was called Runcol and was stored at Rhydymwyn in Clwyd, North Wales. In the event of having to retaliate to German first-use, the gas would be delivered by 65-lb (29.5-kg) bombs. These bombs were extremely fragile, so Forward Filling Depots (FFDs) were established nearer to the bomber airfields to minimise transit damage. FFD2, in operation from November 1942 to June 1944, was established at Riseley, code-named 'Lake', adjoining the 8th USAAF Ordnance Auto-Motive Depot at Melchbourne Park (Repair Depot R7). Three 'pots' were built, each holding 500 tons of Runcol, for the supply of filled bombs to the US 1st Air Division's airfields across East Anglia. The site is now fenced around and the only visible remains are the building containing the bleach store and emergency bathhouse, and the pyramidal concrete supports for an unloading gantry. Sandy Lodge was used as an ammunition depot and a pair of BCF huts may still be seen off the Sandy–Everton road.

From July 1942, Sharnbrook was the home of a US Forward Ammunition Supply Depot, run by two companies of the 2107th Ordnance Ammunition Battalion. The munitions were stored in twenty-six, variously sized buildings, set in three rows in a grid of paths and roadways accessed from the High Street. The depot supplied bombs and small arms ammunition to the 8th USAAF's 1st Air Division. The officers were billeted at Brookfield in the High Street with the enlisted men in tents beyond the railway bridge on Station Road. A truck park was established at Colworth North Lodge, and the administrative and accommodation camps were centred on Cobb Hall, east of the village. Owing to the shortage of storage facilities, bombs were stockpiled all over the place in roadside locations across the county such as Stanford Lane in Clifton, where open-ended Anderson-type shelters lined the verges. Prior to D-Day mortar bombs and 8-inch gas shells were among the ordnance stored in the woods between Woburn and Little Brickhill.

Aircraft Production

Luton was the primary centre of aircraft manufacture in the county. Percival Aircraft had been producing the Vega Gull and the six-seat Q6 through the late 1930s and had designed the Proctor for military use in navigation and W/T training. There was also a four-seat version as a communications aircraft. Once over 200 Proctors had been built at Luton, along with prototypes of its later developments, production moved to Manchester. Percivals now switched to Oxfords, over 1,350 of which were built, and then to Mosquitos, of which they built some 250. Napiers, of Acton in west London, established its Flight Development Unit in Luton in 1940 to work on the 2,000-hp Sabre aero-engine whose development would be fraught with difficulties. The engine finally produced 3,500-hp but, beyond the Hawker Fury prototype, was only fitted into three production aircraft: Hawker Typhoons and Tempests and Blackburn

Melchbourne Hall, administrative offices of the United States Army Ordnance depot.

Melchbourne/Riseley, the bleach store and emergency bathhouse for the chemical weapons store.

Firebrands. Despite the performance of the Typhoon as a fighter-bomber, and the achievements of the Tempest in destroying both V-1 rockets and Messerschmitt Me 262 jet-fighters, by the end of the war, it would be overshadowed by the upcoming jet engines. In 1942, Napiers had been bought by English Electric who built Halifax bombers throughout the war under licence from Handley Page. Also active in Luton were de Havilland's, which dispersed its factories around the town manufacturing aircraft parts in hat factories. Some development work on Frank Whittle's jet engine was carried out at the Vauxhall works. Electrolux made incendiaries for the RAF at their factory in Oakley Road.

In Bedford, Igranic in Elstow Road made parts for de Havilland Mosquitos as well as radios and electric motor control systems. J. P. Whites, Carpenters & Joiners of the Pyghtle Works in Bromham Road made Hamilcar gliders and components such as propellers for Mosquitos. Several Dunstable firms were also engaged in making parts for aircraft. These included the Grice & Young factory in Mathew Street, whose Dope Shop in Nicholas Way sealed linen for aircraft, with four further sites making parts for Mosquitos and Horsa gliders, as well as undercarriages for Percival Proctors. Thermo Plastics in Station Road made plastic radomes for aircraft. Henry Hughes of London had been recognised for its invention of aeronautical instruments in the First World War by being awarded a substantial cash prize. In 1935, it was taken over by Smiths but continued to make high-quality marine and aircraft instruments. Possibly as a consequence of the destruction of its London offices in the 1941 blitz, the company set up a shadow factory in Dunstable. The Empire Rubber Company, which had opened a factory in London Road, manufactured hoses and connectors for the aircraft industry as well as respirators for the services. Gossard's of Leighton Buzzard manufactured parachutes and barrage balloons. Winton Hayes Ltd of Biggleswade appears in a list of Vickers-Armstrong's dispersed sites in 1944, providing storage facilities as well as jigs and tools.

Anti-Invasion Defences

Following the evacuation of British and Allied troops from France in May and June 1940 there was a strong expectation of enemy invasion and plans were hurriedly drawn up to organise resistance. Given that much of the Army's equipment had been left in France the two key problems were lack of mobility and the absence of A/T weapons. Until the factories could remedy this, it was necessary for General Ironside to think in terms of static, linear defences and improvised artillery support. A coastal crust of obstacles, minefields, coast artillery batteries, and infantry strongpoints would be backed up by inland stop lines. These would consist of anti-tank barriers, usually natural waterways strengthened by concrete emplacements. The main stop line, the GHQ Line, ran from Weston-Super-Mare along the Kennett Canal and the Thames to Reading, then south of London to the Medway before turning north across the Thames and up through Essex, Cambridgeshire and Lincolnshire to the Humber. It would notionally reach as far as the River Tay, but north of the Humber defences were limited to prepared bridge demolitions. These stop lines were intended to delay invading forces until the Navy could arrive from its Scottish bases, and mobile forces could gather to throw the invaders back into the sea. Only with the air superiority gained in the Battle of Britain would this scenario have the slightest chance of succeeding.

Bedfordshire lay behind the fortifications of the GHQ Line within a defence zone, which harboured the reserve striking force, largely consisting of units reforming after Dunkirk, and TA divisions. These were distributed along a line stretching from Northampton through Bedford down to north London and out to Aldershot. The 2nd (London) Division, TA, was based in the county for a while with one of its artillery components, 117 Field Regiment, at Hasells Hall near Sandy. The division's three field regiments should have had seventy-two 25-pounder guns between them but could muster just four 18-pounder guns and eight 4.5-inch howitzers, all of First World War vintage. The situation in regard to the division's establishment of forty-eight A/T guns was even worse as its sole A/T regiment had just two out of its sixteen guns. This duplicate, second-line 117 Field Regiment would spend the whole of the war in the UK. By the autumn of 1940, the local position had improved as 2nd London Division had moved to a fresh deployment in the West Midlands and IV Corps, with its HQ in Chesham (Buckinghamshire), now consisted of a relatively well-equipped 43rd Division and the 2nd Armoured Division with an assortment of around 300 light tanks. While distant from the coast, the possibility of an airborne landing north of London had to be defended against by ensuring that communications were protected against such enemy action.

Defences of Nodal Points

Behind the GHQ Line, strategy was thus based on defending towns that constituted important road, rail, or waterway junctions. Initially labelled as 'Anti-tank islands', this designation was subsequently altered to 'Nodal Points'. Additionally, both within and outside these locations, vital bridges, airfields, and munitions factories were designated 'Vulnerable Points' (VPs) and closely guarded. While defences were constructed and guards provided by regular troops at first, once the Home Guard was up and running, these duties were delegated to these local forces, and to building contractors under the direction of RE officers.

The Nodal Points in Bedfordshire included Luton, Bedford, Dunstable, Ampthill, Biggleswade, Potton, and Sandy. The first three required quite extensive constructions whilst at the others a more compact nucleus could be defended. Small numbers of the simplest Type FW3/22 pillboxes were constructed at all six of these sites. At Elstow such a pillbox has recently been restored by local effort. A larger Type FW3/24 pillbox stands in Luton's Stockwood Park guarding the road from London. Supported by trenches on the other side of the road and an advance observation pit, a pillbox stands at the top of the hill where the Bedford road runs down into Ampthill. Like many of Bedfordshire's pillboxes, it is constructed entirely of local Phorpres bricks but does enjoy the benefit of a concrete roof. Similar pillboxes were sited to protect the southern approaches to Bedford at both Kempston and Fenlake, and Potton was given at least eight, all these being provided with associated A/T obstacles.

The shortage of anti-tank weapons prompted the development of alternatives to the conventional but scarce 2-pounder gun. Spigot mortars were developed in the county (see below) and at least two each were emplaced in Bedford, Ampthill, and Dunstable with three at Potton. The weapon was mounted on a stainless-steel pintle on top of a framework of tubular steel embedded in a domed concrete cylinder the size of an oil-drum standing in a pit lined with recesses to hold the bombs. The optimum range was around 100 yards and either 14-pound (6.4-kg) anti-personnel or 20-pound (9-kg) A/T bombs were available. Spigot mortars were mounted at the junction of Goldington Road and Kimbolton Road in Bedford and further east along Goldington Road. One survives in a garden on Woburn Street in Ampthill and there was a second in the Market Place. An example may be seen in the lawn fronting flats on the corner of Chiltern Road and West Street in Dunstable and others were emplaced in Linslade Wood. A portable version mounted on short lengths of scaffold pole with spade grips for stability, was available, so many more of these locally produced weapons may have been issued. The object of all these A/T improvisations was to halt a column of tanks so that close-quarters weapons such as sticky-bombs and SIP (Albright & Wilson, or self-igniting phosphorous) grenades might be used. The flame-fougasse consisted of 40-gallon (180-litre) barrels of a petrol/diesel (gas-oil) mixture that could be ignited by detonating a small charge. Its purpose was to engulf enemy armoured vehicles in flame thereby flushing out their crews. The most effective tactical application was to link it with a roadblock in a defile or cutting, planting the barrels horizontally in the roadside bank. Suitable cuttings exist on the A6 road below Barton-le-Clay where flame-fougasses are known to have been installed. Roadblocks generally consisted of a combination of 4-foot (1.2-metre) concrete cubes, and 'hairpins', which were formed by bending lengths of rail to be slotted into prepared sockets in the ground, closing the central gap between the blocks and thus sealing the roadway. Smaller, cylindrical concrete blocks could be rolled under tanks to foul their tracks. Often knife-rests were used to create checkpoints as at the top of Everton Hill controlling access to RAF Tempsford or the simple pole mounted on trestle-table legs used in Barton-le-Clay. The railway bridge on the Wing Road out of Linslade had a movable barrier defended by a sandbagged machine-gun post. More evil in intent were Ampthill's

Elstow, the recently conserved pillbox at the Interchange Retail Park.

Luton, Stockwood Park, a pillbox defending the southern approaches to the town.

wire obstructions. Here, hawsers were threaded through steel rings fixed into walls each side of the four roads entering the town centre. While unlikely to stop a tank they would have been quite capable of decapitating motorcyclists, very often employed as reconnaissance troops, and quite capable of being landed by glider. Pairs of these rings can still be seen in Ampthill's Church and Bedford Streets and one odd one in Woburn Street. They were sited in conjunction with roadblocks formed of two rows of heavy hairpin A/T Rails. Their concrete sockets were provided with cast-iron covers or wooden plugs to keep the water out and to ease the passage of traffic. An A/T Block was excavated at the south end of Bedford's Harpur Street in 1997. Other A/T blocks and rails have been recorded in the county but the majority have long been removed.

Many of the Home Guard's weapons and munitions needed secure storage. There was a standard design of store with separate compartments for inflammables and explosives. Examples at Ampthill and Potton have been demolished, along with one with the regulation two doors behind the Old Bedford Road drill hall in Luton. The structure behind Dunstable's parish hall may represent such a store and two more in Yielden may be further, surviving variations.

Dunstable, West Street, a spigot mortar commanding the approaches to the town, its pedestal buried with only the stainless steel pintle now showing; there was a gun position in the cemetery opposite.

Right: Ampthill, Church Street, one of a pair of rings that held hawsers suspended across the road as an obstacle to speeding (enemy) motorcyclists.

Below: Yielden, a Home Guard storehouse cum shelter; its twin stands beside the church.

The Defence of Vulnerable Points

From early days in the summer of 1940, airfields were seen as particularly vulnerable, either as the direct targets of airborne landings, or for enemy troops landed elsewhere but seeking to capture a base for the landing of reinforcements. The German invasion of Russia in the spring of 1941 took much of the danger of a full-scale invasion away and the expenditure of labour and materials on fixed defences had more or less stopped by then. The exception was airfield defences, especially after the airborne assault on Crete, where securing airfields for flying in reinforcements was the prime objective of the paratroops. Such was the level of German casualties that Hitler forbade any repeat but British military planners were unaware of that injunction. Uncharacteristically, the Air Ministry had sought the advice of Maj.-Gen. Taylor, inspector general of Fortifications & Works at the War Office, who had come up with a scheme that allocated defences to airfields on the basis of their functions and locations, especially regarding their proximity to ports or specific VPs. He assigned Tempsford, Thurleigh, and Twinwood Farm to Class IIa, while Barton-le-Clay, Cranfield, Luton, Henlow, and Cardington were all placed in Class III. This classification determined the number of pillboxes to be provided and the size of the Army garrison that would man them. Notionally, an airfield such as Thurleigh would have between fifteen and twenty-four pillboxes, some facing the flying-field and some the outer approaches, manned by 225 troops supported by armed RAF groundcrew. Henlow as a Class III airfield would have between ten and sixteen pillboxes similarly oriented inwards and outwards with a garrison of 191 soldiers. It is unlikely that with only a few notable exceptions anything like these numbers were built. Many airfields will have been defended by fieldworks—weapons pits, wire, and mines. Podington was too late for the scheme anyway and USAAF bases tended to favour mobile defences using 0.5-inch Browning machine guns, removed from aircraft and mounted on jeeps. There are, nevertheless, a number of examples of fixed defences on Bedfordshire airfields. These are mainly pillboxes built to the Air Ministry's own designs. Examples of a hexagonal pillbox with an open square annexe built on to the entrance face and intended to house an LAA mounting can be seen at Cranfield (three), Henlow (two), and Cardington (one). Barton-le-Clay has an unusual combination, not seen anywhere else, of pillbox and shelter-magazine at three of the corners of the airfield with a probable fourth pair destroyed. The technical site appears to have been defended by two further pillboxes. All the surviving structures are sunken into the perimeter banks and hedges. The pillboxes are entered through low doorways at one corner accessed by steps, thereby allowing a loophole in each face. The shelters are rectangular and also entered down steps. On many airfields, the defence was co-ordinated from a Battle HQ, which after 1941 was built to a standard design (11008/410). Neither of the two known Bedfordshire BHQs, however, conforms to this design. Now missing the top of its cupola, that at Cranfield is recorded as '11747/41', while Luton's differs even more from any other BHQ. Here, an

L-shaped building with thick concrete roof and two entrances stood above ground level. On top of the roof, a hexagonal cupola with six observation slits stood in the angle. The early fighter stations around London are known to have been given one-off BHQ designs, but Luton's is unique. Pillboxes have been recorded at some of the county's airfields but in nowhere near the numbers in Taylor's plans. Some thirteen pillbox sites have been reported around RAF Henlow in various surveys but only three at Cranfield and none at Thurleigh. Twinwood Farm has one F. C. Construction pillbox, the 'Mushroom' or Oakington pillbox, circular with a domed top and a continuous rail inside to carry two Vickers machine guns. The roof is cantilevered on a central column with three leaves acting as anti-ricochet screens.

The surviving defence plan for Tempsford was probably drawn up late in 1941 or early the next year, dates suggested by the presence of Oakington pillboxes and the RAF Regiment, both appearing around that time. It shows in great detail the precautions taken against possible airborne assault. Located at each corner of the airfield is a Defended Locality (DL), two of which contain Oakington Pillboxes, and all four contain a sunken Nissen hut as shelter and magazine. Each of the four is surrounded by up to four V-shaped weapons pits for riflemen and machine-gunners commanding both the flying-field and the approaches. The airfield's defence force consists of a squadron of the RAF Regiment with its HQ in one DL and a Flight HQ in another. Each of these four DLs is manned by two sections armed with three to five Medium or Vickers machine guns, two Sten or Tommy guns and around sixteen rifles. Additionally, positioned at intervals around the airfield are six LAA posts each equipped with a single 0.300-inch light machine gun—a Lewis gun from the USA firing non-standard ammunition. Two further posts appear on the plan as 'not constructed'. The technical site, to the rear of the watch office, was ringed by fifteen 'shelter trenches' each manned in emergencies by twenty-five 'semi-trained airmen, armed mainly with No. 36 Hand Grenades'.

VPs of different types received whole range of defences. River crossings were seen as especially meriting fixed defences. A ruinous pillbox guards the bridge over the Ivel in Biggleswade, and similar pillboxes stood at the next bridge to the north and by the railway. At Sandy, the bridges were guarded by pillboxes and A/T obstacles, and the transmitter site was guarded by an Allan Williams turret, a sunken, revolving dome-shaped steel turret fitted for light automatic weapons, with a pillbox standing near the approach road. A string of pillboxes at Great Barford (two), Blunham, Shefford, and Roxton was built to secure the river crossings and at Bedford and Bromham A/T rails were held ready to block the bridges over the Ouse. An isolated pillbox at Arlesey may represent a searchlight site since in the early years of the war such sites were treated as resistance points. A pillbox at Staploe may have been built to protect the nearby HAA site, and what appears to be a guardhouse alongside the Langford–Edworth road could represent the camp entrance for the adjacent HAA battery. The Meteorological Office in Dunstable

RAF Cardington, one of the pillboxes with an annexe for a light anti-aircraft machine gun, peculiar to Bedfordshire airfields.

RAF Luton, the unique airfield Battle HQ.

RAF Barton-le-Clay, one of the sunken Air Ministry type pillboxes.

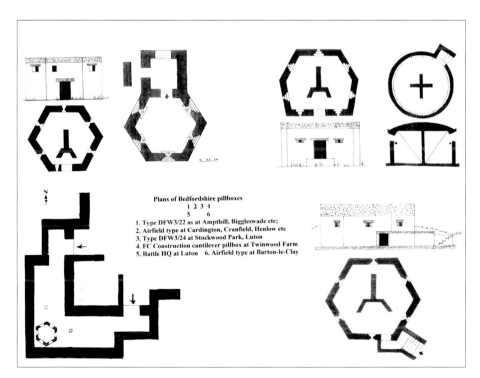

Plans of Bedfordshire pillboxes
1 2 3 4
5 6
1. Type DFW3/22 as at Ampthill, Biggleswade etc;
2. Airfield type at Cardington, Cranfield, Henlow etc
3. Type DFW3/24 at Stockwood Park, Luton
4. FC Construction cantilever pillbox at Twinwood Farm
5. Battle HQ at Luton   6. Airfield type at Barton-le-Clay

Plans of Bedfordshire pillbox types.

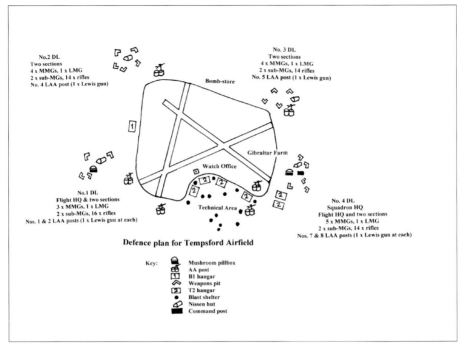

RAF Tempsford's airfield defence plan.

Above left: Elstow, one of the Royal Ordnance Factory's double-decker pillboxes, now demolished. (*Adrian Armishaw*)

Above right: Luton, a protected guard-post at Skefco's ball-bearing factory on Leagrave Road.

was surrounded by wire fences patrolled by Air Ministry civilian police. Later in the war, these were uniformed and armed with service revolvers. The Royal Ordnance Factory at Elstow had its own fixed defences. A ring of seven two-storey pillboxes, of a design found at other ROFs, was planned in March 1942. Owing to a lack of labour, however, only one was completed and the rest were aborted, but many of the factory's buildings had loop-holed turrets that doubled as defence posts and fire-watching positions. The entrance to Luton's Skefco ball-bearing factory on Leagrave Road is protected by a guard-post with long horizontal slits.

Armoured Trains

Although the Royal Navy had stored large numbers of guns from obsolete warships and made these available to the anti-invasion forces in 1940, there remained the twin problems of how they could be mounted and how they could be made mobile. One solution was to mount them on specially designed armoured trains, twelve of which were assembled and assigned patrol routes along the invasion coast from Scotland to Cornwall, manned by Polish troops. By 1943, the Poles wished to withdraw their troops to be trained for airborne operations and two more trains became available for service in the Eastern Command area. One would be stabled in Hitchin and would operate on the lines between Bedford and Fenny Stratford; the triangle of Sandy–Bedford–Hitchin taking in 12 miles (19 km) of the East Coast main line; and Bletchley–Leighton Buzzard–Luton. The train consisted of two open wagons, with riflemen and teams manning Bren guns on AA mountings, bookending the armoured locomotive, and at each end, a gun-truck mounting a 6-pounder Hotchkiss QF gun, previously mounted in First World War tanks. A number of Bedford 30-cwt trucks that had been converted into improvised armoured vehicles in 1940, had become surplus to requirement and some were allocated to the armoured trains as backup. With the expected redeployment of the Poles, the Home Guard had been lined up to take over the manning but by May 1943, Train 'A' at Hitchin, along with most of the others, had been withdrawn. In a general attempt to reduce labour and operating costs on the railways, a number of services were shut down for the duration and these included three halts closed on the Bedford to Fenny Stratford line; passenger services withdrawn from Girtford Halt; and Dunstable London Road restricted to freight traffic; but a new short length of line was opened linking Girtford Halt with the main line north of Sandy below Tempsford.

The Bedfordshire Home Guard

From the first days of the Local Defence Volunteers in May 1940, the organisation, renamed as the Home Guard, would steadily grow into a large, well-trained force, which would take on much of the responsibility for defending the country thereby enabling the Regular Army to fight in foreign parts. The eight battalions of the Bedfordshire Home Guard, wearing the Bedfordshire & Hertfordshire Regiment's cap-badge, and 'BDF' on their shoulder-flashes, were part of the East Anglia North Area, under the local control of the East Central sub-District HQ in Bedford. They were organised in two sectors: the Northern Sector with the 1st, 5th, and 8th Battalions based in Bedford, the 2nd in Biggleswade, and the 3rd in Ampthill; and the Southern Sector, comprising the 4th and 7th Battalions in Luton and the 6th in Dunstable. In addition, LAA Troops attached to the 4th and 7th Battalions defended factories in Luton; the Meteorological Office (ETA) raised its own unit in Dunstable; detachments of 'E' Company, 34th (GPO) Battalion (HQ Cambridge) were based in Bedford and Luton; and, from 1943, the HQ of the East Central Home Guard Transport Column was in Dunstable with component units in Northampton, Peterborough, High Wycombe, and St Albans. An Area HQ was in Dunstable; the Southern Sector HQ was at 4 Dunstable Road, Luton; and the drill hall in Luton was HQ of the 4th and 7th Battalions. Officers were often either local worthies or 'dug-outs' from previous wars. The 6th Battalion was commanded by Lt-Col. Part, lord lieutenant of Bedfordshire. The Gravenhurst platoon of the 2nd (Biggleswade) Battalion was commanded by Lt-Col. Michael Bowes Lyon, the elder brother of Queen Elizabeth. The Pertenhall platoon of the 5th Battalion was commanded by the former Maj.-Gen. Loch who had retired in 1935 and was consequently known locally as the sergeant-general. The Vauxhall company was commanded by Maj. Brett, one of several assistants to the managing director whose peacetime role, probably sales or marketing, had disappeared with the war. Many NCOs were former regulars and the younger members would have received useful preparation from them prior to being called up.

The Home Guard carried out guard duties on a variety of VPs. In the early days individual factories such as Igranic in Bedford formed their own companies, arming their employees with whatever was available, such as 0.22-inch rifles from local shooting clubs. Vauxhall in Luton was able to exploit its army contacts, gained through its multiple contracts, in order to access weapons and equipment otherwise unobtainable. Once there was greater organisation, local units approached the guarding of many more potential targets, ranging from the railway tunnel at Ampthill to permanent roadblocks outside Nodal Points, in a much more systematic way. Certain targets required extra protection at particular times. During the weeks leading up to D-Day, the 1st Battalion's 'E' Company was based on the Elstow ROF. Other targets needing to be guarded included the Eastern Command supply depots at the Portland Cement Works in Arlesey and at Lidlington Station serving No. 11 Main Supply Depot at Marston Mortaine run by No. 297 Pioneer Company.

Although members turned out for guard duties at VPs, they also spent much of their muster time in training activities. Drilling constituted most members' introduction to the Home Guard, but once rifles became available, many of them from Canada and the USA, shooting became first priority. There were indoor miniature ranges in many buildings used by the Home Guard as well as outdoor ones, from which members might graduate to the full-size outdoor 600-yard (554-metre) ranges, which were dotted across the county (see Appendix VIII). Given that the primary function of the Home Guard was to defend against enemy invasion, their training had to include the tactics of fighting in all environments, both rural and urban. Dunstable Home Guard trained up on Totternhoe Knolls, and Leighton Buzzard guardsmen were involved in a street-fighting exercise held in Bedford in June 1942. An invasion exercise held in Bedford in September 1942 saw one Regular and three Home Guard battalions attacking the town. The Home Guard battalion defending it were deemed to 'have held their ground well'. In December 1942, Dunstable hosted Exercise Watling, to test the town's defences. The 34th (GPO) Battalion set up a Post Office Home Guard Training School in Sandy. The Meteorological Office Forecasting Department's Home Guard unit was formed in May 1940 and equipped with 0.300-inch, five-round magazine, US P14 rifles made at Remington's Eddystone Arsenal in Pennsylvania. Grenade practice was carried out in a local chalk-pit and 0.22-inch rifle shooting in the Dunstable Rifle Club range underneath a disused retort house at the local gas works. Their officers had all served in the Army in the First World War. It would appear that the ETA Home Guard was separate from the Dunstable unit as they were only involved in one exercise together. This was a total disaster in which they clashed with each other while the 'enemy' slipped away unnoticed. Vauxhall Motors' Home Guard, 'J' Company of the 4th Battalion, gathered in the car showrooms in Kimpton Road. They very quickly acquired 0.303-inch SMLE rifles, Tommy Guns, and Lewis guns. Many of the members being engineers, they developed their own grenade projector. Their commanding officer even managed to borrow a Churchill tank for one exercise, successfully defending the factory and inflicting a surprise defeat, officially declared a 'draw', on the regulars charged with its capture. Grenade practice was carried out in a deserted quarry on Dunstable Downs. In May 1943, the local Home Guard battalions paraded through Bedford to mark the third anniversary of their formation.

Each Nodal Point was required to have a defence plan based on a variety of likely scenarios. Most of these plans incorporated an estimate of the forces available: Luton fielded 4,000 men; details of early warning: in Luton, OPs were located in the Water Towers at Hart Hill and Tennyson Road, and Dunstable maintained a lookout on Edlesborough Mill; the weapons available such as the Spigot Mortars we have seen deployed in several centres; and the organisation of Defended Localities (DLs) and Keeps. DLs were centres of resistance, usually with all-round defences and often formed around an important roadblock or a VP. Each Nodal Point would have several DLs and one or more Keeps, which were HQs and final resorts. In Luton, there were DLs at Stopsley, the airport, Vauxhall Motors, Kingsway, Skefko, Commer Cars, Kents, Wardown Park, and the Castle Street–Windsor Street Crossroads, with a tank-stop in George Street. There were four designated Keeps: the town hall, post office, telephone exchange, and police station under which lay the town's Emergency HQ.

Air Defence: Guns and Searchlights

Although the responsibility for AA defence had been lodged with the TA from the 1920s, the outbreak of war saw the TA subsumed into the Regular Army so all units involved with AA guns and searchlights were simply designated as RA regiments for the guns, and RE battalions for the searchlights. The RA soon took the searchlight units into their ranks, but some of the organisational terms lasted for a while. Only in May 1940 was very much done to marshal the AA defences of the area. Operational Order No. 3 from 40th AA Brigade was despatched to Col. Reinhold at Bedford sub-Area HQ on the Embankment on 14 July 1940. It concerned the defence of AA and S/L sites, which would become defensive strongpoints. A concrete pillbox was to be constructed on each site along with slit-trenches measuring 4 feet and 6 inches (1.4 metres) in depth, with a width of 2 feet (61 cm) for air-raid protection. The defences would be completed by barriers of barbed-wire and weapons pits. A Lewis gun on an AA mounting would provide protection against low-level strafing attack. This early in the war, searchlights were placed singly at 3-mile (4.8-km) intervals, and were seen as being permanently positioned. Shortly, clusters, and then other permutations, were used as night fighters were equipped with radar. Personnel were often accommodated in tents, but at Arlesey, the WI let their hall to the Army for billets.

In July 1940, the only installation in Bedfordshire defended by HAA guns was the RAF W/T station at Leighton Buzzard, VP No. 130. In May, four of the extremely scarce mobile 3.7-inch HAA guns had been sent, manned by 409 Battery of 78 HAA Regiment in 40 AA Brigade. They were emplaced on two sites, 'A' and 'B', and in October, an increase to eight was recommended but is unlikely ever to have been implemented. In July, the site was manned by two troops of 245 Battery, relieved in January 1941 by 262 Battery. The address of Battery HQ was c/o the GPO. Ironically, owing to the immense investment made in camouflaging the station, the gunners were forbidden to open fire on enemy aircraft unless under direct attack, for fear of drawing attention to the importance of the site. German aerial reconnaissance appears to have identified the presence of aerials but failed to recognise their significance. An elaborate decoy complex further confused the bombers.

In Bedford, four sites were identified for HAA batteries but were never armed. However, in July 1942, in response to a bombing raid on the town, a battery of four mobile 3.7-inch HAA guns was deployed, probably only temporarily as a morale booster. Four HAA sites were built around Sandy to defend the secret Tempsford airfield, the BBC transmitter, and the fuel depot, but none was ever armed. A number of searchlight sites were established: three by May 1940 at Edworth, Goldington, and Wilden, manned by troops still belonging to the 36 AA Battalion RE; and at least four others later on, manned by 467 Battery, 73 S/L Regiment, one of which was on Podington airfield. Only LAA guns could be allocated to other targets in the county, mainly either airfields or essential industries, classified as VPs. Little Barford power station was bombed in February 1941 and a number of Lewis guns manned by a troop from 118 Battery, 30 AA Regiment, were mounted. From May 1940 the Skefco Ball Bearing Co. Ltd, VP No. 546, in Leagrave Road, Luton, was defended by just eight Lewis guns, reduced to six in the October. However, by May 1943, as more effective LAA guns became available, and as the Home Guard were trained in their use, this important factory was provided with four 40-mm Bofors LAA guns, manned by 'A' Troop, 230 LAA Battery, 4th Battalion, Bedfordshire Home Guard. Similarly, at Vauxhall Motors Ltd, twin Lewis guns were mounted on the roof of the car showroom, again manned by the Home Guard. Staying in Luton, Percival Aircraft Ltd at the airport (VP No. 138) also enjoyed Home Guard AA protection. In Dunstable, the AC-Delco factory was provided with LAA guns. In May 1944, 40 AA Brigade moved its HQ to Lyndhurst in the New Forest in order to support Operation Overlord, the D-Day landings, providing AA cover for the advanced RAF airfields.

RAF Cranfield (VP No. 517) was defended by ten Lewis guns in May 1940, increased to fourteen in the July. The airfield was also provided with a canopy of six searchlights. In January 1943, these defences were taken over by the RAF Regiment. A single searchlight was deployed at RAF Henlow in May 1940, along with sixteen Lewis guns, retained by subsequent LAA units until the RAF Regiment took over in July 1943. RAF Tempsford, in the absence of the HAA cover proposed for Sandy, was forced to rely on six single Lewis guns until well into the war when close-defence 20-mm Oerlikon LAA guns were supplied, mounted in pits around the airfield. However, as at RAF Stanbridge, gunners were under instruction to fire on enemy aircraft only in a dire emergency to avoid revealing the existence of the airfield.

Fooling the Bomber: Decoys and Camouflage

Much ingenuity went into finding ways of stopping the enemy's bombers from hitting their intended targets, particularly those deemed significant in terms of military operations, morale, war production, or communications. Hayward Tyler and Vauxhall in Luton both employed camouflage techniques to blend in with the surrounding urban landscape. At 'Q Central', the central communications hub for the armed forces and intelligence services, the entire site was draped with netting and many of the site's facilities were dug into the brick-pits, leaving only the large number of radio masts visible from the air. Fortunately, the true importance of the site remained a closely-guarded secret from friend and foe alike. In addition to the netting, a dummy installation was built only 500 yards (460 metres) to one side of the real thing. This was designed, like many other such decoys, by the film technicians of Sound City, and included buildings, a road, and a car park, complete with cars that would be shunted around by the maintenance crew, who also kept the netting looking neat and seasonal. The all-grass airfields could be disguised as arable fields by having false hedge lines painted across them. Since these measures could only be short-lived, various longer-term techniques of mowing and sowing were developed. Concrete runways needed to be camouflaged more effectively, so fresh concrete would be sprayed with a dark liquid to take the shine off it, and other hard standings and perimeter tracks were surfaced with a mixture of bitumen and woodchips. Much of the exploratory work on airfield camouflage was carried out at Cranfield, an airfield that itself was an example of the regularity of layout, which was so conspicuous from the air. The highly secret Tempsford was camouflaged as a derelict farm by the celebrated magician and illusionist Jasper Maskelyne, working for the War Office Directorate of Camouflage based at Leamington Spa in Warwickshire. The Meteorological Office in Dunstable, codenamed 'ETA', was camouflaged by installing steel uprights, which carried cables over the buildings. These supported wire netting, which was sprayed with dull paint. ETA's shadow establishment at Princes Risborough in Buckinghamshire was camouflaged by painting tennis courts on its roof. The tower of Luton's town hall was camouflaged in order to limit its use as a marker for enemy bombers aiming for, particularly, the Vauxhall works.

Another way of avoiding being bombed was to trick the enemy into dropping his bombs somewhere else. Two types of decoy airfield were built. The 'K' site used fake aircraft to simulate daylight operational use. The aircraft mock-ups were built by the film industry and then moved around by a resident ground crew. The 'Q' site was for night-time operation and made use of lights. A brick and concrete control bunker was built to house the crew and a generator. Simulated runway lights were switched off a moment or two after the sound of approaching aircraft had been heard. A Chance light, mounted on the end of the blockhouse, would be rotated to simulate a taxiing aircraft. Most pre-war airfields were given at least one such decoy site. Cranfield's was at Hardmead, across the Buckinghamshire border, Henlow's was at Astwick, and Cardington's at Cople. All three were 'Q' sites as was a fourth decoy at Swineshead serving RAF Chelveston over the Northamptonshire border. As well as the military targets such as airfields and W/T stations, civil and industrial targets were also given their own, often individually designed, decoys. Bedford had two: Cardington's one at Cople, repurposed for its new application, and a new site at Moggerhanger. These were 'QL' sites using lights to simulate built-up areas and thus attract the attentions of bombers seeking suitable targets. A development of this was the SF (special fires or Starfish) site, which used a large grid of fires, seeded with inflammatory materials that would suddenly flare up, all designed to simulate a settlement or factory blaze. This would, it was hoped, act as a lure for the incoming bombers. Luton had two such sites at Bendish and the appropriately named Flamstead in Hertfordshire. By the autumn of 1942, a range of sophisticated lighting systems had been developed to fit specific situations, and were installed in some existing Civil Series decoy sites. These included systems that would simulate railway marshalling yards (MY), the lights of factories (FL), or the glows from locomotives or furnaces (LG). Bendish had started out as a Starfish site but was then adapted to simulate the marshalling yards and factory lighting associated with Luton's railway yards, and Flamstead used similar tricks to draw bombers away from, specifically, the important Vauxhall vehicle plant. Cople applied those same techniques to protecting the Igranic Works in Bedford, and Moggerhanger posed as Bedford's factory quarter. While it is obviously impossible to measure the success of decoys, it should be noted that the majority of such sites did attract enemy bombs that might otherwise have fallen on those real targets that the decoys were designed to protect. Most of the airfield decoys were closed down in 1942, but the Civil Series sites remained in operation well into the next year. The brick-built control bunker for the Cople decoy site may still be found on the western edge of Sheerhatch Wood overlooking Cardington airfield.

Cople, the brick-built control bunker for the bombing decoy on the edge of Sheerhatch Wood, overlooking Cardington airfield.

The Royal Observer Corps (ROC)

Bedford remained the HQ of 12 Group ROC (it gained its 'Royal' in 1941) starting the war with nineteen posts spread across Bedfordshire with nine posts and parts of Buckinghamshire and Northamptonshire with four and six respectively. All these aircraft-spotting posts were located on, generally east-facing, vantage points. That at Riseley must have been fairly typical. Here, there is a small, gabled timber shed, tucked behind a high brick L-shaped wall. The wall gives shelter against the east wind in this exposed position, and probably supported a viewing platform where the observers would have stood their watch. The shed contained the very minimum of home comforts, and a telephone line linked the post to the central control in the telephone exchange in Bedford. At Ampthill, there was an aircraft-spotting post on Cooper's Hill and another, not manned by ROC personnel, on the hill above the church at Barton-le-Clay. While in the previous war, spotters had lacked the means to communicate sightings to anyone who might act speedily on their information, things were better in this one. An example may be found in a 1941 action when a Dornier bomber was reported to central control at Bedford. Here, it was realised that three Hurricanes from RAF Wittering were airborne and in a position to intercept. The fighters were consequently vectored onto the bomber and shot it down, the whole action over within half an hour. In 1942, the hitherto entirely visual and aural spotting

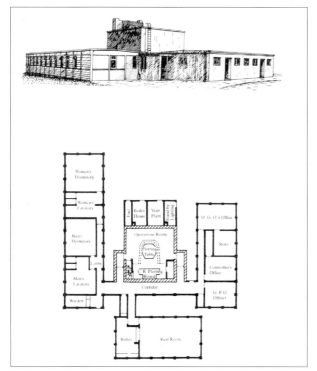

Biddenham, Days Lane, Bedford Royal Observer Corps Group HQ, a standard design assembled from prefabricated Seco hutting, in 1943. (*Defence of Britain Project handbook*)

procedures were enhanced by the recent improvements in GCI Radar, which was a way of directing fighters on to targets picked up on the screen. Each ROC Centre was linked to a pair of GCI stations, Bedford being linked to Comberton in Worcestershire and Langtoft in Lincolnshire. In 1943, the Bedford Group HQ was moved to a new centre in Day's Lane, Biddenham, a little way to the west of the town. This was constructed of prefabricated Seco hutting, taking the form of a horseshoe-shaped single-storey complex of administrative and domestic rooms, wrapped around a two-storey operations block. On the ground floor was the plotting table with, above it, a balcony running around three sides of the upper floor from which the controller could co-ordinate plots and incoming reports in order to inform the fighter stations. From 1943–5, No. 12 Group ROC took in the three National Air Raid Warning Districts of Banbury, Market Harborough, and Northampton.

War Production

Learning from the experience of the First World War when it took a long time for industry to attain an effective war footing, the government took measures to ensure that firms moved more rapidly into tailoring their output to the demands of a war economy. An added motivator for preparation was the fear of air raids and many employers initiated measures to protect their buildings and workforce. Bedfordshire was home to a wide range of key industries: aircraft and vehicle manufacture; plastics; ball-bearings; explosives; pumps; and instruments. To keep this enterprise going, large numbers of workers were required and, in Luton alone, 22,000 women registered for work. As in the First World War, dedicated factories were established to supplement existing industry in meeting the needs of the armed forces. Lord Melchett of Colworth House, the chairman of ICI, was given the task of establishing eight Royal Ordnance Factories (ROF) across Britain. Some industrial concerns were fundamental to all engineering production. Britannia House, the Skefco factory in Luton's Leagrave Road, had been built in 1911, with attics added in 1930. It housed 4,000 workers making millions of ball-bearings. The firm moved out to Sundon Park after the war and the building is now a business centre. AC-Delco manufactured spark plugs in Dunstable; Alliance Castings' foundry in Icknield Road, Luton, supplied many of the local factories; and the Empire Rubber Company in Houghton Regis and Dunstable made respirators for service and civilian use. Waterlows printed propaganda leaflets and ration books by the million. Other work included the manufacture of pumps for the PLUTO Project and a wide range of contracts for MAP. Firms like Sterling Foundry Specialities in Bedford met one-off engineering requirements. The Ministry of Works Storage Depot at ROF Elstow was responsible for distributing flat-pack *Seco* huts to RAF stations and elsewhere.

Munitions

The Elstow ROF, Filling Factory No. 16 was managed by J. Lyons & Co. Given that the prime task of the ROF was filling shells and bombs with high explosives, the danger of explosion was a prime consideration for the management. A thirty-two-page book of rules, mainly safety procedures, was quickly introduced to a workforce totally fresh to the business of producing dangerous munitions. The ROF produced the first 4,000-lb (1,818-kg) bombs for the RAF as well as 2,000-lb (909-kg) bombs, and 'A' Mines for the Royal Navy. It produced 5 million bombs in fourteen months during 1942–3. Having built up plentiful stocks, the Cordite Group (or department) was then shut down. Hydrogen Peroxide for use in these explosives was produced in Luton. The writer H. E. Bates produced a history of the ROF in 1946. The Diamond Foundry in Luton produced 750,000 shells for 25-pounder guns, and also ammunition for the sub-artillery weapons of the Home Guard. Electrolux made incendiary bombs for the RAF and depth charges for the Navy. Coty, the cosmetics company had, by 1941, moved its English operations to Leighton Buzzard with its offices at 41 High Street. They adapted their face powder machinery to grind the chemicals for use in explosives and manufactured magnesium parachute flares for firing from 2-inch mortars.

Elstow, a wartime storage shed on the Royal Ordnance Factory site, now demolished.

Weaponry

Besides being involved in the production of conventional weapons, Bedfordshire appears to have attracted the inventors of alternative weaponry. Before the war, Maj. Northover of Bisley House, Kensworth, outside Dunstable, had established a factory in Perivale in north London to manufacture his clay-pigeon shooting equipment. Recognising its vulnerability to enemy bombing once war had broken out, he moved it to Kensworth as the Bisley Clay Target Company, in Isle of Wight Lane. He then adapted the projector to fire self-igniting phosphorous (SIP) bombs, also known as Albright & Wilson (A&W) bombs. This became the Northover Projector, one of the staple sub-artillery weapons of the Home Guard, and thousands were manufactured in Dunstable. One was successfully demonstrated in Luton, firing at a lorry being towed by a tank as a target. Lt-Col. Blacker had been at school in Bedford and had acquired an interest in explosives during the First World War. He developed a spigot gun, which fired a hollow charge thus maximising the explosive effect. His invention became the Blacker Bombard or 29-mm Spigot Mortar with anti-tank and anti-personnel bombs. He next began work on a handheld anti-tank weapon that would be completed by Col. (later Maj.-Gen. Sir) Millis Jefferis of Military Intelligence's research department, later MD1, and would be known as the Projector Infantry Anti-Tank or PIAT. Lord Melchett of ICI sent the blueprints for the PIAT to the USA and a manufactured prototype was returned. The weapon went into production and thousands were manufactured, many by Adamant Engineering of Dallow Road, Luton, who also produced spigot mortars. Maj. Cecil Clarke, another explosives *aficionado* set up a business in Tavistock Street, Bedford, after the end of the First World War. Lo-Lode made trailers and caravans which often incorporated innovative features, which caught the attention of Stuart Macrae of MD1. When war broke out, Clarke experimented with underwater explosives and developed a limpet mine that he tested in Bedford Modern School swimming-baths and in the Ouse. One of his inventions, intended for the Resistance movements of continental Europe, was tested by breaking into the heavily guarded Luton Power Station and planting dummy bombs before escaping, only to return with fake authority to inspect the place for security lapses. He invented all sorts of kit for SOE as well as the Great Eastern Ramp, a rocket-fired 60-foot-long (18.5-metre-long) bridging ramp, mounted on a Churchill tank body. These improvised weapons all met specific needs and most were judged to have proved their worth. On a more conventional level, in 1941 Hayward Tyler of Luton took over Messrs J. Balmforth's premises to manufacture a quarter of a million 20-mm Oerlikon LAA guns.

Tanks and Military Vehicles

Vauxhall Motors in Luton, with a further works in Dunstable that opened in 1942, employed 12,000 workers and produced over 200,000 Bedford 30-cwt and 4WD Bedford QL trucks. The 30-cwt trucks carried out all sorts of functions for the Army and the RAF. Some were even converted into armoured vehicles for airfield defence in 1940. Tractors were built to tow the articulated Queen Mary trailers that the RAF used for moving large aircraft parts, and the RAF also used Bedford bowsers, holding 950 gallons (3,400 litres) of aviation spirit, on fighter airfields. A standard conversion of the thirty-six-seater charabanc became an ambulance. Trucks were tested in Wardown Park Lake. Commer and Karrier produced vehicles in their Biscot Road factory in Luton.

Special prototype A24 Cromwell Cruiser tanks were built by Vauxhall and the plans passed to other factories including Morris, Rover, and Leyland for volume manufacture with Rolls-Royce engines. In 1940, Vauxhall was invited to redesign a new infantry tank, the A22 Churchill. They went on to build 5,500 of them from 1941, testing them in the brick-pits at Stewartby. Despite its disastrous debut at Dieppe in 1942, the up-gunned Churchill would become the main battle tank throughout much of the war. It would also be the basis for some of the Funnies of the 79th Armoured Brigade, so influential in the D-Day landings, which included the Bridgelayer and the Armoured Vehicle Royal Engineers (AVRE) carrying a 12-inch (29-cm) Petard for reducing concrete fortifications on the Atlantic Wall. Another of these specialised vehicles, for destroying minefields, was the Matilda Flail-tank, powered by a paired Bedford truck engine and gearbox mounted on each side of the vehicle. Vauxhall also designed a self-propelled 3-inch gun on a Churchill chassis as a tank-destroyer but only a very few were produced. A number of German half-tracks had been captured in North Africa and delivered to Luton for Vauxhall's engineers to strip down and analyse. Vauxhall then produced six prototypes of their own version, the Traclat, which was a three-quarter-tracked artillery tractor powered by twin Bedford 3.5-litre engines and designed to tow 25-pounder guns and 17-pounder A/T guns. Although 12,000 were ordered, production was overtaken by events in 1945 and cancellation resulted. Also in Luton, Messrs J. Balmforth's premises were taken over for the manufacture of Churchill gun-turrets, and George Kent made steering gear for tanks. In Dunstable, Bagshawes made caterpillar tracks particularly for Bren-gun or Universal carriers. At Harlington, the Gordon Highlanders practised firing Wasp flame-throwers on the 100-yard range. The Wasp, developed by the Canadian Army from the Ronson, was mounted on the Gordons' Universal carriers, which duly landed on the Normandy beaches on the evening of D-Day. Other flamethrowers came with strong Luton connections. One was the Crocodile, a version of the Vauxhall-built Churchill tank. This was one of the Funnies, specialist vehicles developed to clear beach defences on D-Day. The flamethrower was mounted in the tank turret with the tank of gasoline towed behind in a trailer. The other was a prototype AEC Matador six-wheel-drive cross-country chassis carrying a flamethrowing pump powered by Napier's Lion engine. This was later developed into the Basilisk, an armoured car armed with a flamethrower.

Products for the Royal Navy

Several Luton firms manufactured a range of items for the Royal Navy. In 1941, Hayward Tyler of Luton was placed on the Admiralty's Essential Works schedule and, that year, took over Messrs J. Balmforth's premises to manufacture 20-mm Oerlikon LAA guns and pumps for oil-tankers. Hudsons Foundry made parts for Coastal Motorboats- MTBs and MGBs; George Kents made Clear-View Screens for all types of warship as well as torpedo-firing mechanisms; Electrolux made depth-charges; and Napier's Lion engines were used in MTBs.

Agriculture

Almost as important as munitions was the production of food to feed the civilian population and the growing numbers of troops gathering for the invasion of the Continent. The Women's Land Army (WLA) had been raised towards the end of the First World War but, this time, was mobilised by the County War Agricultural Committee at an earlier stage of the conflict. The committee was based at Phoenix Chambers in Bedford's High Street, and the HQ of the Bedfordshire WLA was 2 St Paul's Square, Bedford in 1939, moving to 42 Harpur Street in 1942. Training centres were set up at Luton Hoo, Ravensden House, and Toddington Park. There were also farm camps at Sharnbrook and Blunham. Ampthill Park was used as a tented agricultural camp where volunteers harvested sugar-beet. From 1942, WLA Hostels were set up for girls away from home who could be deployed wherever they were needed. These hostels were either houses requisitioned for the purpose such as Kensworth House, Cople House, or Clifton House, or a standard design of a T-shaped hutment with a dormitory with twenty two-tier bunks in one wing; a kitchen, dining room, Warden's suite, and recreation space in another; and ablutions in the third. Five such hutted hostels, usually accommodating up to forty girls were built in Bedfordshire including at Milton Ernest, Leighton Buzzard, and at Bolnhurst where its remains cling to life. Houses could often house many more with Cople House holding a maximum of ninety-seven girls. As well as these groupings, land-girls were lodged in ones and twos in farms and smaller houses such as the Grange and Grange Farm, in Upper and Nether Dean. There was social provision at Bedford Girls' Club in Harpur Street, Bedford. The War Agricultural Committee maintained a Tractor Repair Facility in Newnham Street with its Transport Office in Turners Yard, Goldington Road, with a driver-training school in Ginns Yard. Many of the girls worked in the fields alongside Italian POWs. At its peak, the Bedfordshire WLA contingent numbered many hundreds, and what is often forgotten is that their operations continued on as late as 1950. This important aspect of the Home Front is comprehensively covered in a book by Stuart Antrobus.

Air Raid Precautions (ARP)

Although Bedfordshire escaped much of the onslaught of the Blitz, there were raids that caused significant numbers of casualties. An early attack came on 26 May 1940 when Little Barford power station was bombed. In August 1940, fifty-one bombs fell on the Vauxhall Motors plant in Kimpton Road killing thirty-nine people, and two parachute mines landed opposite Kempston Barracks. During the course of the war, there were incendiary attacks on RAF Cardington and Shortstown and a bombing raid on Chicksands. Bedford was bombed on 23 July 1942 resulting in fatalities and damage to housing. A total of 107 people were killed in Luton by German bombing and 1,500 houses destroyed or severely damaged. Between 21 June and 18 December 1944, ten V1 Doodlebugs fell on Bedfordshire, and between 6 November 1944 and 23 March 1945, at least three V2s fell on Bedfordshire. One V2 landed on Biscot Road, Luton, destroying the canteen at Commer Cars and the houses along one side of adjacent Curzon Road killing nineteen and injuring 196. During the course of the war, Luton was subject to 900 air-raid warnings and twenty-six actual raids.

Bedfordshire lay in Civil Defence 'Eastern' Region 4 with its HQ in Cambridge, and sub-Area HQs in Bedford, Ipswich, Chelmsford, and Norwich in 1941. Once all the local fire services had been brought under one umbrella, the county belonged in National Fire Service Region No. 15 with its HQ in Taplow, Buckinghamshire. Within this NFS Region, Luton became the centre of an area covering 600 square miles (960 square km). The Fire Service had centres in Church Street and Oxen Road with Fire Stations at Chaul End, Biscot Road, the Diamond Foundry, and the Vauxhall Motors Works. The town recruited 650 Air Raid Wardens, organised in four groups with a total of eighty-four sectors. Luton, with its essential industries, was protected against air-raids by 25,000 oil-burners, operated as smoke generators by a company of the Pioneer Corps. There was an ARP base in the Old Vicarage Coachhouse in Biscot Road, and all the emergency services: NFS/AFS, Ambulance, ARP, Civil Defence, and Bomb Disposal attempted to integrate. The Special Constabulary HQ was at 9 (later 15) Gordon Street.

In Bedford, the St Leonard's Hall in Victoria Road was converted to an ARP HQ and Control Centre, with a network of ARP wardens' posts, including one at street level in the Bunyan Schools, and a training centre in the Mission Hall in Greyfriars Walk, later used by Toc H. The Control Centre for the South Bedfordshire element of the County Emergency Committee was in the Dunstable Council Offices. Other towns also set up their ARP infrastructure. In both Ampthill and Leighton Buzzard, the Public Assistance Institutions were converted into Control Centres, First Aid Posts, and Cleansing/Decontamination Centres. The police station in Biggleswade became the ARP Control Centre and HQ and 'The Lawns' became a First Aid Post. Park Farm in Dunstable was requisitioned as an ARP depot and the Parish Hall was used as a base for watchers when fire-watching became compulsory there in 1942. The Kempston Methodist Sunday School became a First Aid Post, as did Clifton church hall. An Ambulance Depot was set up at Sandy. In Potton, Linden Lodge was a Rescue Party Depot then a First Aid Point; there was a purpose-built ARP Wardens' Post in the Market Square, and an improvised one at Home Farm in Horne Lane; and the Chequers Inn at Brook End was used to garage an ambulance in 1944. The ARP post at Upper and Nether Dean was initially at the Grange, and then at Bryant Cottage. Although many smaller centres managed to get by relying on volunteers, the larger towns needed to organise paid ARP personnel. Bedford was reported as spending £1,500 a week on wages.

When completed, the four Air Raid Shelter Tunnels of Luton's Ministry of Home Security schemes stretched a total length of 0.9 miles/1,600 yards (1.5 km) at Upper George Street, High Town, Beech Hill, and Albert Road. The Beech Hill tunnel entrances were blocked up at the end of the war but left with breakaway slabs that, in an emergency, would allow reinstatement within twenty-four hours. Other towns made a variety of provision, as in Biggleswade where the basements of houses were converted into air-raid shelters. Two very different air-raid shelters have been excavated. One, in the back garden of the Old Rectory, Hills End, Eversholt, was excavated in 1997. Completely buried in a natural

Bedford, Victoria Road, St Leonard's Hall, a Voluntary Aid Detachment auxiliary hospital in the First World War, and the town's Air Raid Precautions HQ and Control Centre in the Second World War.

grassy bank behind the house was an Anderson-type shelter with cast-concrete walls with a vaulted roof of heavy-duty corrugated, galvanised steel sheets. It was entered via a flight of nine steps descending between concrete blast-walls. In the floor was a manhole cover over a drainage sump and at the far end was an escape shaft fitted with a fixed iron ladder and a hinged manhole cover. The house, part of the Woburn estate, was occupied during the war by Rex Leeper and his wife. He was involved in planning psychological warfare operations and was part of the team managing the Woburn Abbey intelligence effort. The other, a covered trench type shelter, was excavated in Dunstable next to a sports centre. It consisted of two long and two short corridors with bays and entrance, built of prefabricated reinforced concrete panels, and measured 78 by 31 feet (24 by 9.5 metres). Individual factories took their own protective measures. Skefco in Leagrave Road, Luton provided tunnels underneath Britannia House and built a fire-watchers' post on the roof. In Leighton Buzzard, two cellars in the High Street were converted into shelters to accommodate 300 people, and communal shelters were built in Billington and proposed for the area around Stanbridge Road.

Prisoners of War (POW) Camps

From early in the war, significant numbers of POWs were housed in Bedfordshire, many of them Italians, captured in the colonial possessions of East Africa. They were organised into Italian Working Companies (IWC) and assigned a variety of labouring and agricultural tasks. These POWs were accommodated in camps and guarded by men of the Pioneer Corps. Camp No. 42 at Ducks Cross consisted of over forty permanent huts for prisoners in a wired compound with a further thirty or so huts in a separate area for staff, stores, and medical centre. Some of these huts survive as an industrial estate, one with a sign reading 'Interpreters' painted over the doorway, while others display the remains of graffiti. By 1945, the population stood at 800. At Cockayne Hartley, POWs were held in twenty Nissen huts behind the Old Rectory with a mess in the Rectory itself. The camp at Clapham's Green Lane was tented and as this directly contravened the Geneva Convention, the guards had to give up their huts to the POWs and move into the tents. The gliding club at Dunstable, where several of the camp buildings survive, held POWs from 1941–5. The present petrol store was built as cells for uncooperative prisoners. Other large POW camps were established at Potton, Old Woodbury, Harrold Hall, Clifton, and Ampthill Park. Not all prisoners were held in camps as smaller parties were put up in hostels. In 1942, fifty Italian POWs working on the land and housed in a hostel in Leighton Buzzard were moved away as they were considered a threat to the security of 'Q Central'. Italian POWs worked with land-girls (WLA) at Upper and Nether Dean, and Ravensden

Ducks Cross, one of the surviving huts at POW Camp No. 42.

Dunstable, the fuel store of the gliding club was built as the punishment cells of the POW Camp.

House was home to the WLA and then to POWs. The IWCs were assigned to the ammunition dumps at Sandy Lodge and the Command supply depots around Marston Mortaine. In a unique event in 1943, an Italian POW killed a guard, taking his rifle and going on the run. He was cornered and shot in an exchange of fire by Private J. Shelton of the 5th Battalion Home Guard who was rewarded with the BEM. Steven Risby points out that his commander, the former major-general, would have been familiar with writing a convincing commendation and that such an award would be good for the morale of home guardsmen carrying out often tedious duties.

Military Hospitals, Welfare, and Hospitality

As in the First World War, the available provision of hospital beds and medical services were quickly outstripped by demand. In 1939, the only military hospitals were that at RAF Henlow, opened in 1935, and the small hospital at Kempston Barracks. To supplement the civil hospitals in Bedford and Luton and the isolation hospitals at Biggleswade and Steppingley, a number of large houses were converted for use as auxiliary hospitals. These included Old Warden Park and Ickwell Bury. In Leighton Buzzard, Stockgrove Park was taken over by the 200-strong 1st (1st London) Casualty Clearing Station, RAMC (TA), soon to be renumbered as No. 10 CCS and posted to France. In 1941, the RAMC moved to Heath House on Plantation Road. As wounded troops recovered, they underwent convalescence at places like Luton Hoo, Oakley House in Bedford, and Kempston Barracks. Anticipating heavy casualties in the D-Day landings, two new military general hospitals were set up: the 81st in Leighton Buzzard and the 86th in Luton.

With the vast majority of the British Army at home between Dunkirk and D-Day, and a million US servicemen in the country from 1942, there was an enormous demand for entertainment and for hospitality for young men far from home. Village halls, Armed Forces clubs, voluntary groups such as the WVS and the WI, and individual families all contributed to meeting these needs by providing refreshment, opportunities for rest and recreation, and a chance to escape the rigours of warfare. Service personnel and civilians alike were entertained in the American Red Cross Clubs in Luton's George Street and Bedford's Goldington Road. Refugees were taken in and a national camp was established at Heath & Reach.

6

Bedfordshire from 1945 to the Present: The Cold War and Beyond

While it can be argued that Britain's transition from a warfare state to a welfare state was not as speedily achieved as many have supposed, the balance did swing away from the control economy of the war years. Nevertheless, peacetime conscription and a succession of wars and emergencies all took place in the context of the Cold War.

The Regular and Territorial Armies after 1945

In 1947, the TA was reconstituted but would take a long time to recruit its required establishment. By 1949, 248 Field Squadron RE at Bedford was complete having reached its complement of sixty-nine officers and men, but the 5th Battalion, with seventeen officers but only ninety-eight ORs was way short of the 237 necessary to train the new intake of National Servicemen. Although, overall, the CTA had only recruited 59 per cent of its establishment, over the next twenty years, both regulars and territorials would still be affected by a succession of cuts. In 1947, the 305th (Bedfordshire Yeomanry) Medium, later Light, Regiment was formed, and in 1961, it amalgamated with the Hertfordshire Yeomanry to form 286th (Hertfordshire and Bedfordshire Yeomanry) Field Regiment, RA, TA. In 1967, it was reduced to just 201 Medium Battery (V), 100th (Yeomanry) Regiment, RA, in which guise it received the freedom of Dunstable, before being placed in suspended animation in 2014. In 1958, the Bedfordshire and Hertfordshire Regiment and the Essex Regiment amalgamated to become the 3rd East Anglian Regiment. In 1964, a further amalgamation, with all three East Anglian Regiments and the Leicestershire Regiment produced the Royal Anglian Regiment. The 5th (TA) Battalion, despite merging with the Hertfordshire (TA) Battalion in 1961, was disbanded in 1967, continuing only as part of a catch-all volunteer battalion of the Royal Anglians.

Along with the reorganisation of individual units, there was a rationalisation of premises. The Cipher and Switchboard Operating Troops of the WRAC moved to the Luton Territorial Training Centre in 1949 leaving the gunners in sole possession of Dunstable drill hall, and there were plans to build a dedicated centre for the REME Brigade Workshops at the Vauxhall works. In 1955, Luton got a new drill hall, still in use (2019) as an Army Reserve Centre with a recently-formed squadron of the Army Air Corps. In Biggleswade, the Shornmead Street drill hall was given a new miniature range in 1949. The Gwyn Street drill hall in Bedford was demolished for the new bus station, but not until 1983 was Bedford given a new TA Centre, on the Kempston Barracks site and currently (2019) home to a Royal Logistic Corps transport squadron.

At Chicksands, the Priory itself had served as the Operations Centre of the RAF 'Y' Station until 1945 when it became the officers' mess. In 1950, the site was leased to the USAF as a listening station and remained in service throughout the Cold War as one of its three main strategic interception sites in Europe, the other two being in Turkey and Italy. Targets were not only Warsaw Pact air force signals but also the military and diplomatic signals traffic of NATO allies. Chicksands was the centre point of a network of communications that collected information from intercept centres in Britain and Iceland and from relay stations in (West) Germany, Turkey and Morocco. It connected GCHQ in Cheltenham and the National Security Agency in Fort Meade; the strategic command centres of the USAF and RAF in South Ruislip and High Wycombe; and had the capability of reaching the President's desk in Washington within ten minutes. One resident unit was the 6950th Electronic Security Group whose sister unit was based at Kirknewton outside Edinburgh. Chicksands was designated as one of ten 'Comint Communications Relay Centres' and the first to be commissioned in 1956. Its star bit of kit, the 'Elephant Cage', consisting of two concentric circles, 433 yards (400 metres) across, of 115-foot-high (35-metre-high) FLaRe 9 aerials, was built in 1963, from prefabricated parts imported from the US. It was one of five (or possibly nine) such structures worldwide and a component of 'Iron Horse', the HF/DF target-locating system and secure global communications system. It was shut down in 1995, deactivated in 1996, and dismantled in 1998. From the 1950s, the CIA is reported to have sponsored stay-behind undercover resistance groups to be activated in the event of a Soviet invasion of Western Europe, under the code-name Gladio. They would initially be armed by NATO but would then be subject to their own national governmental controls. While the extent of British involvement remains uncorroborated, Chicksands has been reported as housing a NATO stockpile of weapons for the use of Gladio cadres.

Returned to British control, the base became HQ of the Intelligence Corps and the Defence Intelligence and Security Centre (DISC). It is currently named the Joint Intelligence Centre (JIC) and carries out signals intelligence work and training for intelligence personnel from all branches of the armed forces. The old

RAF Chicksands, a building from the post-war era, possibly a gymnasium.

RAF Chicksands, a complex probably dating from the US Army's use of the site.

RAF Chicksands, the massive Elephant Cage aerial array is now marked only by concrete pads; this one is from the outer ring.

Gilbertine priory building, retaining some mediaeval work but largely the product of Wyatt's gothicisation of 1813, serves as the Intelligence Corps' officers' mess. Up on the hill behind the base, the concrete pads for the Cage can still be seen. The base itself contains a mix of medieval, Gothic, wartime, 1950–60s, and more recent structures. Many have been repurposed and others are still being added. Large roofed shelters have been shown to be nothing more sinister than barbecue areas from the time of the US occupation.

Currently (2019) cadet organisations are thriving. The duke of Gloucester inspected the Combined Cadet Force contingents from six Bedford schools in 2018, celebrating the centenary of King George V's inspection of the town's two Junior OTC. Bedford School's CCF is now affiliated to the Intelligence Corps. There is a Sea Cadets contingent in Bedford and six squadrons of the Air Training Corps in the county including one at Shortstown and one at Luton Airport with others at Oakley, Biggleswade, Dunstable, Flitwick, and Stanbridge. The ACF contingent in Bedford has a smart new Cadet Centre in Kimbolton Road; that at Sharnbrook still sports the badge of the 9/12th Lancers; and Chicksands has its base on the Intelligence Corps site. There are further detachments at Sandy, Shortstown, Stotfold, Lidlington, Leighton Buzzard, and Stanbridge.

Sharnbrook, the cadet centre/village hall with the 9/12th Royal Lancers' badge.

Post-1945 Aviation

At the end of the war, the county's airfields faced a variety of different futures. RAF Cardington saw the amalgamation of the Training Aids Development Unit and the Balloon Development Unit as the RAF Research and Development Unit through to 1966 when it moved to Wiltshire. The RAF Recruit Depot took in thousands of National Servicemen and career airmen until 1953. No. 279, later No. 217 MU, absorbed units from Wellingborough and Kinloss supplying all the Armed Services' Compressed Gas needs from 1948–2000, by which time its staff was predominantly civilian. Its two enormous hangars still dominate the landscape and the HQ building has recently been renovated as apartments and a conference centre. In April 1946, at RAF Stanbridge, 60 and 26 (Signals) Groups were amalgamated as RAF 90 (Signals) Group, being absorbed into RAF Support Command in 1973. Podington was returned to the Air Ministry in July 1945 for storage but was finally closed in 1960, being reborn in 1966 as Santa Pod Raceway. RAF Stanbridge continued to operate as an important communications hub through to its closure in the new millennium. Tempsford became a sub-site for storing Mosquitos and Harvards, from 1946–47, and then transferred to Technical Training Command and was put under care and maintenance until the land was finally sold in 1963. Luton reverted to its pre-war status as a municipal airport gaining new buildings including a control tower in 1952. Its municipal hangars still fulfil their original function and the two T2s and Bellman added during the war survive along with a handful of ancillary buildings. No. 95 MU, running No. 2 FFD at Riseley, was taken under RAF Cardington's wing in 1953. It disposed of its mustard gas and Runcol through the mid-1950s by burning it, much to the discomfort of the local inhabitants. It then took on a more conventional role as bomb-storage for RAF Bassingbourn before closing in 1958.

In 1945, flight development was at its peak in Britain and the Royal Aircraft Establishment at Farnborough (RAE) needed more space than was available locally. Space was especially needed for flight-testing the new giant Bristol Brabazon airliner. Thurleigh and Twinwood Farm, only 4 miles (6.4 km) apart, had both ceased their flying operations in the summer of 1945, and together represented the perfect home for the newly created National Experimental Establishment for aeronautical research and development (NAE). The NAE, initially independent of the RAE, needed a 2-mile runway so one of Thurleigh's was extended to 10,500 feet (3,230 metres) by John Laing, and was intersected by a second runway, 6,750 feet (2,077 metres) long. Both new runways had a depth of 36 inches (92 cm) mainly of concrete. Two of the original runways were retained, one for use by the Naval

RAF Stanbridge, one of the several houses in the surviving married quarters' estate, which served the RAF station.

Air Department (NAD) and the other for VTOL (Vertical Take-Off and Landing) aircraft. It had been planned to lay a 5-mile runway linking the two airfields and the road into Thurleigh village was actually sunk into a cutting to enable this, but the steady development of jet engines rendered this unnecessary. Wind-tunnels from the Luftwaffe research station in Germany were brought back to a site at the north end of Twinwood Farm and reassembled. The immense power and water needs were supplied by Little Barford Power Station and the Air Ministry's own wartime pumping station at Sharnbrook. Thurleigh's dominant location was perfect for radar tracking with a 150-mile (240-km) radius. A tower on each side of the main runway carries the kinetheodolite system for tracking aircraft up to 30 miles (48 km) from the airfield. The NAD runway was in use from 1954–70 and was equipped with steam catapults and arrester wires. Later, a ski-jump was built to test the use of Hawker Harriers on aircraft carriers. Although the Brabazon was never put into production, there was plenty of other work for the NAE. Much of this was carried out by the Aerodynamics Flight Division's experimental and modified aircraft, which solved problems caused by natural conditions: gusts of wind, slush, and ice, turbulence, and storms; or into conditions caused by performance, such as flying in the wake of other aircraft. They also simulated the climb noise and sonic booms generated by Concorde. The Blind Landing Experimental Unit (BLEU) arrived from Martlesham Heath (Suffolk) in 1957 to continue the exploration of fully automated landing systems. Between 1955 and 1965, over 20,000 successful landings using the Bedford-developed Autoland system had been achieved by every type of aircraft from Canberra and Comet to Trident and Vulcan, many of them at Thurleigh. In 1955, the NAE had been taken over by the RAE Farnborough and RAF Thurleigh officially became RAF Bedford. The RAE then directed operations until the airfield was decommissioned in 1994. The experimental flying moved to Boscombe Down and the defence research and development work reverted to Farnborough.

In November 1953, the first British atomic bomb, the Blue Danube, packaged in the old Tallboy bomb casing, was delivered to an active RAF base. This air-launched bomb would be delivered by the V-bombers stationed at a dozen bases, mainly in the east of the country. In 1962, the V-bomber force remained spread across these bases, permanently rotating four of their aircraft on Operational Readiness Platforms (ORP), ready armed and at fifteen minutes' notice to take off. Were the outbreak of war to become imminent, then many of these aircraft would be dispersed to appropriately equipped airfields across Britain. Bedford (Thurleigh) was one of five widely scattered dispersal airfields equipped to take four aircraft. A further twenty-two airfields could accommodate two V-bombers each. Some dummy Blue Danubes in spherical concrete casings with a diameter of 5 feet (1.3 metres) have turned up on the ROF Elstow site.

By 1966, a new, smaller, but infinitely more powerful weapon, the WE177, had been developed with much of the non-nuclear work being carried out in Luton by Hunting Engineering. This new bomb could be delivered by many smaller aircraft

Left: RAE Bedford, a kinetheodolite tower for tracking aircraft on test flights.

Below: RAE Bedford, a rare ORLIT hut, which was one of a group accommodating flight crews on the V-bomber dispersal ready to take off at fifteen minutes' notice.

such as Buccaneers, Jaguars, and Tornados, all of which had taken part in trials at NAE Bedford. In the north-east corner of RAF Bedford lies a group of huts, which held the Vulcan crews on fifteen-minute alert. Bedford was on the list of eleven Colocated Operating Bases (COB) where, in the event of war, USAF units would move in beside RAF squadrons. It is likely that USAF F-111 fighter-bombers armed with nuclear weapons would have been based there alongside the V-bombers of the RAF. The RAF's primary responsibility for the nation's nuclear deterrent ended in 1969 when the Polaris nuclear submarines came into service with the Royal Navy.

In order to fulfil its new role, the airfield's buildings had been upgraded. A new tower was built in 1957, four storeys high with a Visual Control Room or 'glass-house' on top. It accommodated air traffic control, the meteorological office, and the flying wing offices, with an adjacent fire station. Two of the twenty-three-bay wartime T2 hangars were relocated on the airfield, now numbered as Hangars 4 and 5. A new Maintenance Hangar (Hangar 1) was built around 1955 with a clear span of 218 feet (67 metres) and a clear height of 50 feet (15.4 metres). It is flat-roofed, with sliding doors at each end, and constructed from aluminium. Hangar 2 was constructed for BLEU with a 150-foot (46-metre) clear span and a clear height of 35 feet (10.8 metres). The earliest of the three new hangars is the Aero Flights Hangar (Hangar 3) with a clear span of 131 feet (40 metres) and outward sloping sides. A number of workshops, laboratories, simulator buildings, stores, and computer suites surround these major structures.

The Twinwood wind-tunnel site to the south of Thurleigh would eventually contain six distinct elements. Work started in 1949 and took over ten years to complete. The first element to be commissioned was the 3 by 3-foot (92 by 92-cm) Transonic Speed Tunnel followed by the Vertical Spinning Tunnel and the High Speed Laboratory all completed by 1952. In the next year, the 13 by 9-foot (4 by 2.75-metre) Low Speed Wind Tunnel came on stream, and in 1956, the 8 by 8-foot (2.46 by 2.46-metre) High Speed Wind Tunnel became operational. The 3 by 4-foot (92 by 123-cm) High Supersonic Speed/Hypersonic Tunnel was the last to be completed in 1961. These tunnels would remain in operation for between twenty-five and forty-five years. The Low-speed Wind Tunnel is currently (2019) used by Red Bull Racing to test the aerodynamic properties of their cars. The 125-foot-high (38.5-metre-high), Vertical Spinning Tunnel Building, with a diameter of 16 feet (5 metres), in Building No. 36/37, is now used by 'Bodyflight Bedford' providing not-so-cheap thrills for the more adventurous of the general public. The south-east corner of the site has been taken over by the Yarl's Wood Immigration Removal Centre but most of the complex remains, in 2019, as a monumental but dystopian post-industrial wasteland.

After a brief hiatus when RAF Cranfield operated as Aircrew Holding Units, demobbing and repatriating Commonwealth aircrew, the Empire Test Pilots' School from Boscombe Down took up residence, remaining there until 1947. Cranfield had been chosen back in 1944 as the site of the new College of

RAE Bedford, the maintenance hangar (Hangar 1) was built around 1955 with a clear span of 218 feet (67 metres) and a clear height of 50 feet (15.4 metres). It was originally built with the Bristol Brabazon airliner in mind.

RAE Bedford, the new control tower built in 1957.

Right: Twinwood, the Vertical Spinning Tunnel Building now used by 'Bodyflight Bedford'.

Below: Twinwood, the low-speed wind tunnel used by Red Bull Racing.

Aeronautics, which opened in October 1946 using existing buildings as living accommodation, laboratories, and lecture rooms, the latter centred on the airmen's dining room, Stafford Cripps Hall. The RAF based aircraft here for servicing the RAF No. 23 (Training) Group HQ at Stanbridge. In 1954, the Fairey Development Flight was based at Cranfield and carrying out test firings of their Fireflash air-to-air missile using Gloster Meteor jet fighters. This beam riding missile, deployed in small numbers in 1957, would quickly be superseded by the de Havilland Firestreak. The college prospered, gaining international attention, and university status was achieved with the award of a Royal Charter in December 1969. The new Cranfield Institute of Technology continued to work very closely with RAE Bedford to develop modifications to both military and civil aircraft, activities that continue to this day. The campus retains a large proportion of its Expansion Period buildings, complemented by some impressive modern additions.

In 1945, RAF Henlow housed signals and engineering development units, and in 1947, the RAF Technical College was set up to train officer cadets, some of whom would be sent on to university as engineering officers. It took in additional armament and radio sections throughout the 1950s, running to five wings before amalgamating with the RAF College at Cranwell in 1965. An Officer Cadet Training Unit, catering for a wide range of candidates, arrived in 1966, staying until 1980. This was followed by a number of staff training courses, preparing RAF officers for higher command. New building included extensions to both officers' messes, and Henlow is now home to the Joint Arms Control Implementation Group and the RAF Centre for Aviation Medicine. Although slated for closure in the near future, this has now been put back to 2023 and plans for a research and training centre with a focus on human performance under water and in space is planned. Despite some regrettable demolitions, a fine collection of First World War era, 1920s, and Expansion Period structures survive. But for a small estate of RAF housing, RAF Stanbridge has disappeared under housing developments.

Defence against the Nuclear Attack

Once the Soviet Union had atomic weapons, it was realised that, although the nation's air defence system had lately proved itself capable of stubborn resistance, some form of civil protection programme would be necessary if only to reassure the population. The ROC, so successful in the last war, was resurrected; voluntary medical organisations were alerted to the new situation; a new Auxiliary Fire Service was established; and an entirely new Civil Defence Corps was recruited. The government set about nuclear-proofing itself by establishing both metropolitan and provincial underground control centres for civil and military use, serviced by secure communications systems. It also ensured that legislation was put in place to provide for a robust response to any breakdown of law and order.

Royal Observer Corps (ROC) and UK Warning and Monitoring Organisation (UKWMO)

In 1948, the Midland Area carried out an exercise involving dozens of observer posts and over 100 aircraft. It was observed by the RAF top brass from the Bedford Centre. In 1949, the Ampthill post was selected to conduct an experiment using radar to track incoming aircraft. The equipment was assembled at RAF Henlow and senior observers received some training in preparation for the trial. Despite the success of the experiment, the RAF hierarchy decided that it was not the job of observers to use radar, so the equipment was never issued. The observers' role, then, continued to be one of visually spotting aircraft, a task that would become increasingly difficult as aircraft would come in faster and faster and at ever lower levels. In 1953, a complete overhaul of the ROC was carried out and Bedford, reporting to RAF Watnall in Nottinghamshire, now found itself controlling No. 7 Group with seventeen clusters totalling around fifty posts under command. During the Second World War, observers had often applied DIY to the construction of one-off posts, but between 1952 and 1955, a custom-built aircraft-spotting post was introduced centrally. Designed and built by ORLIT, a specialist manufacturer of prefabricated structures, this was made up of concrete panels measuring 10 feet (3 metres) by 6 feet 8 inches (2 metres), one half being open to the sky, and the other half roofed over with corrugated-iron sheets, allowing plotting instruments to be used. It could either sit at ground-level (Orlit A), or be raised up on 6-foot-high (1.8-metre-high) concrete legs accessed by an integral concrete ladder (Orlit B), and by 1955, some 400 had been supplied across the country. The sorry remains of an Orlit A post can just be discerned at Renhold. Riseley appears to retain its wartime timber hut behind an L-shaped blast-wall, which appears to predate the Cold War period but may have remained in use.

In 1954, a fundamental change in the role of the ROC took place after the need for a system of plotting the spread of radioactivity after an atomic bomb-burst had been identified. The ROC with its network of posts and its expertise in recording and reporting was seen as the ideal agency for this task. Given that its primary role hitherto was becoming increasingly impossible to fulfil, this was a sensible way of exploiting the skills, experience, and commitment of all those trained men and women. By 1961, aircraft-spotting in any systematic way had become a thing of the past although not totally abandoned for a further four years. The corps' two major roles were now reporting the location and power of nuclear bursts, and the spread of radioactive fallout. In the reorganisation of 1965, No. 7 Group transferred to the Northern Area as the Eastern Area was broken up. Following the cutback in provision in 1968 when a number of posts were closed, thirty-two active, regularly-manned posts survived in the Bedford Region as part of the UKWMO Midlands Sector, until final stand-down in 1991.

In order to carry out this new monitoring role, ORLIT was commissioned to design an underground post. This consisted of a concrete box, measuring 20 feet by 8 feet by 8 feet (6 by 2.5 by 2.5 metres), and accessed via a trap door and steel rungs set in the side of a 14-foot-deep (4.5-metre-deep) shaft. The three-man crew was equipped with instruments that would record the ground zero of a nuclear blast and supply data relating to fallout. On the surface, all that can be seen is the entry hatch, a ventilator, and the tops of the Bomb Power Indicator and the Fixed Survey Meter Probe. The roof was protected by a 7.5-inch-thick (19-cm-thick) slab of reinforced concrete and 3 inches (7.6 cm) of earth. Substantial parts of the surface structure can be seen at Carlton/Pavenham, Renhold, and Riseley, while only a manhole cover is visible on Cooper's Hill, Ampthill. In 1962, the old Group HQ in Day's Lane, Biddenham, was replaced by a protected, semi-sunken building on two levels, with the main floor on the lower, overlooked by a balcony. Data relating to locations of bomb-bursts and direction of fallout would be displayed on glass screens and transferred to the plotting table. With an establishment of forty ROC personnel and ten from the Home Office, it had to be able to operate for a week under lockdown conditions, so was furnished with generator plant, sleeping quarters, kitchen, air conditioning, air filters, communications equipment, and storage for water and food. As with all nuclear bunkers, questions would arise regarding whether the designated occupants would leave their loved ones to the perils of either instant liquefaction or lingering radiation sickness.

Carlton/Pavenham, the access hatch of the underground Royal Observer Corps monitoring post.

Civil Defence (CD)

As the implications of the Cold War began to be revealed, the Civil Defence Act of 1949 required local authorities to organise for community protection against nuclear attack. Provision would include a co-ordinating HQ and then four sections: Warden; Rescue; Welfare; and Ambulance and First Aid. Some counties also raised a Signals Section. This skeleton was fleshed out by industrial initiatives and by the existing voluntary organisations such as the W(R)VS, the St John Ambulance, the Red Cross, and the AFS with its distinctive 'Green Goddess' fire engines, dark green with red pump-faster stripes along the side. Despite the much-heralded four-minute warning, it was officially felt that any move to war would be gradual, allowing adequate time to mobilise, so to save money, the Civil Defence Corps was stood down in 1968.

Bedford began recruiting for the CD Corps by setting up an office in the town hall in 1949, and talks on 'The Bomb' were delivered throughout 1950 to raise public awareness. The recruitment target was 3 per cent of the population, a figure that would never be remotely approached, with the best achieved being 0.25 per cent. A general meeting was held in the Shire Hall, and in November 1951, the Manor House in Kempston was, in one account, donated, and in another, bought as the Bedfordshire Divisional CD HQ and Control Centre with offices and storage for vehicles and equipment. It was suggested in 1952 that the room beneath the stage in Bedford Corn Exchange could be used as a protected CD Control Centre but this was rejected and a CD Training Centre was set up in Albert Street. This took the form of two halls, at right angles to each other, on the south side of the street, long since redeveloped. Sirens were installed but recruitment was slow. In 1952, there were 127 men and 125 women enrolled in Bedford's CD Corps, but the next year, recruits were still being sought. Luton began recruiting separately from the county division in early November 1950, appointing administrative staff at its HQ at 9 Gordon Street, and though Stockwood Park was proposed as an operational HQ, a CD Centre at 51 Guildford Street was officially opened in October 1953 when 75 Guildford Street was also reported as belonging to Luton CD. Vauxhall Motors, Percival Aircraft, Skefco, and Hunting Engineering along with a further six firms contributed members, particularly First Aiders. By the end of 1952, membership stood at 525 rising to 709 in September 1954 when the corps mounted a searchlight tattoo in front of a crowd of 6,000 spectators. In 1953, it had formed a motorcycle despatch rider section and a Mobile Column.

Recruitment to the Bedfordshire CD Corps was promoted in Leighton Buzzard and Biggleswade, and in 1950, the Dunstable CD Corps formed with its HQ in the Maltings, in High Street North. A CD information and recruitment meeting was held in the Wingfield Club hall in Church Street, Ampthill, in November 1950. November 1956 saw a joint exercise involving CD members from Bedford, Luton, Biggleswade, Sandy, Leighton Buzzard, Kempston, Leagrave, and Dunstable using the derelict buildings and wide open spaces of Tempsford airfield.

CD Corps across Britain required specialist vehicles and Vauxhall produced a number of them, the best known being the 'Green Goddess'. This was the Bedford RLHZ Self-Propelled Pump, over 1,000 of which were produced between 1953 and 1956 primarily for use by the newly raised AFS. Its function was to pump large quantities of water from rivers and lakes to fight a nuclear conflagration. They remained in use into this century before most were sold abroad to developing countries in 2005. The OY Series of 3-tonners had been developed in 1939 for the British Army, and a version fitted with a solid body and carrying ladders and other standard rescue equipment was produced for the CD Corps Mobile Column Rescue Sections.

The Bedford ROC No. 7 Group Control in Biddenham had ceased its role in 1991, and the Home Office was responsible for both the ROC buildings and the Regional Government Headquarters (RGHQ) programme. With an unsatisfactory RGHQ under a government office block in Hertford, the Home Office was looking for a viable alternative as the third centre in No. 4 Eastern Region. The Bedford building was in good order but, geared to accommodate only sixty people, it was smaller than would have been preferred. The central well was therefore roofed over to provide more space for the planned establishment of 134, and the building became RGHQ No. 4.2 in 1992. However, the whole programme would almost immediately be phased out as part of the emerging Peace Dividend. In the event of war, it would have housed civil service and local government administrators tasked with keeping the wheels turning and then getting life up and running again after the emergency. This included restoring food supply, public health, transport, and public utilities. A second group included representatives of the military, the police, civil defence, the BBC, and of other emergency services. These would maintain law and order, carry out rescue and salvage tasks, and communicate orders and advice to anyone out there unfortunate enough to have survived. Local councils were required to compile emergency plans detailing the wartime responsibilities of their peacetime staff. Education personnel would have to set up feeding stations and hospitals in schools, and technical services workers would handle burials. The requirement on local authorities to establish and maintain ideally a nuclear-proof bunker, but at the very least, a secure emergency control centre, existed well into the 1980s and Bedfordshire County Council's new County Hall, now the Borough Hall, opened in 1970, was designated as the county's wartime HQ. In Luton, the 0.9 miles (1.5 km) of the old Ministry of Home Security tunnels, built before the Second World War, remained ready to be reopened at twenty-four hours' notice, as public shelters. In 1954, plans were started to get an underground control centre for the town. A single storey surface blockhouse was indeed opened in 1954 and had a training centre added on top and a three-bay garage alongside. It continued in use after 1968 but was replaced by minimal facilities in the town hall in the 1980s when CD requirements were renewed by the Thatcher government but was eventually demolished. The Mid-Bedfordshire Council offices sit just outside

Elstow, Ministry of Supply and Ministry of Works storage sheds on the ordnance factory site.

the wire of the highly secure Chicksands complex so may have negotiated access to emergency facilities there. New such protected local authority control centres continued to receive government subsidies right through the Thatcher years. The Ministries of Supply (MoS) and of Agriculture, Fisheries and Food (MAFF) and their successor departments maintained stockpiles of, respectively, equipment and food across the country, with MAFF, in Region 4, having a food depot on Tempsford airfield and ranks of A-frame storage sheds on the ROF Elstow site.

Communications

Established installations such as RAF Stanbridge continued to play an important part in the military communications framework, but a wholly new network of line of sight Microwave Towers was constructed to inform important strategic planning decisions by conveying information from all sources but particularly from the early-warning radar systems. The cover for the Microwave Towers, the most familiar of which is the GPO (BT) Tower in London's Tottenham Court Road, was the rollout of colour TV. A site at Dunstable, known as Zouches Farm, standing over 650 feet (200 metres) above sea level, had been chosen pre-war for an experimental relay station for TV signals from Alexandra Palace to Birmingham. After the hiatus caused by the war, in 1947, it was again chosen as a repeater station on the London-Sutton Coldfield link, standing between Harrow Weald and Charwelton (Northamptonshire). In 1949, a square-section guyed lattice mast was erected. This was followed by a self-supporting tower with pairs of dishes in 1962. By 1965, this had been fitted with new dishes and a second freestanding tower with horn antennae had been added, linked to the Anglia TV studio in Luton. From 1956, Charwelton had been incorporated in Backbone, the core of the microwave communications network within the national system of nuclear defence, marking the point at which the London–Birmingham line intersected with the main North–South line. The system was continuously evolving as refinements were made to the equipment and at Dunstable, the horn antennae had been dismounted by 2003 and the main dishes six years later. The current tower stands 226 feet (70 metres) tall and is used for analogue and digital radio transmissions. The mast at Chaul End near Caddington reservoir appears to cater for mobile phones. Telephone landlines were held to be more secure than radio so were considered important in the government's communications systems. The larger telephone exchanges, such as Bedford, had protected basements in which were located terminals for the Emergency Manual Switching System. Along with the microwave network, the Home Office set up dedicated Hilltop radio stations, primarily for internal security, to enable the police to control any disorder arising from the breakdown of normal life after a nuclear attack. This system was also used by the emergency services until their own radio systems had

Dunstable, Zouches Farm, the microwave tower, part of the early-warning system.

been developed by the 1970s. There are two Bedfordshire Hilltop radio stations recorded in sub-Region 4.2. One was at Oakley Hill, now marked by a mobile phone mast standing around 170 feet (52 metres) above sea level; and the other at Streatley, where there are still two aerials standing just above the 490-foot (150-metre) contour line. The ROC posts supplemented their landlines with VHF radios to relay information to control centres.

In the aftermath of a nuclear strike, it would become essential for roads to be kept clear of refugees and open for official traffic using armed soldiers of the TA. The Military Road Route System (MRRS), based on a survey carried out in 1975, defined those through routes and key transport hubs which would become subject to martial law. In Bedfordshire, the M1, code-named BAT, formed part of the designated route from the outskirts of London (pre-M25) via Luton Airport to Leeds. Although, in theory, provided they kept away from the MRRS people were free to drive wherever they were able, in practice this was far from true. First, all supplies of fuel would have been requisitioned by the military, the emergency services and government agencies. Even with a full tank, driving to its maximum range would be impossible. Not only would the available roads be clogged with immobilised vehicles, but the Essential Service Routes (ESR) network was designed to keep open the many routes needed by the emergency services and the distributors of emergency food and medical supplies. Guarded by armed police and soldiers who would restrict access to official traffic, they effectively sealed off the exit routes from cities ensuring that escape would prove impossible. In Bedfordshire, the ESR Scheme covered the M1, A1, A421, A422, A45, and the A428. Most of these routes bypassed large towns and cities for obvious reasons (the main one being that they would almost certainly have been obliterated) so Luton can be seen to be intentionally isolated and effectively blockaded. Bedford, however, sits astride an ESR, clearly an oversight given the proximity of RAE Bedford, with its RAF Vulcans and USAF F-111s; the Sandy and Crawley Crossing fuel depots; the electronic monitoring base at Chicksands; a myriad of other prime targets within a 25-mile (40-km) radius; and clearly itself identified as the likely recipient of a Russian first strike. This would inevitably place it fair and square in the Fallout Front from either air- or ground-bursts. A 1980 comparison of the British and Russian appreciations of nuclear targets reveal only marginal predictive differences. The British saw Bedford as a target while the Russians chose Chicksands as their bull's-eye. This would have made little difference to anyone living within 10 miles of either. These emergency scenarios, apparently rooted in an unbelievable level of suspended disbelief, retained currency well into the 1980s, and journalists like Duncan Campbell were prosecuted under the legislation underpinning the Official Secrets Act for taking his Emperor's Clothes approach. Much of this infrastructure would, of course, be useful were Britain to suffer a disaster of any type whether natural or manmade, but such planning does tend to benefit from a reasonable foundation of reality.

Munitions Production

While we tend from a distance to think of the later 1940s and 1950s as a time of reconstruction, the cost of rearmament ran at a high of 10 per cent of GDP, an unprecedented level in peacetime, and more than five times the level currently seen as appropriate by NATO. Many of those companies that had produced munitions during the Second World War continued to do so. We have already seen the defence work going on at RAE Bedford and Hunting Engineering's contribution to the WE177 atomic bomb. Napier, part of English Electric since 1942, had worked on converting Lancasters to Lincoln airliners in the 1960s at their base in Luton Airport, continuing to produce aero engines, particularly for helicopters, with Rolls-Royce from 1961, before moving to GEC and then Siemens. In 1949, English Electric set up its Navigational Projects Division in Luton. This would develop the guidance system via a range of simulators, followed in 1955 by the Automatic Computing Engine (LACE) series of analogue computers, production of which was moved to Stevenage after 1962. This was instrumental in designing Red Shoes or Thunderbird SAM missile for the British Army. Its RAF equivalent, Red Duster, better known as Bloodhound, was also a BAC development, and vital to the defence of the RAF V-bomber bases against attack by conventional bombers.

A number of short-range tactical battlefield and intermediate-range missiles were in development in the late 1950s. English Electric's missile division in Stevenage had manufactured the Corporal with a range of 55 miles (89 km), and so anticipated having responsibility for its successor. Its new missile, Blue Water, expected to be in service in 1961, would be an improvement on Corporal in that it would have a guidance system, would be air-portable, and would have a smaller, more powerful, 10-kiloton nuclear warhead. The 25-foot-long (7.7-metre-long) missile would be fired from a modified Bedford RL launch vehicle, which would transport the missile, raise it into its firing position, and fire it, crewed by just two gunners. There was also an air-launched version for use by the TSR-2 also produced by General Electric as a replacement for their Canberra. It was expected that Blue Water would be bought by the Bundeswehr and then be rolled out across NATO. In the event, although the trials had gone well, the West Germans decided to buy a different rocket, the US MGM-29 Sergeant. At the same time, an improvement in co-operation between the Army and the RAF was removing the need for dedicated ground-based battlefield weapons as fighter-bombers could, once again, assume the role of aerial artillery. Unwilling to bear the cost of these developments alone, the government decided to cancel the order for both Blue Water and TSR-2, and, as a consequence, General Electric closed its Luton factory in 1962.

Vauxhall extended its range of trucks for the military with a range of S-type 7-ton vehicles, including, as we have seen, the Green Goddesses of the CD Corps and the AFS. The TK, TL, and TM range of trucks were supplied to the British Army into the 1980s along with a solely military 4×4 version known as the MK, of which nearly 12,000 had been produced by the end of 1977. Although the Army wanted to maintain its relationship with Bedford and was impressed by the 4×4, 4-ton General Service truck's performance, the contract was awarded elsewhere for mainly political reasons. The TM 6×6 Truck, produced from 1974–86 with a payload of 13.75 tons (14,000 kg) and available in a number of different conformations, was the largest supplied to the Army. In 1987, the trucks division, based in Dunstable, was sold to David Brown's AWD company that continued production of the TK for the Army. Via Caterpillar and Marshalls of Cambridge, the Bedford name lived on with trucks for the military until 1998, and the last Bedford trucks had been replaced by the Army only in 2014. AC Sphinx officially became AC Delco in 1952 and the AC Delco Division of General Motors in 1974.

In 2014, the then defence minister, visiting Blue Bear Systems at Milton Ernest, identified a 'corridor of defence contractors who make an important contribution to the multi-billion pound defence industry' between Luton and Bedford, and added that he thought 'there's every reason for Bedfordshire to continue being an important contributor to defence'. Lockheed Martin in Ampthill 'is in the forefront of complex mission systems integration, system design and development, and the implementation of electronic architecture' to provide the 'battle-winning solutions' that make it a 'partner of choice for the British Forces'. A trawl of the internet reveals that AXIS Electronics of Bedford Heights produces 'high reliability equipment for Land, Air, Unmanned, Sea and Sub-Sea applications' supplying the MoD and the US DoD. Further information from the same source suggests that companies in Cardington, Cranfield, Dunstable, Luton, and Bedford all continue to supply goods or services to the defence establishment.

A Bedford Green Goddess fire tender designed for use by Civil Defence and the Auxiliary Fire Service in national emergencies. (*photographed at RAF Scampton*)

APPENDIX I

Iron Age Hillforts

Aspley Heath, Danesborough Camp, SP921348
Billington Camp, by church, SP940225
Bolnhurst, Manor Farm hillfort, TL085598
Dunstable Maiden Bower, enclosure, SP997225
Leagrave, Waulud's Bank, earthwork enclosure TL062246
Leighton Buzzard (golf course) Craddock's Camp, SP9127
Luton, Dray's Ditches, TL086266
Luton, Grim's Ditches TL088264
Mowsbury, hillfort, TL065533
Puddle Hill, Houghton Regis, enclosure, SP999234
Ravensburgh, Barton-le-Clay, hillfort, TL099295
Sandy, Galley Hill, promontory hillfort in RSPB grounds, TL185478
Sandy, Caesar's Camp, NE of railway station, TL180493
Sandy, The Lodge, promontory fort in RSPB grounds, TL1847
Sharpenhoe Clappers, promontory fort, TL067302
Stotfold, Fairfield Park, Bronze Age enclosure and later settlement, TL204348/204354
Thurleigh, Bury Hill Camp/Castle, TL052584

Medieval Castles, Fortified Manor Houses and Tudor Strong Houses

Castles

Ampthill: quadrangular castle of *c.* 1420, demolished by 1649	TL024383
Bedford: motte and bailey developed as stone castle, destroyed 1224	TL053496
Bletsoe: courtyard castle, licensed 1327	TL024584
Cardington, Exeter Wood: low motte, built by the Beauchamps	TL100443
Chalgrave: low motte and insignificant bailey; ploughed out	TL008275
Clophill, Cainhoe: motte and three baileys built by d'Albinis in C11	TL096373
Eaton Bray, Park Farm, fortified manor from 1221	SP961210
Flitwick, The Mount: small motte inside bailey with outer bailey	TL027343
Luton 1: motte and bailey built 1139 by Robert de Wauderi	TL092207
Luton 2: motte and bailey built 1221 by Fawkes de Breaute	TL096211
Meppershall: motte and two baileys in existence 1135	TL133359
Odell Castle: motte and bailey with stone keep, destroyed 1623	SP966578
Old Warden Castle, Biggleswade: ringwork and bailey, ploughed out	TL184445
Old Warden, Quince Hill: much-reduced ringwork and bailey	TL137446
Podington: small motte and bailey, mostly destroyed	SP943628
Renhold, Howbury: ringwork, overgrown	TL107513
Ridgmont Castle, Segenhoe: ringwork and bailey, fragmentary remains	SP970385
Risinghoe: motte and bailey of C11 built by the lords of Bedford	TL090509
Someries: strong house with brick gatehouse and chapel of 1470s	TL119201
Steppingley, Seymours Mount: possible ringwork	TL001351
Sutton, John of Gaunt's Hill: possible motte, now on golf course	TL221487
Thurleigh: motte and bailey castle with village enclosure	TL052584

Tilsworth, Warren Knoll: small, damaged motte	SP975244
Toddington, Conger Hill: motte with large flat top, bailey under farm	TL011289
Totternhoe: motte and three baileys on prominent site	SP979221
Wrest Park: moated strong house of C15	TL092354
Yielden: motte and two baileys with water defences	TL014670

Moated Sites

Arlesey, Etonbury	TL191378
Astwick	TL215385
Barton-le-Clay, Faldo Farm	TL074319
Biggleswade	TL207438
Biggleswade, Scroup's Farm	TL186430
Biggleswade, Hill House	TL171444
Biscot, Moat Farm	TL078240
Bolnhurst, Greensbury Farm	TL074590
Bolnhurst, Greensbury Farm	TL069591
Bolnhurst, The Old Rectory	TL087592
Bourne End, Eyreswood Farm	SP964459
Bourne End, Boxhedge Farm	SP963453
Bourne End, Ivy Hall	SP958451
Brogborough	SP977401
Bromham Hall	TL017513
Bushmead, The Camps	TL118603
Carlton	SP945545
Colmworth, Manor House	TL108585
Cople, Wood End Farm	TL109466
Cotton End	TL100457
Cranfield, Boxhedge Farm	SP958451 and 963453
Cranfield, Moat Farm	SP967434
Dunton	TL226446
Everton, Woodbury Hall, Story Moats	TL205520
Flitwick, Ruxox Farm	TL048360
Gossards Green, Moat Farm	SP967434
Great Barford, The Creakers	TL105530
Great Barford, Birchfield	TL121541
Hardmead	SP935476
Harlington	TL04 31
Harlington, Old Park Farm	TL030295
Henlow, Old Ramerick	TL173350

Higham Gobion	TL105333
Hockliffe	SP966269
Holme	TL186430
Houghton Conquest, The Old Rectory	TL045409
Houghton Conquest	TL045414
Houghton Conquest, Limbersey Farm	TL062392
Houghton Regis, Calcutt Farm	TL012254
Keysoe, Park Farm, Hardwick End	TL061626
Keysoe Row, College Farm	TL070615
Lidlington, Thrupp End Farm	SP988396 and 987397
Lidlington	SP978401
Luton, Limbury	TL078240
Luton, Someries	TL109201
Marston Mortaine, Beancroft Farm	SP990420
Marston Mortaine	SP993413 and 995413
Maulden	TL053389
Maulden, Bolebec Farm	TL053388
Maulden, Limbersey	TL062384
Meppershal, Rectory Farm	TL137362
Meppershall adjacent to Castle	TL134359
Milton Ernest, Yarl's Wood	TL038560
Mobbs Hole	TL264438
Moggerhanger	TL144489
Mowsbury Hill	TL066533
Newton	TL227446
Northill	TL144463
Odell, Wold Farm	SP946598
Old Warden, Abbey Farm	TL119440
Pertenhall	TL096658
Pertenhall, Sowmead's Spinney	TL072645
Potsgrove	SP951297
Potsgrove	SP940313
Renhold, Hill Farm	TL107513
Ridgmont	SP986359
Riseley, Lodge Farm	TL032628 & 032626
Roxton, Birchfield Farm	TL121540
Roxton, Palaceyard Wood	TL130545
Sharnbrook	SP989595
Sharpenhoe, Bury Farm	TL065308
Shelton	TL034686
Shillington, Apsley Bury Farm	TL118323
Shillington, Apsley End	TL122335

Shillington, Bury End	TL119350
Shillington, Pirton Grange	TL123329
Stagsden, Burdely's Manor, Bury End	SP984508
Stagsden, Grange Farm	SP966492
Stagsden, Wick End Farm	SP988501
Staploe, The Camps	TL118603
Staploe, Bassmead Manor/Farm	TL140612
Steppingley, Wake's End Farm	SP993348
Stevington, Moat Farm	SP972521
Stotfold, Astwick	TL215385
Swineshead, Moat Farm	TL057659
Tempsford Park	TL162539
Tempsford, Biggin Wood	TL181528
Tempsford, Gannock's Castle	TL160530
Thurleigh, Blackburn Hall	TL041586
Thurleigh, Bolnhurst, Mavourn Farm	TL072576
Thurleigh, Greensbury Farm	TL074590 and 069591
Tilsworth	SP976242
Upbury, Pulloxhill, Gagmansbury Farm	TL074344
Westoning Manor	TL028325
Westoning, Wood End	TL017322
Wilden, Sevick End	TL096543
Willington, Danish Camp	TL113508
Woodbury, Story Moats	TL204514
Wootton, Bourne End Farm	SP978453
Wyboston	TL160567
Wyboston, Chawston	TL152562

Ecclesiastical Defences

Dunstable Priory: fifteenth-century gatehouse to outer court
Elstow Abbey: fifteenth-century detached tower
Melchbourne: preceptory of Knights Hospitallers
Sharnbrook: preceptory of Knights Templar from 1199

Regular, Militia, and Volunteer Forces, 1815–1918

Rifle Volunteer Corps (RVC) 1860–87

1st Bedfordshire RVC Administrative Battalion, HQ Bedford (1860–6), Toddington (1866–70), Woburn (1870–1887)
1st Corps, Bedfordshire RVC, Bedford
2nd Corps, Bedfordshire RVC, Toddington
4th Corps, Bedfordshire RVC, Dunstable
5th Corps, Bedfordshire RVC, Ampthill
6th Corps, Bedfordshire RVC, Luton
7th Corps, Bedfordshire RVC, Biggleswade and Shefford (HQ from 1871)
8th Corps, Bedfordshire RVC, Woburn
9th Corps, Bedfordshire RVC, Britannia Works, Bedford, 1864–72

3rd Volunteer Battalion, Bedfordshire Regiment (1887–1908)

'A' and 'B' Companies, Bedford
'C' Company, Toddington
'D' Company, Dunstable
'E' Company, Ampthill
'F' and 'G' Companies, Luton
'H' Company, Shefford
'I' Company, Woburn (Luton from 1894)

The Bedfordshire Yeomanry 1908–18

HQ and 'A' Squadron: Bedford
'B' Squadron: Biggleswade and Shefford

'C' Squadron: Dunstable and Leighton Buzzard, Woburn and Ampthill
'D' Squadron: Godmanchester and St Neots, Kimbolton, Ramsay, Somersham, (all in Huntingdonshire) and Sutton and Chatteris (Isle of Ely)

5th Battalion, Bedfordshire Regiment 1908–18

'A Company: Bedford
'B', 'C', and 'F' Companies: Luton with Dunstable and Leighton Buzzard
'D' Company: Biggleswade with Sandy, Arlesey and St Neots
'E' Company: Ampthill with Olney (Buckinghamshire)
'G' Company: Fletton with Yaxley (both Huntingdonshire),
'H' Company: Huntingdon with St Ives and Ramsey (all Huntingdonshire)

By 1914, many of the potential recruits to the Bedfordshire Regiment had been diverted to the Huntingdonshire Cyclists, an unattached unit under Eastern Command. The Cyclists' eight companies were based on Huntingdon (two), St Ives, St Neots, Ramsey, Fletton (two), and Yaxley, all now in Cambridgeshire.

World War I Anti-Invasion Deployments, 1917–18

The 11th (Provisional) Battalion (TF), Bedfordshire Regiment from 1917 belonged to 225 (Mixed) Brigade, which included 19th (Provisional) Battalion, Royal West Surrey Regiment; 18th (Home Service) Battalion, Essex Regiment, which replaced the 15th Battalion in May 1918; 32nd (Provisional) Battalion, Middlesex Regiment. The 2/9th (Cyclist) Battalion, Hampshire Regiment, was attached from April 1918. The brigade was based at Pakefield, Great Yarmouth, Gorleston, and Lowestoft throughout 1917–8.

The 1st (Volunteer) Battalion, Bedfordshire Regiment (VF), from 1917 was allocated to 215 Brigade, which included 13th (Provisional) Battalion, Lincolnshire Regiment, only until July 1917; 18th (Provisional) Battalion, Warwickshire Regiment, only until December 1917; 15th (Provisional) Battalion, Sussex Regiment; and the 51st (Graduated) Battalions of the Durham Light Infantry and the Royal Fusiliers. The brigade was based initially in Bedford and then moved to Ipswich in May 1917, remaining there for the duration.

The 2nd (Volunteer) Battalion, Bedfordshire Regiment (VF), in 1917 was allocated to the Northamptonshire Composite Brigade, based in Northampton. It is unclear with which battalions they would have been brigaded, but at least part of the 4th Reserve Brigade was located at Northampton, and contained the 53rd Battalion, KRRC, and the 53rd (Young Soldier) Battalion, Rifle Brigade.

APPENDIX IV

Command Centres, Barracks, Army Camps and Billets, Training Centres

1800–1914

Ampthill Park: venue Bedfordshire Regiment and TF Summer Camp etc. 1895–1914
Bedford Castle: Militia Depot, 1804–56 (now within Higgins Museum)
Bedford, Goldington Road: Militia Barracks, 1856–77, demolished (TL058052)
Bedford: Bedford Park: camp for troops in transit
Bedford, Russell Park: TF camp
Bedford, Clarence Paddock: Bedfordshire Yeomanry training ground
Bedford, Horne Road and Cardington Road: EARE training grounds
Dunstable, outdoor rifle range in Pascombe Pit
Kempston Barracks, 1874 depot of the Bedfordshire Regiment
Luton, Popes Meadow: TF camp
Luton Hoo: Hertfordshire Yeomanry summer camp, 1914
Toddington, miniature indoor range built 1907
Woburn Abbey: Yeomanry base, 1901–14
Woburn, George Street, Bedford Arms Hotel: Militia Barracks and drill hall

First World War

Ampthill Park: Bedfordshire Regiment training depot, 1914–16
Ampthill Park: No. 9 Regimental Command Depot, 1916–19
Ampthill: No. 126 Company, Canadian Forestry Corps
Bedford: HQ 1st Army: Highland, Welsh & West Riding Divisions, and 2 Mounted Brigades, 1914
Bedford: Highland TF Division billeted in town, August 1914 to February 1915 to May 1915

Bedford, Haynes Park: training camp, infantry & RE (Signals)

Bedford: 38 Reserve Park and No. 11 Auxiliary MT Company ASC, 1915–20

Bedford: No. 3 Company (HT) ASC Train, 72nd (HD) Division

Bedford: Nos 432–3, 656 AGR Labour and 586–587 EMP Labour Companies, 1917

Biggleswade: RE camp

Dunstable: RE Signal Depot

Dunstable, Brewers Hill Farm: 'Canvas City', camp in 1915

Elstow: No. 2 Infantry Officers' School, TF

Flitwick: camp for detachment No. 126 Company, Canadian Forestry Corps

Harrowden: TF camp and rifle range

Haynes Park: Signals Service Training Centre (RE)

Houghton Regis: No. 588 EMP Labour Company, 1917

Howbury Hall: tented camp for Scottish, then Welsh troops

Kempston Barracks, depot of the Bedfordshire Regiment

Kempston, Grange Camp (now Hillgrounds housing)

Luton, Stockwood Park: HQ 46th (North Midland) Division, 1915

Luton, Stockwood Park: North Midland Divisional Veterinary Hospital

Luton, Beech Hill: Army Remount Depot

Luton Hoo: HQ Central Force and 3rd Army 1914

Luton, Biscot: TF camp and RFA training camp with ASC unit, 1914–19

Luton, Dallow Road: rifle range

Maulden: camp for detachment No. 126 Company, Canadian Forestry Corps

Millbrook: rifle range (now within vehicle test circuit)

Mowsbury, Cleat Hill, rifle range used by Highland Division (TF), 1915

Warden Hill: rifle range used by 139 Brigade, 1915

Woburn, Bedford Arms Hotel, annexe of Ampthill Camp

Woburn: RE camp

Yielden, Rifle Range Farm (TL005655) 'Ordnance Field 147'; used by CTA, 1917

1919–1939

Haynes Park: Signals Service Training Centre (RE)

Second World War

Ampthill: D-Day camp in former ROF Hostel, 1944

Arlesey, WI Hall: billets for searchlight unit

Bedford, 27 The Embankment: HQ Bedford sub-Area, Eastern Command

Bedford, 8 Rothsay Gardens, HQ No. 9 Group, Pioneer Corps

Dunstable, Bennetts Brewery, Chiltern Road, and Tavistock Hall, High Street North: HQ East Central Area, Eastern Command

Dunstable: Meteorological Office Central Forecast Office (ETA), 1940

Dunstable, 22 Priory Road, later HQ No. 9 Group, Pioneer Corps

Harlington: 5/7 Gordon Highlanders, 51st Highland Division, March 1944

Heath and Reach, The Grange/Heath Cottage: WAAF billets

Kempston, Grange Camp (TL032486)

Leighton Buzzard: 'Q Central', Air Ministry RAF Communications Centre, central telephone/teleprinter exchange; HQ RAF No. 26 (Signals) Group, 1939

Leighton Buzzard, Plantation Road, Oxendon House and Carlton Lodge in Heath Road: HQ RAF 60 (Signals) Group

Leighton Buzzard, Grovebury Road, Workhouse: WAAF billets

Leighton Buzzard, Plantation Road, The Heath: RAMC training centre

Leighton Buzzard, Plantation Road, Woodlands: WAAF billets

Leighton Buzzard, Stockgrove Park: No. 10 CCS, RAMC; 66 (Lowland) Medium Regiment, RA; Commandos; billets for WRNS from GC&CS

Leighton Buzzard, 3 High Street, Albion (temperance) Hotel: WAAF billets

Linslade, Stoke Road, Bossington House: WAAF billets

Linslade, Castle House: billets for RA personnel

Linslade, Church Road, The Hollies: billets for ATS

Linslade, Lake House: billets for KRRC personnel

Luton, Luton Hoo: Advance HQ Eastern Command, 1941

Milton Ernest Hall: HQ 8th USAAF Communications Section & Maintenance

Podington Camp (SP945625)

Potton Manor (now the Manor): army camp later POW camp

Sandy, Hasells Hall: requisitioned January 1941 for 117 Field Regt, RA, 2nd London Division, then II Corps Junior Leaders' School

Sandy, Baptist Schoolroom Small Hall: troop billets to May 1941

Stopsley: tented army camp

Woodbury Hall near Sandy: billets for troops pre-SOE use

Yelden, Rifle Range Farm 'Ordnance Field 147' (TL005655)

Drill Halls and TA/Army Reserve Centres

Note: the War Office conducted a survey of drill hall provision in 1958 recording the number of premises in use in 1910 and 1933; this survey is referenced below.

Ampthill

One drill hall in use 1910 (*2) and in 1933 (*4).

*1 Houghton House, base for 5th Corps Bedfordshire Rifle Volunteers with a rifle range near Reddings Wood, 1860.

*2 King's Arms, Market Place, drill room in 1885, later Band Room.

In 1887, 'E' Company, 3rd Volunteer Battalion, Bedfordshire Regiment.

*3 Dunstable Street, drill hall in gymnasium erected 1889 opposite Russell House; in use 1912–22.

In 1914, drill station 'C' Squadron Bedfordshire Yeomanry; base for 'E' Company, 5th Battalion, Bedfordshire Regiment.

*4 No. 3 Woburn Street, drill hall in a converted house, 1922.

In 1922, 'B' Company, 5th Battalion, Bedfordshire Regiment.

*5 Woburn Street, drill hall, 1937; two-storey front block with hall behind.

In 1937, 'B' Company, 5th Battalion, Bedfordshire Regiment.

In 2019, ACF.

Arlesey

No dedicated building found.

In 1914, drill station for 'D' Company, 5th Battalion, Bedfordshire Regiment.

Bedford

Two new TA Centres in use in 1933 (6* and 7*).

*1 Castle Lane, ex-Militia Depot, 1st Corps, Bedfordshire RVC.

In 1877, HQ 1st Corps, Bedfordshire RVC.

*2 No. 155 Tavistock Street.

In 1885, HQ and orderly room, and 'B' Company, 1st Bedfordshire RVC.

In 1887, 'A' and 'B' Companies, 3rd Volunteer Battalion, Bedfordshire Regiment.

*3 Nos 44 and 46 Gwyn Street, HQ 3rd Volunteer Battalion, Bedfordshire Regiment; drill hall opened in January 1904.

In 1911, 'A' and 'B' Companies, 3rd Volunteer Battalion, Bedfordshire Regiment.

*4 No.18 Hassett Street, East Anglian Royal Engineers.

In 1907, HQ 1st and 2nd Field Companies, EARE.

*Training locations for EARE: River Street, The Paddock; Cauldwell Street, Harness Room; Cardington Road, Mounted Section; Priory Street School, NCOs' lecture rooms, 1911.

*5 No. 10 St Paul's Square, HQ East Midlands Infantry Brigade (TF).

*6 Nos 32, 34, 40, etc. Ashburnham Road (west side), drill hall, 1912; demolished in mid-1980s; replaced by *9, now Braemar Court.

In 1914, HQ and 'A' Squadron, Bedfordshire Yeomanry; HQ, 1st and 2nd Field Companies EARE; HQ and Nos 1–4 Sections East Anglian Divisional RE Signal Company; 'B' Section. Eastern Mounted Brigade Field Ambulance, RAMC.

In 1922, 417 Howitzer Battery, 105 Bedfordshire Yeomanry Brigade, RFA; East Anglian REs.

In 1949, 305 (Bedfordshire Yeomanry) Medium Regiment RA, TA; HQ 61 Army Signal Regiment, Royal Signals; HQ 248 Field Squadron, RE, TA.

*Drill grounds for EAREs: Horne Road and Cardington Road, 1914.

*Meadows behind Clarence PH used for training by Bedfordshire Yeomanry, 1914.

*7 Ashburnham Road (east side), drill hall, 1922.

In 1922, HQ and 'A' Company 5th Battalion, Bedfordshire & Hertfordshire Regiment.

In 1949, HQ 5th Battalion, Bedfordshire & Hertfordshire Regiment.

*8 No. 95 Ashburnham Road (off east side) TA Association offices.

*9 Kempston Road, TAC 1983; in use; incorporating stone crest from *6.

In 2019, 201 (Bedford) Transport Squadron, 158 Regiment, Royal Logistic Corps.

*10 Kimbolton Road, Cadet Centre, recent build, in use.

Biggleswade

One drill hall in use in 1910 (*1) and one in 1933 (*3).

*1 Bonds Lane (off Hitchin Street), drill hall in use 1894–1921; hall with pitched roof and ventilator; former frontage along building line; 1931–40, Brittains Furnishers

In 1894, 'I' Company, 3rd Volunteer Battalion, Bedfordshire Regiment.

In 1914, 'D' Company, 5th Battalion, Bedfordshire Regiment.

*2 Shortmead Street, drill hall; large hall behind frontage, 1921, demolished 2004.

In 1914, base for 'B' Squadron, Bedfordshire Yeomanry.

*3 Shortmead Street, 1930s; two-storey front block; latterly United Services club– 'Millennium House', apartments; garage/workshops demolished 2004.

In 1922, detachment of 'B' Company, 5th Battalion, Bedfordshire Regiment; 418 Battery, 105 (Bedfordshire Yeomanry) Brigade, RFA.

Dunstable

One drill hall in use 1910 (*2), and two in 1933 (*4 and *5).

*1 Saracens Head PH, shooting gallery and drill shed, 1860.

*2 Church Street, Assembly Rooms 1872; RVC Drill Hall & Armoury, now a shop.

In 1887, 'D' Company, 3rd Volunteer Battalion, Bedfordshire Regiment.

*3 Town hall, HQ and drill hall for Bedfordshire Yeomanry from 1902; Park used for mounted drills.

*4 No. 164 High Street North, Tavistock Hall, Yeomanry HQ, 1912 (now Tesco).

In 1914, base for 'C' Squadron, Bedfordshire Yeomanry; drill station 'F' Company, 5th Battalion, Bedfordshire Regiment, and for 'A' Section, Eastern Mounted Brigade Field Ambulance, RAMC.

*5 Victoria Street, drill hall by 1933; hall with two-storey block at each end.

In 1932, 419 Battery, 105 (Bedfordshire Yeomanry) Field Brigade, RA, TA.

In 1968, 201 (Hertfordshire & Bedfordshire Yeomanry) Medium Battery RA (V).

In 2019, ACF.

Leighton Buzzard

One drill hall in use 1933 (*2).

*1 Town hall served as drill hall 1860–1933.

In 1885, section of 'D' Company, 3rd Volunteer Battalion, Bedfordshire Regiment.

In 1914, drill station for 'F' Company, 5th Battalion, Bedfordshire Regiment, and for 'C' Squadron, Bedfordshire Yeomanry.

*2 Drill hall, West Street, built by 1933; now RBL Bossard Hall.

In 1922, 'D' Company, 5th Battalion, Bedfordshire & Hertfordshire Regiment.

Luton

One drill hall in use 1910 (*3) and one in 1933 (*5).

*1 Cheapside, Plait Hall in use as drill hall 1869–1914, and Armoury/Stores to 1887; Waller Street, Plait Hall also used on occasion by RVC.

In 1885, base for 6th (Luton) Corps, Bedfordshire RVC.

*2 Park Street, HQ, Armoury, stores, Volunteer drill hall and Volunteer Social Club, in use 1887–1918; from 1918 ex-Servicemen's club.

In 1887, 'F' and 'G' Companies, 3rd Volunteer Battalion, Bedfordshire Regiment.

In 1894, 'C', 'F', and 'G' Companies, 3rd Volunteer Battalion, Bedfordshire Regiment.

In 1903, 'C', 'F', and 'G' Companies, 3rd Volunteer Battalion, Bedfordshire Regiment.

In 1910, 'B' and 'C' Companies, 5th Battalion, Bedfordshire Regiment (TF).

In 1914, 'B', 'C', and 'F' Companies, 5th Battalion, Bedfordshire Regiment (TF).

In 1916–18, training base for 2nd Volunteer Battalion, Bedfordshire Regiment (VF).

*3 Grove Road, drill hall, by 1910, until no later than 1926; with offices, staff house, single-storey hall and garage behind.

In 1914, base for 'B', 'C', and 'F' Companies, 5th Battalion, Bedfordshire Regiment.

HQ and 'A' Section, Eastern Mounted Brigade Field Ambulance, RAMC; drill station No. 2 Field Company, EARE.

*4 No. 46 Castle Street.

In 1920, HQ Luton companies, 5th Battalion, Bedfordshire & Hertfordshire Regiment.

*5 No. 40a Old Bedford Road, drill hall in use 1924; two-storey block wrapped around lateral hall; Romney hut, explosives and inflammables store, brick office, etc.; miniature range; then Leisure Centre but demolished after 2005.

No. 28 Old Bedford Road, drill hall flat.

In 1922, 'C' Company, 5th Battalion, Bedfordshire & Hertfordshire Regiment.

420 Battery, 105 Bedfordshire Yeomanry Brigade, RFA; 249 Field Company, RE.

In 1949, 162 Infantry Brigade-Group Signals Squadron; Cipher and Switchboard Operating Troops WRAC.

*6 Vauxhall Works: planned REME Brigade Workshops, late 1940s.

*7 Marsh Road, TAC/Army Reserve Centre, 1955; two-storey front block with royal crest over door; garages etc. to rear.

In 2019, 678 (Rifles) Squadron, Army Air Corps.

Sandy

*1 Girtford, London Road/West Road, Sandford Rise/Braybrook: pre-First World War iron-framed, concrete and brick, prefabricated building, demolished; Home Guard use in the Second World War and post-war use by CD.

In 1914, drill station for 'D' Company, 5th Battalion, Bedfordshire Regiment.

Shefford

One drill hall in use in 1910 (*1) but none in 1933.

*1 North Bridge Street, drill hall; site redeveloped.

In 1885, 'H' Company, 3rd Volunteer Battalion, Bedfordshire Regiment.

In 1914, drill station for 'B' Squadron, Bedfordshire Yeomanry.

Toddington

HQ 1st Bedfordshire Rifle Volunteers, 1866–70 (? Toddington Manor, home of Major Wm. Cooper Cooper).

In 1887–94, 'C' Company, 3rd Volunteer Battalion, Bedfordshire Regiment.

Woburn

HQ 1st Administrative Battalion, Bedfordshire Rifle Volunteers, 1870–80 and 8th Corps, Bedfordshire RVC, 1860–1887.

*1 Nos 1–3 George Street, Bedford Arms Hotel, drill hall, range, clubroom, and armoury.

In 1887–94, 'I' Company, 3rd Volunteer Battalion, Bedfordshire Regiment.

In 1914, drill station for 'C' Squadron, Bedfordshire Yeomanry.

In 1922, detachment of 'B' Company, 5th Battalion, Bedfordshire & Hertfordshire Regiment.

Military Airfields and Other Aviation-Related Sites

*Barton-le-Clay, opened 1935 as a home for Luton Aircraft Limited; then operated as Bedford School of Flying; requisitioned 1939 as a RLG for Cranfield; No. 5 Ferry Pool, ATA, Relief Training Ground, 1940–45.

*Bedford NAE/RAE: experimental and development work for military and civil aviation, 1945–1994.

*Bedford, Marsh Leys Farm: Automobile Association LG (SP021450).

*Biggleswade, 75 (Home Defence) Squadron LG in use the summer of 1917.

*Cardington 1917 Admiralty airship development; Royal Airship Works, 1919; Directorate of Airship Development, 1932, from Air Ministry; No. 2 ASU, 1933.

Balloon Development Establishment then Unit, 1938; No. 2 RAF Depot, 1937; No. 1 Balloon Training Unit, 1937; No. 2 Recruit Centre & Aircrew Medical Board 1939; RAF Recruit Depot, 1945–53; Balloon Development Establishment until 1966; No. 279/217 MU Compressed Gas production unit, 1948–2000.

*Cardington: Airstrip for Training Aids Development Unit (TL082462).

*Cranfield, opened 1937 as Expansion Period bomber station/SFTS; No. 14 SFTS until 1941, then No. 51 OTU until 1945; Empire Test Pilots' School, 1945–7; RAF College of Aeronautics, 1946–69; Cranfield Institute of Technology chartered 1969.

*Crawley Crossing: Aviation Fuel Depot, spur from Sandy.

*Dunstable: Automobile Association LG with maximum run of 630 yards (580 metres) (TL035233).

*Dunstable, London Gliding Club, inaugurated 1930; hangar built 1935; requisitioned as POW camp 1941–5.

*Dunstable: 887 Military Police Company (Aviation) Detachment 'A', 8th USAAF.

*Eaton Bray, Mead Farm acquired 1938 as second airfield for Bedford School of Flying; requisitioned but not used and handed back at end of the Second World War.

*Elstow, Race Meadows Way, racecourse designated Royal Automobile Club LG.

*Flitwick, Maulden Road Industrial Estate, 75 (HD) Squadron LG, 1916–17.

*Goldington, Bedford: HQ 75 (HD) Squadron, RFC, 1916–17; Night LG, March 1917, Day LG, July 1917.

*Henlow 1916 Depot; opened 1918 as No. 5 Eastern Area ARD & ERD; Officers' Engineering Course (from Farnborough) 1924; RAF School of Aeronautical Engineering 1936–1970s; RAF Parachute Test Unit, 1923; Aircraft Riggers School, 1935; MT Training School 1937; No. 2 RAF Depot 1937, moved on to Cardington; No. 13 School of Technical Training 1939; No. 13 MU and No. 6 Repairable Equipment Unit, 1939; No. 14 (ex-13) School of Technical Training 1940; No. 26 MU RAF Repair Depot (Rail siding); School of Aero Engineering became RAF Technical College 1947: Radio Engineering Unit, 1950; Engineering & Armament Division, 1951; Empire Radio School, Signals Division, 1960; RAF Technical College of HQ and 5 Wings, 1960: Basic Studies; Electrical Weapons Systems; Mechanical Engineering; Engineering; and Cadet Wing, 1965 to Cranwell; OCTU, 1966–80 and Aircrew Officer Training School, from Church Fenton, 1969, then to Cranwell; RAF Officers' Command School, 1976, from Tern Hill; RAF Officers' Basic Staff Course, 1997, from Bracknell; Civilian Technical Training School, 1980 (with Bedford College).

*Leighton Buzzard airfield, not developed at Eaton Bray (qv).

*Leighton Buzzard, Corn Exchange: 'Q Central', HQ RAF No. 26 (Signals) Group, 1939–43.

*Leighton Buzzard, Plantation Road, Oxendon House and Heath Road, Carlton Lodge HQ RAF 60 (Signals) Group, 1939.

*Leighton Buzzard, RAF Stanbridge, HQ RAF 23 (Training) Group and parent to RAF Edlesborough's HF transmitters, 1945–1987; central RAF Supply Control System under RAF Henlow, 1997–2013; closed and demolished 2016; housing.

*Luton, Leagrave, Oak(ley) Road, Hewlett & Blondeau factory flying field, 1915–18; planned RFC Home Defence airfield off Oak(ley) Road, not taken up, 1916.

*Luton, Percival aircraft factory, 1936; No. 29 E&RFTS, 1938; No. 24 E&RFTS; No. 264 (Fighter) Squadron, 1940; No. 5 Ferry Pool, ATA, 1940–43.

*Melchbourne Hall, USAAF Station 572 (R7) Ordnance Maintenance, 1942–44.

*Milton Ernest Hall (TL018558) Advanced Air Service HQ, later HQ Strategic Air Depot Area; HQ 8th USAAF Communications Section; Pierced Steel Planking (PSP) airstrip for use by senior officers and liaison aircraft.

*Oakley: AMWD Repair Depot.

*Old Warden (TL150447), airfield taken over by MAP for the repair of light aircraft including Proctors and Harvards, 1940.

*Podington 1942 satellite of Chelveston; USAAF Station 109 from 1943–5, operating B-17 bombers, often on clandestine (Carpetbagger) missions.

*Putnoe, Elms Farm: Emergency LG, First World War.

*Riseley, USAAF Station 541 Quartermaster Stores from 1943–5; RAF No. 95 MU, chemical weapons and bombs, until 1958.

*Sandy Aviation Fuel Depot, nodal point on national pipeline network; in use.

*Sharnbrook, USAAF Station 583, 1942–44, storage and distribution of bombs and chemical weapons (SP991599).

*Stagsden Airfield (SP972463), satellite airfield for Cranfield, airstrip on the ridge between Stagsden West End and Old Farm; never any permanent structures.

*Tempsford, opened 1941 as bomber station; used for wireless and communications development; flew sorties for SOE dropping agents and supplies and associated missions; closed to flying 1947 and sold off 1961.

*Thurleigh opened in 1941 with Nos 12 and 18 OTUs; then USAAF Station 111 from 1942–5 as HQ 40th Combat Wing; 306th Bomb Group 8th USAAF flying B-17s. From 1945 operated as NAE/RAE Bedford (qv); base for BLEU and NAD; dispersal site for V-bombers to 1963.

*Twinwood Farm opened in 1941 as a landing ground for SFTS from Cranfield, then developed as a bomber airfield in 1942 serving No. 51 OTU used by Beaufighters and Blenheim Is until 1945; then planned as part of NAE/RAE complex.

*Woburn Park, No. 34 SLG opened by July 1941 under No. 6 and then No. 8 MU. Initially, holding fighters and training aircraft, then four-engined bombers; prior to D-Day, up to 200 Stirlings were fitted with glider-towing gear; after 1945 surplus aircraft were broken up; site closed in May 1947, (SP970340).

Second World War Anti-Invasion Defences

Nodal Point and Vulnerable Point Defence

* denotes some survivals; a survey co-ordinated by Trevor Ball and Steven Coleman in 1999 recorded many sites for the Defence of Britain Project, and much of the data below, especially regarding removals and demolitions, draws both on that survey and the 30 miles from Harrington site list.

*Ampthill: roadblocks, *spigot mortars, *pillbox, and trenches, HG Store, *five out of original eight hawser rings for wire obstructions.

Arlesey: (TL207360) pillbox, demolished.

Barton-le-Clay: flame fougasse and knife-rest roadblock.

Bedford: pillboxes, *spigot mortars and A/TBs.

Bedford: ?A/T rail at SW corner of St Mary's church.

Biggleswade: pillboxes at TL187444, 190436 and *187453; spigot mortar and A/T obstacles.

Blunham: (TL155519): pillbox demolished by 1999.

Bromham: (TL001506 and 024518) A/TRs demolished by 1999.

Clapham: (TL025519) A/T obstacles destroyed.

Dunstable: pillbox on Station Road and possibly another in Green Lane; *spigot mortar on corner of Chiltern Road and West Street; gun emplacement in Grove House Gardens; roadblocks.

Elstow, Exchange Retail Park: *pillbox (TL040468) recently restored.

Elstow (TL050472) trenches.

Elstow, ROF defences, pillbox, and guard posts demolished.

Great Barford: pillboxes (TL134514 and 122516) demolished.

Houghton Regis: pillbox (TL011238) demolished.

Kempston pillbox and A/T obstacles (TL021472) demolished by 1999.

Luton, Leagrave Road: *Skefco factory guard post.

Luton, Stockwood Park: *pillbox (TL091195).

*Potton: seven pillboxes, spigot mortars, A/T obstacles, and Home Guard Store mainly demolished.

Roxton: pillbox (TL156545) demolished.

Sandy: pillboxes and A/T obstacles (TL176482 and 163489) demolished.

Sandy: Allan Williams Turret (TL206493) destroyed.

Shefford: pillbox (TL143394) demolished.

Staploe: pillbox (TL155588) demolished.

Streatley: A/T obstacles (TL075288) destroyed.

Sundon: spigot mortar (TL040261) demolished.

Sutton: pillbox (TL213477) demolished.

Yielden: *two Home Guard Stores/shelters (TL011672 and 014672).

Airfield Defences

Barton-le-Clay: *three out of six pillboxes and *three out of four shelter/ magazines remain.

Cardington: *one of three pillboxes remains.

Cranfield: *two of at least seven pillboxes remain.

Henlow: possibly *four of at least thirteen pillboxes remain.

Luton: *BHQ may survive but pillbox(es) demolished.

Tempsford: both pillboxes demolished.

Twinwood Farm: *one 'mushroom' pillbox remains.

Bedfordshire Home Guard: Units and Locations

East Anglia North Area, East Central sub-District HQ Bedford.

Bedfordshire Zone, Northern Sector: 1Bn Bedford, 2Bn Biggleswade, 3Bn Ampthill, 5Bn Bedford, 8Bn Bedford.

Bedfordshire Zone, Southern Sector: 4Bn Luton, 6Bn Dunstable, 7Bn Luton.

34 (GPO) Battalion, detachments of 'E' Company at Bedford & Luton.

Dunstable, Meteorological Office (ETA) Home Guard.

LAA troops.

'A' Troop, 230 LAA Bty. Skefco Ball Bearing Co. Ltd Luton (4th Bn Beds HG).

'A' Troop, 231 LAA Bty Vauxhall Motors Ltd Luton (7th Bn Beds HG).

'B' Troop, 232 LAA Bty Percival Aircraft Ltd Luton (7th Bn Beds HG).

Dunstable, HQ East Central Home Guard Transport Column.

Premises used by Bedfordshire Home Guard

Headquarters and Training Facilities

Bedford, HQ Bedfordshire Zone, Northern Sector, 95 Ashburnham Road (CTA).

Clifton, Elm Farm, local HQ.

Dunstable, later Southern Sector HQ.

Dunstable, 'H' Company, 6th Battalion's First Aid section in Nissen hut at Delco.

Dunstable, shop on Church Street near Book Castle, local HQ.

Dunstable, Old Golf Clubhouse 'Guest House', local HQ.

Dunstable, Periwinkle Lane near Water Tower, local HQ.

Eaton Bray, Chequers PH, local HQ.

Hockcliffe, Red Lion PH, local HQ.

King's Walden, parish room and pump house on Church Road, local HQ.

Leighton Buzzard, West Street: Bossard Hall (formerly Drill Hall and Parade Hall), HQ 'E' Company, 6th Battalion.

Luton, No. 4 Dunstable Road, Southern Sector HQ.

Luton, No. 40a Old Bedford Road, drill hall, HQ of 4th and 7th Battalions, Home Guard

Pertenhall Manor, local HQ.

Sandy, Girtford Manor, local HQ.

Willington WI hall used by 'C' Company, 4th Battalion.

Rifle Ranges

Clapham, range in gravel pits.

Clifton, range at Ireland near Southill.

Cople Range.

Dunstable Gas Works, Rifle Club.

Luton Hoo, Riddy Lane, and Fancott.

Newton Bromswold (TL008658) range.

Stewartby, range in very deep knot-hole in brick-pits.

Streatley, training area in quarry.

Toddington indoor range.

Yielden Range.

Air Defence in the Second World War

Searchlight (S/L) Sites

Ampthill, Cooper's Hill S/L site, TL028377.
Arlesey, The Bury S/L site.
Barton-le-Clay S/L site.
Biddenham, Day's Lane (TL028502) S/L site, 467 Battery, 73 S/L Regiment.
RAF Cranfield: canopy of six S/Ls manned by 426 Troop, 58 S/L Battery, 1943.
Chellington, Great Moor Farm (SP951555) S/L site, 467 Battery, 73 S/L Regiment.
Edworth (TL226410) S/L site No. 4 Section, 346 Company 36 AA Battalion in No. 201 Company Area, 1939.
Goldington S/L site.
Hobbs Green, Podington airfield, (SP976604) S/L site, 467 Battery, 73 S/L Regiment.
Luton, Manor Farm (TL107244) S/L site.
Pavenham, Home Farm Close (SP995552) S/L site, 467 Battery, 73 S/L Regiment
Wilden, S/L site, No. 1 Section, 424 Company 36 AA Battalion in No. 202 Company Area, 1939.

HAA Sites

*Leighton Buzzard Radio Station ('Q Central', VP No. 130): Four 3.7-inch HAA mobile guns of 409 Battery, 78 HAA Regiment, 40 AA Brigade, on Site 'A' (SP956245) and Site 'B' (SP939224) from May 1940 until at least February 1941; in June 1940, manned by two sections of 245 Battery, 78 HAA Regiment, 40 AA Brigade; in January 1941 taken over by 262 Battery.
*Bedford, four HAA sites, numbered H1-4, all reported unarmed in June 1942: H1 Brickhill/Putnoe (TL062520); H2 Queens Park (TL029492); H3 Haynes,

Eastcotts, Rook Tree Farm (TL097433); H4 Carlton, Braehead Cottages (SP971557); H5 Bedford, four 3.7-inch HAA mobile guns sent in response to raid 23 July 1942.

*Sandy, four HAA sites all reported unarmed in June 1942: H1 Staploe (TL150591); H2 Blunham (TL167517); H4 Langford (TL208400); (H3 Gamlingay, Cambridgeshire, TL253525).

LAA Sites—Industry

*Dunstable, Watling Street, AC-Delco factory, LAA guns.
*Little Barford power station (TL203561) Lewis guns of 414 Troop, 118 Battery, 30 LAA Regiment on 25 February 1941.
*Luton Skefco Ball Bearing Co. Ltd (VP No. 546), (TL077225) in May 1940; eight Lewis guns, reduced to six in October, of 445 Troop, 145 Battery, 36 LAA Regiment; in May 1943 and July 1944, four 40-mm Bofors LAA guns of 'A' Troop, 230 LAA Battery, 4th Battalion, Bedfordshire Home Guard.
*Luton, Vauxhall Motors Ltd twin Lewis guns of 'A' Troop, 231 LAA Battery, 7th Battalion, Bedfordshire Home Guard, mounted on car showroom roof.
*Luton Percival Aircraft Ltd (VP138) guns of 'B' Troop, 232 LAA Battery, 7th Battalion, Bedfordshire Home Guard.

LAA Sites—Airfields

*RAF Cranfield (VP No. 517), two sites (SP953419 and SP948430) in July–October 1940; fourteen Lewis guns, ten on 20 May 1940, of 32 Troop, 117 Battery, 30 LAA Regiment, 40 AA Brigade; canopy of six S/Ls manned by 426 Troop, 58 S/L Battery on 27 January 1943; taken over by RAF Regiment February 1943.
*RAF Henlow (VP530), three sites (TL166359, TL168366, and TL162367) in May 1940; 12 Lewis guns in May, increased to 16 of 330 Troop, 117 Battery, 30 LAA Regiment, 40 AA Brigade; also S/L of 41 AA Brigade on airfield; in January 1942 one troop of 300 Battery, 96 LAA Regiment with Lewis guns; in May, sixteen Lewis guns of 'C' Troop, 363 Battery, 111 Regiment; in July 1943, RAF Regiment takes over LAA guns.
*Luton Airport, LAA cover for only the Percival Aircraft Works.
*RAF Tempsford, Everton (TL185520) LAA gun position; six LAA 0.300-inch Lewis guns in 1941; 20-mm Oerlikon LAA guns manned by RAF Regiment and ground crew from 1942, but removed by 1944, probably for anti-V1 screen.

Bombing Decoys

*Astwick (TL202396), 'QF' site for RAF Henlow, 1941–42.

*Bendish (TL163205), 'C' Series, 'SF' site for Luton, 1941–2, then 'MY/FL' site for Luton railway yards, 1942–3.

*Cople (TL126473), 'QF' site for RAF Cardington, 1941–2; then 'C' Series 'QL' and 'MY/FL' site for Igranic Works, Bedford, 1942–3; control blockhouse survives.

*Flamstead (TL085127, Hertfordshire), 'C' Series SF site for Luton 1941–3, and 'QL' and 'MY/FL' site for Vauxhall works, 1942–3.

*Hardmead (SP923483, Buckinghamshire), 'Q' site for RAF Cranfield, 1941–2.

*Leighton Buzzard (SP938242), 'M' Series site for W/T station, 1941–2.

*Moggerhanger (TL126511), 'C' Series 'QL' and 'MY/FL' site for Bedford factories, 1942–3.

Swineshead (TL062635), 'Q' site for RAF Chelveston (Northamptonshire), 1941–2.

ROC Posts 1939–1991

NB. Posts in *italics* have been demolished

Ampthill (TL027378), u/g, only a manhole cover is visible on Cooper's Hill.

Bedford (TL084435), Second World War and TL066518 u/g 1960s.

Carlton/Pavenham (SP973557), ROC Post, 1937 and 1964 (see Turvey below).

Renhold (TL083533), ROC u/g post and ORLIT on footpath 100 metres west of Wilden Road.

Riseley (TL047626) ROC Post, 1937 and 1964 u/g on path to east of Keysoe Road.

Sandy (TL152495).

Shefford (TL153381 and TL158388).

Toddington (TL009263).

Turvey (SP957526) ROC Post, 1937 resited to SP973557 in 1953 and u/g 1960s.

The Secret War: Intelligence, SOE, and Communications

Second World War

Ampthill, Park House: used as clandestine print-works by Army.

Aspley Guise, The Shrubbery: PWE black propaganda.

Aspley Guise, Larchfield: accommodation for PWE personnel.

Aspley Heath, Braystone House and the Mount, PWE black propaganda research station (Free French) The Mount, Rookery and Dawn Edge, black propaganda research station (German); Dawn Edge also recording studio.

Bedford, Ardor House: code-breaking school MI18; then Japanese School serving GC&CS Bletchley Park to 1942.

Bedford, 7 St Andrews Road: Japanese School for Bletchley Park, June 1942.

Bedford, 52 de Parys Avenue: Japanese School for GC&CS Bletchley Park, 1943.

Bedford, Albany Road: Arabic school for GC&CS Bletchley Park.

Bedford, 171–5 Tavistock Street (home of Cecil Clarke) and Dean Street: LoLode sponsored by MI(R)c, later MD1, to carry out weapons R&D.

Biggleswade: BBC 'H' transmitting station between Wrestlingworth and Tadlow.

RAF Cardington: RAF Balloon Establishment and SOE parachute school.

Chicksands Priory: base for RAF 'Y' Service intercept work, 1939–45; main collection point for SIGINT bound for Bletchley Park in the days of ULTRA.

Dunstable: Meteorological Office's Central Forecast Office (ETA) serving Air Ministry and Intelligence requirements, and with RAF Central Forecasting Office, 1940; 'Y' Service intercept site joined GC&CS, 1941.

Eversholt Old Rectory: home of PWE Director and meetings venue.

Everton: Woodbury Hall: SOE radio-operator training, then POW camp.

Everton: Old Woodbury: GEE trials unit, 1942, with RAF Tempsford.

Everton: camp for WAAF personnel working at RAF Tempsford.

Great Brickhill, Duncombe Arms PH: billets for GC&CS personnel.

Hasells (now Hazells) Hall: holding accommodation for SOE and Special Forces personnel prior to flying from RAF Tempsford.

RAF Henlow: RAF Communications School and Parachute Test Unit; supply drop testing for SOE from 1940.

Hockliffe, Bunkers Farm: Czech SOE wireless operators (moved from Woldingham) August 1942; linked to STS 43 and 46; two Nissen huts and radio masts.

Holcot Rectory: PWE black propaganda.

Howbury Hall, Waterend, Renhold STS 40, SOE air-landing communications training unit (*Eureka* transmitters/beacons, and Rebecca, air-to-ground radar).

Leighton Buzzard, Stanbridge Road: Air Ministry central telephone/teleprinter exchange built as 'Q Central', RAF Communications Centre.

Leighton Buzzard, Liscombe Park: Plotters School, training centre for Fighter Command Operations rooms and Filter-room staff.

Leighton Buzzard: 'Q Central'—reserve behind HSBC Bank on High Street.

Leighton Buzzard: Corn Exchange basement, stop-gap teleprinter centre (demolished).

Leighton Buzzard, Plantation Road, Oxendon House: HQ RAF 60 (Signals) Group.

Leighton Buzzard, Heath Road, Carlton House: HQ RAF 60 (Signals) Group.

Leighton Buzzard, Stockgrove Park: billets for WRNS from GC&CS.

Luton, Manchester Street: *Luton News* offices of Home Counties Newspapers, used by PWE for printing *Nachrichten* for dropping over Germany.

Milton Bryan: 5-acre compound with guardhouse and huts; PWE black propaganda; Transmitting Station for twenty-four 'Research Units' representing over sixteen nations.

Milton Bryan, Leys Farm: PWE black propaganda research station (Central & Eastern Europe).

Milton Ernest Hall: base for Communications section of HQ 8th USAAF Service Command; providing navigational assistance and radio countermeasures support for operations; house plus Nissen huts; also possible OSS function.

Netherhill House and Broughton Rectory: PWE black propaganda.

Newton Longville, the Grange and No. 43 Aspley Hill: PWE black propaganda research station (Italy and Southeast Europe).

Potsgrove: SOE/PWE twin transmitting stations, Poppy and Pansy.

Sharnbrook, Colworth House: home of Lord Melchett of ICI, SOE, and MD1 liaison.

Sharnbrook: US Ordnance Depot included Cobb Hall and Colworth North Lodge.

Silsoe, Wrest Park: overspill accommodation for Chicksands Priory 'Y' Service staff.

RAF Tempsford: RAF Wireless Intelligence Development Unit, from January 1942.

RAF Tempsford: base for SOE flights for dropping agents and supplies.

RAF Tempsford, Gibraltar Farm: SOE Briefing Room for pilots and navigators.

RAF Tempsford, Port Mahon Farm: base for pilots on SOE operations.

RAF Tempsford, Waterloo Farm and Hasells Hall: from October 1942 to 1944, CO's offices and officers' mess, and mess for SOE personnel; used by SOE as last stopover for agents flying from RAF Tempsford.

Tempsford Hall: SOE holding camp and training centre.

Tetworth Hall: probable use by SOE associated with RAF Tempsford.

Tingrith Rectory: PWE black propaganda.

Woburn Abbey: Foreign Office Department of Propaganda to Enemy Countries (Electra House), moved to stables 1939 and into main house in 1940.

Woburn Abbey: accommodation for WRNS personnel from GC&CS.

Woburn Abbey: Country HQ of the PWE whose psychological warfare units were housed in Paris House, Foxgrove and Marylands, which became the printing unit of the PID having previously been housed in the redundant hangar of the Flying Duchess; Riding School and stables used by Psychological Warfare Unit; cinema, billiards tables, and dance floor installed in stables for use of staff; Woodcote, a Woburn estate cottage was used for accommodating PWE and MEW (Ministry of Economic Warfare responsible for SOE) staff.

Woburn Park Farm: PWE black propaganda research station (Scandinavian).

Woburn, The Holt: PWE black propaganda research station (Polish & Czech).

Woburn Rectory: PWE black propaganda.

Cold War 1946–1993, and to present

Chicksands Priory: US 6950th Electronic Security Group, 1948–94; HQ Intelligence Corps in Defence Intelligence and Security Centre, 1994; RAF Communications Analysis Training School; RN Special Communications Unit; Defence Special Signals School; Joint School of Photographic Interpretation; Defence Debriefing Team; Defence Intelligence and Security School, etc. currently (2019) Joint Intelligence Training Group.

Dunstable, Zouches Farm: Relay station in 'Backbone' Microwave Tower network.

Leighton Buzzard: HQ No. 90 (Signals) Group (ex-Nos 26 and 60 Groups), 1946.

Oakley: Home Office 'Hilltop' Home Office internal security radio station.

Streatley: Home Office 'Hilltop' Home Office internal security radio station.

Military Hospitals, Hospitality, and Welfare

Pre-First World War

Dunstable military hospital, 1800.
Oakley: 26–28 High Street, cottages for ex-Bedfordshire Regiment soldiers, 1905.

First World War

Ampthill, Eastern Command (rehabilitation) Depot.
Ampthill House Convalescent Hospital.
Ampthill Park Relief Hospital.
Ampthill, Dunstable Street, Wilmington Lodge VAD Hospital.
Ampthill, Dunstable Street, Workhouse: VAD auxiliary hospital.
Battlesden Abbey VAD auxiliary hospital.
Bedford, Britannia and Ampthill Roads, Bedford Hospital.
Bedford, Ampthill Road Schools, VAD Hospital.
Bedford, Kimbolton Road, House of Industry/Workhouse/Hospital.
Bedford Town Hall, hospital supply depot and workroom, 1916.
Bedford, Victoria Road, VAD Auxiliary Hospital (now St Leonard's Hall).
Beeston, Sandy, Council Cottages, Auxiliary Hospital.
Biggleswade VAD Hospital.
Everton, Hasells Hall, military hospital.
Hinwick, Hinwick House (SP935620), Auxiliary Hospital.
Houghton Regis VAD Hospital.
Howbury Hall, Renhold, Auxiliary Hospital.
Kempston VAD Hospital.
Leighton Buzzard Corn Exchange, Auxiliary Hospital.
Leighton Buzzard Workhouse, Auxiliary Hospital, 1915.

Leighton Buzzard, Belgravia Workrooms, Central War Hospital Supply Depot, 1918.

Luton, Bute Hospital.

Luton, Stockwood Park VAD Hospital.

Luton, Wardown House VAD Hospital.

Old Warden, Park House, convalescent hospital.

Sandy, town hall, VAD Hospital.

Shefford, Chicksands Priory, auxiliary hospital.

Steppingley Hospital built (1903–5) as isolation hospital for Ampthill.

Stotfold, Kingsley Avenue, Three Counties/Fairfield Hospital/Asylum built 1857–79, treated shellshock (PTSD) patients.

Tingrith VAD Hospital.

Woburn, Duchess of Bedford's Hospital; fully equipped hospital with operating theatre, 1914.

Woburn Abbey, Riding School served as a convalescent home.

Wrest Park, convalescent hospital from 1914 until 1917 fire.

Hospitality First World War

Ampthill, Flitwick and Maulden, YMCA huts for the Canadian Forestry Corps.

Bedford, Bunyan Canteen, 1914–18.

Bedford Corn Exchange, Central Recreation Room, 1915.

Bedford Park, YMCA hut.

Biddenham, barn as canteen and recreation room, December 1915; now village hall.

Clophill, parish room canteen and recreation room for REs billeted at Haynes Park.

Houghton Regis, YMCA hut, 1916.

Luton, Biscot Mill Camp, YMCA hut.

Luton, Dallow Road, recreation room.

Luton, 5 Upper George Street, Comrades of the Great War Club, 1918.

Military Hospitals 1919–39

RAF Henlow, Station Hospital built 1935.

Military Hospitals Second World War

Ampthill, Workhouse, St George's Hospital from 1942; later The Cedars care home.

Bedford, Britannia and Ampthill Roads, Bedford Hospital.

Bedford, Oakley House Red Cross Convalescent Home/Auxiliary Hospital.

RAF Henlow, station hospital.

Ickwell Bury, The Old House Red Cross Convalescent Home/Auxiliary Hospital.

Kempston, The Grange convalescent camp.

Leighton Buzzard, Stockgrove Park: No. 10 Casualty Clearing Station, RAMC, 1939.

Leighton Buzzard, Stockgrove Park Mansion and The Heath used by RAMC; 81st General Hospital, May to July 1944, then to France.

Luton Hoo, convalescent home/auxiliary hospital.

Luton, 6th General Hospital, October 1940–January 1941, then to Egypt.

Luton, 107th General Hospital, November 1944–January 1945, then to Bangalore.

Old Warden Park, Red Cross Convalescent Home/Auxiliary Hospital.

Stotfold, Three Counties Hospital.

Hospitality Second World War

Bedford, Goldington Road, American Red Cross Club.

Bedford Corn Exchange: venue for concerts, dances, etc.

Bedford, Midland Road/Well (Silver) Street: Pantechnicon department store used by American Red Cross Club; now Wetherspoons.

Bedford Midland Station: Salvation Army Red Shield Club.

Bedford: Swan Lake Hotel and Silver Bar.

Everton Village Hall: canteen for RAF Tempsford etc.

Leighton Buzzard: Corn Exchange.

Leighton Buzzard, Grovebury Road: WVS HQ, quiet rooms, baths, etc.

Leighton Buzzard, High Street, Ravenstone Chambers: Services canteen.

Leighton Buzzard, Lake Street: WVS Services canteen.

Leighton Buzzard, Lake Street, Temperance Hall: Services social club.

Luton, George Street: American Red Cross Club.

Tempsford Village Hall: venue for concerts, dances, etc.

Tempsford, Stuart Memorial Hall: WVS canteen.

Wrestlingworth Memorial Hall: venue for dances, etc.

Military Hospitals 1946–2017

Henlow: RAF Aviation Medicine Training Centre, from North Luffenham 1998.

Henlow: RAF Centre of Aviation Medicine, 1998 from Farnborough.

Munitions Production

Pre-First World War

Bedford: gunpowder works, 1600s.

World War I

General Munitions Production

Bedford, Britannia Works: light railways and steam ploughs.
Bedford, Houghton/Elstow Road, Motor Rail and Tramcar Company: 'Simplex' light, petrol locomotives.
Bedford, Vulcan Works: diesel locomotives for use on industrial light railways.
Leighton Buzzard, Billington Road, Gossard: anti-torpedo nets for Admiralty.
Luton, Chaul End, George Kent: Filling Factory for detonators and fuses.
Luton, Kimpton Road, Vauxhall Motors: trucks for the services.
Luton, Leagrave Road, Britannia Works: Skefco ball-bearings factory.
Luton, Queen Victoria Street, Hayward Tyler: marine salvage pumps.

Aircraft Production

Bedford: W. H. Allen's Queen's Engineering Works: Rhône aero-engines.
Bedford: J. P. Whites, Carpenters & Joiners: aircraft propellers.
Biddenham, Ford End Road, W. H. Allen: new factory; new offices in Hurst Grove.
Cardington, Short Brothers: airship factory, 1915.
Linslade, Morgan & Co.: Vickers, Airco, Sopwith, and Avro aircraft.
Luton, Leagrave, Omnia Works: Farman, Armstrong Whitworth, and Avro aircraft.

Interwar period 1918–39

Cardington: Short Bros airship factory nationalised, as Royal Airship Works, 1919.
Cardington: Directorate of Airship Development, 1932, from Air Ministry.
Cardington: Balloon Development Establishment then Unit, 1938.
Luton: Percival Aircraft from 1936.

Second World War

General Production
Dunstable, London Road and Houghton Regis, The Empire Rubber Company: respirators for the services.
Dunstable, Waterlow's printers: propaganda leaflets and ration-books.
Leighton Buzzard, Cotsmoor: parachutes.
Leighton Buzzard, Grovebury Road, Gossard: barrage balloons for convoy use, dinghies for fighter aircraft, parachutes, lifebelts, distress flares, and sails.
Luton, Icknield Road, Alliance Castings' foundry.
Luton: Diamond Foundry made large-scale cooking units for the Army.
Luton, Leagrave Road, Britannia Works, Skefco: ball-bearings.

Aircraft Production
Bedford, Igranic: parts for Mosquitos.
Bedford, J. P. Whites, Pyghtle Works: components for Mosquitos and Hamilcar gliders.
Biggleswade, Winton Hayes Ltd: jigs and tools for Vickers-Armstrong.
Dunstable, The Empire Rubber Company: hoses & connectors for the aircraft industry.
Dunstable, Grice & Young: parts for Mosquitos and Horsa gliders, and undercarriages for Percival Proctors.
Dunstable, Henry Hughes: marine and aircraft instruments.
Dunstable, Thermo Plastics: plastic radomes for aircraft.
Leighton Buzzard, Gossard: parachutes and barrage balloons.
Luton, Napier Flight Development Unit: Sabre engines.
Luton, Percival Aircraft: Vega Gulls, Q6s, Proctors, Oxfords, and Mosquitos.
Luton, English Electric: Halifax bombers.
Luton, Vauxhall: development of jet engines.
Luton, dispersed Vickers works: aircraft parts.
Old Warden, Shrager Bros: overhaul of Harvards, Proctors, and Magisters.
Tempsford, Vickers: fabric repair work on damaged or poorly finished aircraft.

Munitions

Elstow, Royal Ordnance Factory, Filling Factory No. 16: high explosives.

Leighton Buzzard, Southcott, Coty: magnesium flares for 2-inch mortars, pathfinder, and reconnaissance flares.

Luton, Diamond Foundry: 25-pounder shells and sub-artillery ammunition for the Home Guard.

Luton, Electrolux: incendiaries for the RAF and depth charges for the RN.

Tanks and Military Vehicles

Dunstable, Bagshawes: caterpillar tracks for Universal Carriers.

Dunstable, Boscombe Road, Vauxhall: new factory opened 1942.

Luton, Vauxhall: special prototype A24 Cromwell Cruiser tank.

Luton, Vauxhall: 1940 redesign of A22 Churchill Infantry tank.

Luton, George Kent: steering gear for tanks.

Luton, Messrs J. Balmforth: gun turrets for Churchill tanks.

Luton, Biscot Road, Commer and Karrier: vehicles.

Luton, Napier: Lion engines to power flamethrowers.

Weaponry

Dunstable, Kensworth, Isle of Wight Lane, Bisley Clay Target Co.: development and manufacture of Northover Projectors.

Luton, Dallow Road, Adamant Engineering: Spigot Mortars and PIATs.

Luton, Messrs J. Balmforth: 20-mm Oerlikon LAA guns.

Products for the Royal Navy

Elstow ROF FF No. 16: 'A' mines.

Luton, Hayward Tyler (1941 Admiralty Essential Works schedule), pumps.

Luton, Hudson's Foundry: parts for Coastal Motor-boats (MTBs and MGBs).

Luton, Biscot Road, George Kent: Clear-View Screens for all types of warship and torpedo-firing mechanisms.

Luton, Electrolux: depth-charges.

Luton, Napier: Lion engines for MTBs.

The Cold War

Bedford: National Aeronautical Establishment, 1945–55; then part of RAE.

Bedford: Royal Signals & Radar Establishment, *c.* 1960 (from Malvern).

Bedford: Aircraft Research Association Transonic Wind Tunnel, 1953.

Cardington: Balloon & Training Aids Development Units, 1945–66.

Cardington: R&D Establishment became RAE (Cardington) into 1980s.

Cranfield: rocket-testing, 1950–70s.

Luton: Hunting-Percival, then Hunting, then BAC, mid-1950s, missiles and guidance systems.

Luton: English Electric (additional premises in Stevenage): Thunderbird SAM in the late 1950s.

Luton, Hunting Engineering: construction of centre-section of Blue Danube.

Thurleigh/Twinwood Farm: RAE Bedford.

Depots

First World War

Henlow: Eastern Area (aircraft) Repair Depot, 1914–18.

Interwar Years

Cardington: No. 2 Aircraft Storage Unit, 1933.
Henlow: No. 5 Eastern Area Aircraft Depot, 1918; then Inland Area Aircraft Depot, 1920; then Home Aircraft Depot and Parachute Test Unit, 1926.

Second World War

Arlesey railway station, RASC Duplicate Supply Depot (RASC Rail Siding).
Arlesey, Hitch Road: ordnance depot, later cement works.
Ampthill: Hostel for ROF Elstow, then army camp.
Cardington: No. 26 MU, civilian-manned repair depot.
Dunstable: Ministry of Food cold store (designated as Luton).
Elstow: Royal Ordnance Factory, Filling Factory No. 16, explosives.
Henlow: RAF Service Repair Depot, 13 MU, included RN parachute stocks.
Henlow: 13 MU Service Repair & Salvage Depot.
Henlow: 43 Group Service Repair Depot.
Husborne Crawley (SP959370) Aviation Fuel Distribution Depot, four 500-ton D1 tanks.
Luton: No. 8 MU, Purgatory Area centre, for storage of unassembled aircraft.
Luton: Admiralty Victualling Depot and Salvage Stores, Balmforths Siding.
Luton, Guildford Street, Browns Mill: RAF ammunition storage sub-site, 1943.

Melchbourne Park (AAF-506): USAAF Main Ammunition Storage Depot, 1943; 2003 Ordnance & Armament Unit; 2006 Ordnance Maintenance Company, Chemical Warfare Department.

Melchbourne Park: USAAF Forward Filling Depot (FFD2, chemical weapons).

Milton Ernest: 8th USAAF Advanced Air Depot, 1943 from Honington.

Oakley: RAF Repair Depot.

Riseley: sub-site of FFD2, Melchbourne Park.

Sandy Lodge: ammunition storage.

Sandy: Air Ministry Aviation Fuel Reserve Depot, twenty 4,000-ton C2 tanks.

Sharnbrook: RAF Forward Ammunition Depot, No. 221 MU, 1942.

Sharnbrook, Cobb Hall: USAAF Forward Ammunition Storage Depot, 1943; 2107 Ordnance Ammunition Battalion; 3rd and 4th Companies, 2nd Ordnance Battalion.

Shefford: No. 27 Ammunition sub-Depot RAOC (chemical warfare).

Turvey: depot, later POW Camp.

Wilshamstead: Second World War ammunition factory (TL045445).

Cold War

Cardington: RAF Reserve Ammunition Depot, No. 217 MU, 1953/4.

Riseley: former FFD used as RAF chemical weapons storage site, No. 95 MU, 1946.

POW Camps

First World War

Ampthill; Barton-le-Clay; Bedford Military Hospital; Bletsoe; Broom; Clifton; Houghton Regis; Leighton Buzzard, 20 Market Square; Melchbourne; Meppershall; Milton Ernest; Old Warden, Southill Park; Pertenhall; Podington (?)Camp; Sandy, Blunham; Shillington; Souldrop; Tempsford, administered by Pattishall Camp (Northants); Turvey; Woburn.

Second World War

Ampthill Park—Camp 261; Clapham, Green Lane—Camp 278; Cockayne Hartley, Old Rectory, Village Road—Camp; Colmworth, Dacca Farm, Colesden Road (TL109561), Ducks Cross—Camp 72 for 750 Italian POWs, then work-camp for German POWs; Dunstable, (London) Gliding Club—camp; Everton, Old Woodbury Hall (TL213528)—Camp 561/No. 583 IWC; Harrold, Harrold Hall (SP955566)—Camp 611; Houghton Conquest—Camp 644; Luton Airport—Camp 270; Marston Moretaine, Church Farm (SP997404)—Camp 575; Potton, mansion (now golf course)—Camp 269/No. 628 IWC; Potton, Sutton Park—Camp 628; Ravensden House—POW hostel; Sandy, Tetworth Hall—German POWs kept above garage; Turvey—depot, later POW Camp.

Air-Raid Precautions (ARP) and Civil Defence (CD) in the Second World War

Ampthill, Public Assistance Institution: ARP Control Centre, First Aid Post and Cleansing/Decontamination Centre.

Barton-le-Clay: ARP Heavy Rescue Section.

Bedford, East Hall: First Aid Party Depot.

Bedford, Victoria Road, St Leonard's Hall: North Bedfordshire ARP HQ and Control Centre.

Bedford, Greyfriars Walk, Mission Hall: CD Training Centre.

Bedford, 100 High Street: basement shelter.

Bedford, Queens Park Moravian Church: First Aid Post.

Bedford, St Peter's Emergency Hospital Cleansing Station.

Biggleswade, Police Station: ARP Control Centre and HQ.

Biggleswade, 'The Lawns': First Aid Post and Cleansing Station, and basement shelters.

Billington Manor: ARP Post.

Clifton, Church Hall: First Aid Post.

Dunstable, Parish Hall: base for fire-watchers.

Dunstable, Park Farm: ARP depot.

Dunstable, Bennetts Recreation Centre: shelters beneath field.

Dunstable, Grove House Gardens: shelters beneath field.

Eaton Bray, Bingles, the Institute and St Mary's Church: ARP Posts.

Eaton Bray, Methodist Chapel: First Aid Post.

Eggington House and Plough Cottage: ARP Post.

Eggington, Methodist Chapel school-room: First Aid Post.

Heath and Reach, Village Barn: ARP Post and First Aid Post.

Hockcliffe, the Watling Street PH: ARP Post.

Hockcliffe Men's Club: First Aid Post.

Houghton Regis, Quarry: air-raid shelters.

Kempston, Methodist Sunday School: First Aid Post.

Leighton Buzzard, Grovebury Road, Workhouse/Public Assistance Institution: ARP Control Centre, First Aid Post and Cleansing/Decontamination Centre.

Leighton Buzzard, The Unicorn Hotel, 17 High Street, 42 Church Street, 43 Hockcliffe Street, The Chase in Heath Road, Clent in Billington Road, 121 Vandyke Road, 91 Stanbridge Road, Barclays Bank: ARP Posts.

Leighton Buzzard, 76 North Street: First Aid Post.

Linslade, Springfield Road, coach-house of Perth House: NFS station.

Luton, 9 (later 15) Gordon Street: HQ Special Constabulary, NFS/AFS, Ambulance, ARP, Civil Defence and Bomb Disposal.

Luton: Fire Service at Church Street and Oxen Road; Fire Stations at Chaul End, Biscot Road, Diamond Foundry and Vauxhall Works.

Luton: Upper George Street, High Town, Beech Hill and Albert Road: deep-tunnel Air Raid Shelters.

Luton: Biscot Road Vicarage Old Coach house: ARP base.

Oakley Methodist Chapel School: two rooms as Wardens' Post.

Pavenham Vicarage: Wardens' Post.

Potton, Brook End, Chequers Inn: ambulance garage, 1944.

Potton, Horne Lane, Home Farm: ARP Wardens' Post.

Potton, Linden Lodge: Rescue Party Depot then First Aid Point.

Potton, Market Square: Wardens' Post.

Ridgmont, YMCA Hall: Wardens' Post.

Riseley, 42 High Street, British Legion Room: Wardens' Post.

Roxton, The Institute: Wardens' Post.

Sandy, Public Elementary (C of E) School: CD Mobile Unit Depot and Rest Centre.

Sandy: Baptist Chapel School-room: First Aid & Rescue Party Depot, 1941.

Stanbridge, Five Bells PH and Station Road: ARP Posts.

Stanbridge, Methodist Chapel school-room: First Aid Post.

Tebworth, Old Smithy: ARP Post.

Tilsworth, Woodlands: ARP Post.

Toddington, High Street: ARP Post.

Upper & Nether Dean, The Grange and (later) Bryant Cottage: ARP post.

Woburn, 3 Leighton Street: First Aid Post.

Bibliography

Aberg, F., *Medieval Moated Sites* (York: CBA Research Report 17, 1978)

Abraham, B., 'Satellite Landing Grounds' in *Airfield Review* 91 (Thetford: ARG, 2001) with follow-up letter in *Airfield Review* 92 (reference-Woburn SLG)

Abrams, J., & Shotliff, D., 'The remains of Robert de Wauderi's adulterine castle, Castle Street, Luton', *Bedfordshire Archaeological Journal* 26 (Bedford: 2010)

Adams, M., *Aelfred's Britain, War and Peace in the Viking Age* (London: Head of Zeus, 2017)

Addyman, P., 'A Ringwork and Bailey at Biggleswade,' *Bedfordshire Archaeological Journal* 3 (Bedford: 1966)

After the Battle, *PLUTO: Pipeline Under The Ocean* (Stratford: After the Battle 116, 2002)

Anderson, I., 'The RAE at Bedford: Thurleigh Airfield Post-War, parts 1 & 2' in *Airfield Review* 156 & 157 (Wilden: ARG, 2017)

Antrobus, S., *We wouldn't have missed it for the world: The Women's Land Army in Bedfordshire 1939–50* (Copt Hewick/Dunstable: Book Castle Publishing, 2008)

Bailey, J., 'Calcutt Farm, Houghton Regis, Bedfordshire, a Measured Survey of a Moated Farmstead', *Bedfordshire Archaeological Journal* 10 (Bedford: 1975)

Baker, D., *Bedfordshire medieval moated sites* in Aberg (above)

Baker, D., et al., 'Excavations in Bedford 1967–1977', *Bedfordshire Archaeological Journal* 13 pp. 7-64 (Bedford: 1979)

Baker, K., *Admiralty Shutter Telegraph*, BBC Making History website, 24.06.2014

Bates, H E., *The Tinkers of Elstow* (privately published edition of 300, May 1946)

www.bedfordregiment.org.uk

www.bedsarchives.bedford.gov.uk

Bell, M., *The Archaeology of the Dykes* (Stroud: Amberley, 2012)

Berry, P., 'Bedford Radar Approach Control' (and associated topics) in *Airfield Review* 110 pp39-43 (Thetford: ARG, 2006)

Bigmore, P., *The Bedfordshire & Huntingdonshire Landscape* (London: Hodder & Stoughton, 1979)

Blades, B., *Roll of Honour* (Barnsley: Pen & Sword, 2015)

Bowyer, M., *Action Stations 6: Cotswolds & Central Midlands* (Wellingborough: Patrick Stevens, 1983)

Brown, A. and Taylor, C., *Moated Sites in Northern Bedfordshire*, Vaughan Paper 35 (Leicester: Leicester University Press, 1991)

Brown, A., (ed) *Roman Small Towns in Eastern England and Beyond* (Oxford: Oxbow, 1995)

Brown, P., & Herbert, E., *The Secrets of Q Central* (Stroud: The History Press, 2014)

Brown, R. A., Colvin, H. M., & Taylor, A. J., *The History of the King's Works, Volumes 1 & 2: The Middle Ages* (London: HMSO, 1963)

Burgoyne, Lt-Col. Sir J., *Regimental Records of the Bedfordshire Militia 1759–1884* (London: W. H. Allen, 1884) accessed December 2018 via Google.

Campbell, D., *War Plan UK* (1982, London); *The Unsinkable Aircraft Carrier* (1984, London)

Cocroft, W., *Dangerous Energy* (Swindon: English Heritage, 2000)

Cocroft, W., & Thomas, R., *Cold War: Building for Nuclear Confrontation 1946–89* (Swindon: English Heritage, 2003)

Coles, S., 'Excavation at Castle Street, Luton: The site of Robert de Wauderi's Castle?', *Bedfordshire Archaeological Journal* 25 (Bedford: 2004)

Collett-White, J., 'The Old House at Wrest', in *Bedfordshire Magazine* XXII & XXIII (Bedford: 1991)

Crawley, A., & Freeman, I., 'Bedford—an Alfredian Burgh?', *Bedfordshire Archaeological Journal* 24 (Bedford: 2001)

Creighton, O., & Wright, D., *The Anarchy, War and Status in 12th Century Landscapes of Conflict* (Liverpool: Liverpool University Press, 2016)

Crick, J., & Dawson, M., 'Archaeological Excavations at Kempston Manor, 1994', *Bedfordshire Archaeological Journal* 22 (Bedford: 1996)

Crisp, G., 'The Supply of Explosives and Ammunition to the RAF in WW2', in *Airfield Review* Vol.10 Nos.1 (1988) and 2 (1989) and No.124 (Thetford: ARG, 2009)

Delve, K., *The Military Airfields of Britain: East Midlands* (Ramsbury: Crowood, 2008

Edundson, G., & Mudd, A., 'Mediaeval occupation at 'Danish Camp', Willington', *Bedfordshire Archaeological Journal* 25 (Bedford: 2004)

Edwards, C., 'The excavation of a Second World War air raid shelter at New Venue, Court Drive, Dunstable', *Bedfordshire Archaeological Journal* 26 (Bedford: 2010)

Everitt, A., *The Local Community and the Great Rebellion* (London: The Historical Association, 1973)

Fadden, K., *Ampthill Defences of World War II* (Ampthill: Ampthill & District Archaeological & Local History Society, nd); *An Archaeological Evaluation of a World War II Air Raid Shelter at the Old Rectory, Hills End, Eversholt* (Ampthill: Ampthill & District Archaeological & Local History Society, 1997 & 2010)

Fadden, K., & Turner, M., *The Search for a lost Moat: A Resistance Survey of the Old House at Wrest TL092354* (Ampthill: Ampthill & District Archaeological & Local History Society, 2004)

Foot, W., 'AD60 Boudica: Unlocated battle' in *British Archaeology* 165, (York: CBA, March/April 2019)

Francis, P., *British Military Airfield Architecture* (Yeovil: Patrick Stephens, 1996)

Francis, P., and Crisp, G., *Military Command and Control Organisation* (Swindon: in CD form for English Heritage, 2008)

Galley, R., bedfordhighlanders.blogspot.com (2009)

Godber, J., *History of Bedfordshire 1066–1888* (Bedford: Bedfordshire County Council, 1969)

Gregory, D., *et al.*, *RAF Stanbridge, Leighton Buzzard, Desk Based Assessment* (Swindon: English Heritage, 2011)

Hardisty, O., *Blitzing Vauxhall* (Dunstable: The Book Castle, 2005)

harringtonmuseum.org.uk/Military%20sites%20within2030%20miles%20of%20 Harrington%20Museum.pdf

Hassall, J., 'Excavations at Willington, 1973', *Bedfordshire Archaeological Journal* 10 (Bedford: 1975)

Howarth, P., 'Cranfield Night Fighter OTU' in *Airfield Review* No.106 (Thetford: ARG, 2005)

Howarth, P., 'Luton's First Airfield' in *Airfield Review* No.154 (Sheffield: ARG, 2017)

James, Brig. E., *British Regiments 1914–1918* (Heathfield: Naval & Military Press, 1978)

Johnson, P., *War-torn Skies—Bedfordshire* (Red Kite, 2014)

Keir, W., 'Archaeological Investigations on the western edge of the site of Fulk de Breaute's castle, Park Square, Luton', *Bedfordshire Archaeological Journal* 27 (Bedford: 2017)

Kenyon, J., *Castles, Town Defences & Artillery Fortifications in the United Kingdom & Ireland: a Bibliography 1945–2006* (Donington: Shaun Tyas, 2008)

King, D. J. C., & Alcock, L., 'Ringworks of England and Wales' in Taylor, A. J., (ed.) *Chateau Gaillard lll*, (1966), (Chichester: Phillimore, 1969)

Liddiard, R., *Castles in Context* (Macclesfield: Windgather, 2005)

Luton News., *Luton at War* (Luton: Home Counties Newspapers, 1947)

Lutt, N., *Bedfordshire at War* (Stroud: Sutton, 1997); 'Bedfordshire Muster Lists 1539–1831', *Bedfordshire Historical Society* 71 (Bedford: BHS, 1992)

Maull, A., & Chapman, A., 'A Medieval Moated Enclosure in Tempsford Park', *Bedford Archaeology Monograph* 5 (Northampton: Northampton Archaeology, 2005)

McGlynn, S., *Blood Cries Afar. The forgotten Invasion of England 1216* (Stroud: History Press, 2011)

O'Brien, C., & Pevsner, N., *Buildings of England: Bedfordshire, Huntingdon & Peterborough* (New Haven & London: Yale University Press, 2014)

O'Connor, B., *Churchill's Most Secret Airfield RAF Tempsford* (Stroud: Amberley, 2010, 2013)

Osborne, M., *Defending Britain* (Stroud: Tempus, 2004); *Always Ready, the drill halls of Britain's volunteer forces* (Leigh-on-Sea: Partizan Press, 2006); *Pillboxes in Britain and Ireland* (Stroud: Tempus, 2008); *Grandad's Army: Volunteers in Defence of the British Isles in the First World War* (Stroud: Fonthill Media, 2021)

Petrie, J. (ed.), *The Castles of Bedfordshire* (Donington: Shaun Tyas, 2012)

Pevsner, N., *Buildings of England: Bedfordshire, Huntingdon & Peterborough* (Harmondsworth: Penguin, 1968)

RAF Henlow, *The History of RAF Henlow 1918-Present Day* (Henlow: 1998)

Renn, D., 'Burhgeat and Gonfanon' in Liddiard, R., (ed) *Anglo-Norman Castles* (Woodbridge: Boydell Press, 2003)

Risby, S., *Prisoners of War in Bedfordshire* (Stroud: Amberley, 2011)

Sharpe, J., *A Fiery & Furious People, A History of Violence in England* (London: Penguin Random House, 2016)

Shaw, F., and J. (eds), statement by Peter Cane Vigor in *We Remember the Home Guard* (Hinckley: privately printed in aid of RBL, 1990)

Shotliff, D., 'A Moated Site in Tempsford Park', *Bedfordshire Archaeological Journal* 22 (Bedford: 1996)

Simco, A., *Survey of Bedfordshire: the Roman Period* (Bedford: RCHME and Bedfordshire County Council, 1984)

Smith, T., 'The Anglo-Saxon Churches of Bedfordshire', *Bedfordshire Archaeological Journal* 3 (Bedford: 1966); 'Someries Castle', *Bedfordshire Archaeological Journals* 3 & 5 (Bedford: 1966 and 1970)

Stocker, D., *England's Landscape: the East Midlands* (London: Collins/EH, 2006)

SUBTERRANEA BRITANNICA www.subbrit.org.uk/rsg/sites

Taylor, C., *Fieldwork in Medieval Archaeology* (London: 1974); 'Moated Sites: Their Definition, Form and Classification' in *Aberg*, 1978

Williams, A., 'A bell-house and a burh-geat: lordly residences in England before the Norman Conquest' in Liddiard, R., (ed) *Anglo-Norman Castles* (Woodbridge: Boydell Press, 2003)

Woodley, N., & Abrams, J., 'Inside Fulk de Breautes Thirteenth Century Castle', *Bedfordshire Archaeological Journal* 27, 2015 (Bedford: 2017)

Yates, J., & King, S., *Dunstable & District at War* (Dunstable: The Book Castle, 2006)

Index